TABLE OF CONTENTS

Top 20 Test Taking Tips

1. Carefully follow all the test registration procedures
2. Know the test directions, duration, topics, question types, how many questions
3. Setup a flexible study schedule at least 3-4 weeks before test day
4. Study during the time of day you are most alert, relaxed, and stress free
5. Maximize your learning style; visual learner use visual study aids, auditory learner use auditory study aids
6. Focus on your weakest knowledge base
7. Find a study partner to review with and help clarify questions
8. Practice, practice, practice
9. Get a good night's sleep; don't try to cram the night before the test
10. Eat a well-balanced meal
11. Know the exact physical location of the testing site; drive the route to the site prior to test day
12. Bring a set of ear plugs; the testing center could be noisy
13. Wear comfortable, loose fitting, layered clothing to the testing center; prepare for it to be either cold or hot during the test
14. Bring at least 2 current forms of ID to the testing center
15. Arrive to the test early; be prepared to wait and be patient
16. Eliminate the obviously wrong answer choices, then guess the first remaining choice
17. Pace yourself; don't rush, but keep working and move on if you get stuck
18. Maintain a positive attitude even if the test is going poorly
19. Keep your first answer unless you are positive it is wrong
20. Check your work, don't make a careless mistake

Human Growth and Development

Erikson's stages of development

Erik Erikson described human development as eight stages of psychosocial development. According to him each stage involves a psychosocial crisis, which must be resolved before the person can successfully move on to the next stage. The stages are:
1. Infancy or Trust vs. Mistrust (Hope) – the period from birth to 1 or 1 ½ years.
2. Toddler or Autonomy vs. Shame (Will) – from 1 to 2 years of age.
3. Preschooler or Initiative vs. Guilt (Purpose) – from 2 to 6 years of age.
4. School Age or Industry vs. Inferiority (Competence) – from 6 to 12 years of age.
5. Adolescence or Identity vs. Diffusion (Fidelity) – from 12 (or puberty) to 18 years of age.
6. Young Adulthood or Intimacy vs. Isolation (Love) – from 19 to 40 years of age.
7. Middle Adulthood or Generativity vs. Self-absorption (Care) – from 40 to 65.
8. Late Adulthood or Integrity vs. Despair (Wisdom) – from age 65 till death.

Psychoanalytic and psychosexual development theory

Based on the work of Sigmund Freud, the psychoanalytic theory postulates that all humans have instincts to satisfy their needs for food, shelter, and warmth. Satisfaction of these instincts produces pleasure and leads to the development of sexual drives. The two basic drives are sex and aggression or life and death. Freud divided human development into five stages:
1. Oral birth to 18 months
2. Anal 2 to 3 years
3. Phallic 3 to 5 years
4. Latency 6 years to puberty
5. Genital puberty to adulthood

Incomplete development at any stage he called fixation. The stages are based on his belief that the child focuses on different areas of the body in each stage. These areas are known as erogenous zones and include the mouth, anus, and genitals. Psychological defenses that help a person control or prevent undesirable or inappropriate emotions or behaviors include denial, repression, suppression, projection, displacement, rationalization, reaction formation, regression, and sublimation. Castration anxiety and penis envy are psychological factors that can impact the personality. Other theories include the pleasure principle and the reality principle.

Piaget's theory of development

Piaget described the cognitive development of children using the key concepts of schemas, assimilation, accommodation, and equilibration. Schemas include both the categories of knowledge and the process by which the knowledge is obtained. Schemas change as new experiences add to knowledge. Assimilation is the adding of new information to existing schemas. Accommodation is changing existing schemas to fit new information and experiences. Piaget called the balance between assimilation and accommodation equilibration. Piaget's stages of cognitive development are:
- sensorimotor (birth to 2 years) during which the child learns about himself and his environment through sensory perceptions and motor activities
- preoperational (2 to 7 years) in which language develops and the child is egocentric

- concrete operational (7 to 11 years) during which the child begins to think logically but still has trouble with abstract concepts
- formal operational (11 or 12 years to adulthood) during which the child develops the capability of logical thought, deductive reasoning and systematic planning.

Kohlberg's theory

Building on the work of Jean Piaget, John Dewey and James Mark Baldwin, Lawrence Kohlberg's studies of moral development led him to identify 3 levels of moral development with 2 stages within each level.

- The **preconventional morality level** is the period in which a child is influenced by reward and punishment.
  - Stage 1 - Obedience and punishment orientation, the child sees authority as handing down the rules on right and wrong.
  - Stage 2 – Individualism and exchange, the child begins to perceive that there is not just one right way.
- The **conventional morality level** is the period during adolescence when the person strives to meet standards set by the family and society.
  - Stage 3 –Good interpersonal relationships. During this period, the person is motivated by such feelings as love, empathy and concern for others.
  - Stage 4 – Maintaining the social order, the person becomes more concerned with society as a whole.
- The **postconventional morality level** is the period of self-accepted principles.
  - Stage 5 – Social contract and individual rights, the person begins to think about what makes a good society and what any society should value.
  - Stage 6 – Universal principles, the person has a concern for justice and its impartial application to everyone.

Oedipus and Electra Complexes

According to Freud, the Oedipus complex in boys and the Electra complex in girls occurs during the phallic stage of development, usually between the ages of three and five. The complexes involve the child's usually subconscious sexual feelings toward the parent of the opposite sex. The feelings include jealousy of the same-sex parent and may include a desire for the death of that parent. Successful resolution of the complex is achieved when the child identifies with the parent of the same sex and internalizes the parental values. The process ends in the development of the conscience or superego.

Bowlby and Harlow's theories on attachment and bonding

John Bowlby believes that bonding with an adult before the age of three is vital if a person is to lead a normal social life. According to him, the lack of bonding, or a bond that is severed during infancy, can cause abnormal behavior or psychopathology. His opinion is that the mother should be the primary caregiver for the child with the father in the role of emotional supporter for the mother.

Harry Harlow's work with monkeys led him to believe attachment to be an innate tendency. He saw monkeys raised in isolation develop autistic and abnormal behavior. Placing those monkeys with normally reared ones could somewhat reverse those behaviors.

Imprinting and Konrad Lorenz

Imprinting refers to the way newly hatched ducks and geese instinctively follow the first moving object they see. This is usually the mother but may be any living or non-living thing. Konrad Lorenz worked with goslings and applied his results to the principle of "critical periods." The critical period is the concept that certain behaviors must be learned at specific stages of development or they may not be learned at all. Heredity and environment are both important in critical periods of development.

Categories of human development

The categories of human development are:
- learning, which includes behavioral, social learning and information-processing theories;
- cognitive, which is concerned with obtaining knowledge;
- psychoanalytic, which is the method of investigating psychological phenomena developed by Freud;
- humanistic, which explains development through reasoning and the scientific method.

Human growth and development changes are viewed as qualitative, which involves a change in structure such as sexual development; quantitative, in which measurable changes occur such as in intellectual development; continuous, which denotes sequential changes that cannot be segmented, for example personality development; discontinuous, which are changes in abilities and behaviors such as language that develop in stages; mechanistic, which places behaviors in common groups, such as instinctual or reflexive; and organismic, in which new stages of development use cognition and includes moral and ethical development.

Major theme in Levinson's *The Seasons of a Man's Life*

The book is based on a study Daniel Levinson did with adult males that led him to formulate a comprehensive theory of adult development. He divided life into four periods: preadulthood, early adulthood, middle adulthood, and late adulthood with a major transition occurring as the person moves from each period or stage to the next. He believed the transitions occurred at about 17 to 22 years as the person moved into young adulthood, between 40 and 45 years into middle adulthood, and between 60 and 65 as the person became an older adult. He identified three sets of developmental tasks:
- build, modify, and enhance a life structure
- form and modify the single components of the life structure
- tasks necessary to becoming more of an individual

Maslow's hierarchy of needs, Gesell's maturationist theory, and the behaviorism learning approach

Abraham Maslow, a humanistic psychologist, developed a theory of motivation which he called a hierarchy of needs. According to this theory, a person must first satisfy basic needs such as the need for food and shelter before he can turn his attention to higher needs. In order from basic to higher the needs are: physiological, security/safety, belonging/love, esteem, and self-actualization.

Arnold Gesell advanced the maturationist theory which holds that development is a biological process that proceeds in an orderly, predictable manner, and is independent of environmental influences.

According to behaviorism, learning is a change of behavior brought about by the consequences of behaviors. For example, the child is rewarded for a desirable behavior or punished for an undesirable one. Punishment can be active such as the denial of a privilege or passive in which case the behavior is ignored. The work of John Watson, B.F. Skinner, and Edward Thorndike has been important to behaviorism. Thorndike formulated the "law of effect" which states that a behavior followed by a reward is strengthened and more likely to be repeated.

Work of Jean Baker Miller, Carol Tavris, Nancy Chodorow, Harriet Lerner, Carol Gilligan, and Gail Sheehy

The work of these women deals with the development of women.
- Nancy Chodorow saw psychoanalytic theory as using gender stereotyping with male-imposed standards. In her view, it devalues feminine qualities and contributes to women's status as second-class citizens.
- Jean Baker Miller defined care taking as helping others to develop emotionally, intellectually, and socially. In her opinion, care taking is the main factor that differentiates women's development from that of men.
- Harriet Lerner's writing expressed the idea that women need to achieve a healthier balance between activities that center on others and those that center on themselves. She believes that women need to show strength, independence and assertiveness in their intimate relationships.
- Carol Tavris believes that society "pathologizes" women and judges them according to how they fit into a male world. She sees women as not really different from men but perceived as different because of the roles the male dominated society has assigned to them.
- Carol Gilligan's opinion is that women develop "in relationship" to other women and that their communication patterns are different from those of men. Women make moral judgments based on human relationships and caring, while men use justice and rights.
- In her book, Passages, Gail Sheehy wrote of the transitional, crisis periods between the stages of a woman's life that provide opportunities for growth.

Scheme developed by William Perry

Perry developed his "Scheme of Intellectual and Ethical Development" based on his studies of college students. The scheme consists of four general categories with 3 positions within each category.
- Category 1 is Dualism and is divided into Basic and Full. Students in the basic position believe authorities know the truth, but in the full position begin to realize that not all authorities know all the truth.
- Category 2 is Multiplicity and is divided into Early and Late positions. Students in this category come to believe that any opinion is as good as any other and realize that there is more than one approach to solving a problem.

- Category 3 is Relativism and is divided into Contextual and Pre-commitment. Students here realize that knowledge is subject to change and that opinions develop from values, experience and knowledge.
- Category 4 is Commitment and has three positions: Commitment, Challenges to Commitment, and Post-commitment. In these positions the student focused on moral, ethical and identity development.

Intelligence vs. emotional intelligence

A dictionary definition of intelligence is "the capacity to acquire and apply knowledge." It can also be thought of as the ability to reason, think in abstract terms and understand abstract ideas, plan, and acquire language and knowledge. Piaget's definition specified adaptive thinking or action. Intelligence is not determined solely by genetics; it also involves a person's environment, experiences, and culture. A major criticism of intelligence testing is that it is often culturally biased and measures things some people have not had the opportunity to learn. According to Daniel Goleman, emotional intelligence is self-motivation, self-awareness, empathy, social awareness, and persistence. The emotionally intelligent person also has strong interpersonal skills.

Spirituality influences on personality development

A person may see himself or herself as spiritual even though he or she does not practice any particular organized religion. According to some surveys, more than 90% of the U.S. population believes in some sort of divine power or a force greater than oneself. A person's sense of self, relationships with others, perception of society, and reaction to problems are all influenced by spirituality. Counselors find it helpful to identify a client's spirituality issues and address how they affect his situation. A counselor may find it necessary to examine his own spirituality as he learns about how such issues affect his clients. In some religions, such as Buddhism and Hinduism, the development of the person is included in the belief system.

Ego vs. id

The id is the component of the personality most concerned with primitive instincts such as hunger, sex, and aggression. The id is not concerned with the consequences of actions. The ego is the personality component responsible for balancing the id and the superego or conscience. The ego has most immediate control over behavior and is most concerned with external reality. The id and ego, along with the superego are one part of Freud's theory of personality. He believed people are born with an id, which helps the baby get it needs met. By the age of three, the child begins to develop an ego. Based on the reality principle, the ego meets the needs of the id while taking the child's reality into consideration.

Various theorists

- Adler - Individual psychology: People are essential good. Birth order determines much of a person's behavior.
- Berne - Transactional analysis: Each person has the 3 ego states of parent, adult and child.
- Ellis - Rational-emotive behavior therapy: A person's instincts are both rational and irrational, but different reactions can be taught.
- Frankl – Existential: People are good, rational, and have the freedom to choose their behavior.

- Freud – Psychoanalysis: Biological instincts and development through psychosexual stages control people.
- Glasser - Reality therapy: People have physical needs such as food and shelter plus the need to feel worthwhile and be successful.
- Jung - Analytic psychology: People strive for self-fulfillment.
- Perls - Gestalt: People are whole and complete but are affected by their environment. Learning and change result from how a person organizes experience.
- Rogers - Person-centered: People are essentially good and under the right conditions will move themselves toward self-actualization.
- Skinner - Behavioral/cognitive behavioral modification: Humans are machines that cannot make free-will decisions. Behavior is learned from a person's environment and the reinforcement he receives from others.
- Williamson - Trait-factor: The potential for both good and bad is innate.

Important terms

- Awfulizations - Looking at a situation or anticipating an event with irrational beliefs about how awful or difficult it is.
- Bibliotherapy - The use of books or other written material as part of therapy.
- Centration - In Piaget's preoperational stage, the focus on one feature of an object while ignoring the rest of the object. An example would be seeing an alligator's teeth, but not it's eyes or nostrils.
- Cephalocaudal - means from head to tail and can be used to refer to the head of a fetus developing before the legs.
- EDMR (Eye movement desensitization and reprocessing) – an information processing therapy that uses an eight phase approach to reduce the emotional stress of a distressing event or memory.
- Egocentrism - In Piaget's preoperational stage, it is a child's ability to see the world from only his own viewpoint. The child's viewpoint is current and not influenced by remembering features or details seen at an earlier time.
- Empiricists - maintain that experience is the only source of knowledge. The doctrine of empiricism was formulated by John Locke and is the forerunner of behaviorism.
- Epigenetic - states that an individual is formed by successive development of an unstructured egg rather than by the growth of a preformed entity. Kohlberg, Erikson and Maslow used epigenetic principles in developing their theories of human development.
- Epistemology - the theory of knowledge. Piaget was a genetic epistemologist. His theory was that children learn from their own actions and experiences with their peers rather than from adults.
- Ethology - the study of animals in their natural environment and makes use of Darwinian theory. Ethology research findings can be applied to humans as comparative psychology.
- Genotype - the genetic makeup of an organism.
- In vivo desensitization - a behavior therapy technique in which a person is gradually exposed to something he fears.
- Instinctual - refers to behavior that is innate rather than learned.
- Musterbations - Absolutist thinking by the client; the use of "musts, shoulds, and oughts."
- Nature vs. nurture - the question of whether a person is more influenced by nature (genetic and hereditary traits) or by nurture (learning from parents and others in his environmental and social setting.

- Organicism – the theory that the total organization of an organism is the determinant of life processes. The Gestalt psychologists, such as Kurt Goldstein, subscribe to the theory.
- Paraphrasing - The counselor rephrases what the client has said.
- Parroting - The counselor repeats what the client has said.
- Phenotype - the physical or biochemical characteristics determined by genetics and the environment of an organism.
- Plasticity - the smooth transition of a person from one stage of development to the next.
- Psychodiagnostic - a type of testing that assesses how a patient's thinking and emotions may affect his or her behavior.
- Psychometrics -the design, administration and interpretation of tests that measure intelligence, aptitude and personality characteristics.
- Psychopharmacology - the study of the effects of drugs on psychological functions.
- Resiliency - the ability of a person to deal successfully with adverse conditions and adapt effectively.
- Summarization - The counselor sums up or reviews what has happened in a session or in the course of the therapy.
- Symbolic schema - Piaget's term for language and symbolism becoming a part of play during the preoperational stage when the child is 2-7 years of age. This process allows a child to substitute one object for another such as when a box becomes a car with a paper plate for the wheel.
- Tabula rasa - John Locke's philosophy that a child is born with an unformed mind that develops through experience. This is sometimes referred to as a "blank slate."
- Umwelt, Mitwelt & Eigenwelt - In existential philosophy, the three components of the conscious experience of being alive - Umwelt is biological, Mitwelt is social, and Eigenwelt is psychological.

Social and Cultural Diversity

Cultures

A culture is made up of the customs, values, attitudes and beliefs shared by a specific group of people. Each culture differs in some way from all others.

- Universal: All human beings belong to this grouping since all have the same biology and basic biological needs.
- Ecological: This grouping includes the physical location and climate of where a person lives.
- National: This grouping is by the country in which a person lives.
- Regional: Some countries are subdivided into regions in which details of the culture differ. Such details may involve language (dialect), food, manners, and social mores.
- Racio-ethnic: This grouping is determined by biological differences including skin color and other physical features. It may be used to designate majority (superior) and minority (inferior) groups within a population.
- Ethnic: This grouping is used to designate a social subdivision of a society or larger cultural group. It may include race but more often refers to differences such as religious or ancestral.

Biological and social factors

Parents
Parenting styles can be varying degrees of authoritarian or permissive. Parents provide role models for their children and pass on to them ideas, ideals, values, patterns of behavior and even habits.

Peers
Ideas and behaviors are learned from other children. Peer pressure becomes especially important for teenagers.

Society
The neighborhood, church, and school are other sources for ideas, standards, values, beliefs, and other influences on behavior.

Media
Television can be a strong influence with its views of different lifestyles and presentations of different behavior modes.

Gender identity
Gender identity usually agrees with a person's biological gender, but in some cases does not. A person starts to identify himself or herself as male or female in infancy and the identification is reinforced during adolescence.

Prejudice and various "isms"

The *Merriam-Webster's Collegiate Dictionary* defines prejudice as a "preconceived judgment or opinion. An adverse opinion or leaning formed without just grounds or before sufficient knowledge." Such prejudices can often be described by an "ism" such as racism, sexism, ageism, and anti-Semitism.

- Racism is the belief that one race – usually one's own – is naturally superior to all others and discrimination based on that belief.
- Sexism is the belief that one sex – usually the male – is superior to the other and denial of opportunities and privileges to persons of the "lesser" sex.
- Ageism is the denial of opportunities and privileges to older persons simply because of their age.
- Anti-Semitism is prejudice or hostility toward Jews.
- Size-ism is prejudice toward people who are overweight.
- Heterosexism is the expectation that everyone is, wants to be, or should be heterosexual.
- Ablism is the denial of fair treatment to people who are disabled.
- Classism is the assumption that everyone has access to the income necessary to live above the poverty level.
- Ethnocentrism is the tendency to see the world from the viewpoint of one's own ethnic group or culture.

Cultural norms

Cultural norms are the systems of beliefs, values, and behaviors that are specific to a cultural group. They are the unwritten rules for everyday living; the standards for correct and moral behavior. Children learn the norms from their parents and other close associates. This guides what behaviors are expected of them and what is unacceptable. Not all cultural norms have positive effects.

Culturally different clients

- The uniqueness of each client must be respected. All people have worth and dignity. Factors such as race, creed, and sex must not be used to make assumptions.
- Help clients reach their self-determined goals.
- Learn about the cultures of the clients.
- Understand how the client's culture interacts with the sociopolitical environment.
- In situations where it will be helpful and not violate client confidentiality, utilize network therapy by involving members of the client's immediate family or community support groups.
- Be aware of and sensitive to the role of the family in the life of the client, especially when dealing with a culture in which strong family ties (familism), are important.
- Recognize that the counselor may need to assume various roles such as advocate, change agent, consultant, adviser, and facilitator when performing multicultural counseling.
- Be aware and work to overcome personal biases, stereotypes, and prejudices.

Acculturation, assimilation, cultural encapsulation, and worldview

Acculturation is the process by which a person of a minority group adopts the values, beliefs, and customs of the majority population. It can also refer to the adoption of values and behaviors by a primitive culture through contact with a more advanced culture. *Assimilation* is the process by which immigrants or other minority groups adopt the characteristics of the dominant culture. *Cultural encapsulation* is a form of ethnocentrism in which the person defines reality by his own set of cultural assumptions and stereotypes and is insensitive to cultural variations. *Worldview* is the way a person sees and interprets the world. Worldview can also be described as a philosophy of life made up of attitudes, values, opinions, etc.

Women vs. men in counseling

Early theories of development and personality focused primarily on males and ignored females. More recent feminist theories focus on the marginalization and cultural, political, and economic limitations that historically have been placed on women. Many differences in behavior, attitudes, and expectations between men and women grow out of cultural influences rather than stem from biology. Specific psychological problems are more common to one sex than the other. Some women experience conflict because of the multiple roles expected of them. These roles include those of wife, mother, and career woman. Men are often socialized to be competitive, active, and emotionally unexpressive while many women are socialized to be less aggressive, more emotionally expressive, more co-operative, and nurturing. Men are expected to be responsible for working and supporting a family. Women are expected to be caregivers even when they also hold a job outside the home. Many men deny problems and will not express feelings while many women find it easy to express their emotions. Many men deal with problems in a linear or sequential manner while women tend to be intuitive, global thinkers.

Culture and class

Normative behavior is the expected or conventional behavior in the culture of the client.

Structuring clearly defines the roles of the counselor and client so that there is no misunderstanding of what is expected of each.

Transference is the process by which feelings, thoughts, and wishes are shifted from the client to the counselor. Counter-transference is the shift from the counselor to the client. It is important that client and counselor each maintain his or her own cultural identity.

Personalism is the client getting to know the counselor as a person before a professional relationship is established.

Diagnosis must take the client's culture into consideration. The counselor must not judge the client's behavior on the basis of his own culture. The counselor must also be aware that standardized tests are based on cultural norms, and may not give a true evaluation of a person from another culture.

IDEA

IDEA is an acronym for the Individuals with Disabilities Education Improvement Act of 2004. The legislation provides for:
- free and appropriate public education for everyone between the ages of 6 and 21.
- the least restrictive environment possible for handicapped individuals.
- an individualized education plan (IEP) for each person.
- services for eligible students in private schools.
- funds to communities for services to eligible children between the ages of 3 and 5.

Adults over 60

Due to the American lifestyle and healthcare, life expectancy is now 83 years and more than 12% of the population is 65 or older. Characteristics of older adults include some physical impairment for the majority of people by the age of 70, and for some a degree of intellectual decline. Depression or some other mental disorder affects approximately 10% of older adults, and many do not receive treatment for the problem. Older adults must deal with a number of issues concerned with aging. Ageism can be a major problem for older adults who want to continue working since many younger persons see them as incompetent, forgetful and useless. Older adults may also be faced with the loss of family members and friends, physical problems, changes in their family situation, and retirement with more leisure time but often with less money.

ADA

The Americans with Disabilities Act of 1990 (ADA) prohibits discrimination against qualified and disabled persons by private employers, employment agencies, local and state governments, and labor unions. A disabled person is defined as someone who has an activity-limiting mental or physical impairment, who has had such an impairment, or is perceived as having such a condition. A qualified employee is one who with reasonable accommodation can perform the essential functions of the job. Employers are required to make such reasonable accommodations unless to do so would impose undue hardship on the business.

Older workers

While the mental abilities of older workers remain unimpaired, many do experience some slowing down of such tasks as assembly line work. It is important for them to feel secure in their jobs and to have a sense of affiliation. Many older workers experience more job satisfaction than their younger counterparts, but when an older person loses a job he or she is likely to remain unemployed longer than a younger person. Counselors working with older persons should assist them in the development of positive attitudes toward their worth and dignity. This is especially important when working with someone whose need for counseling derives from unemployment. Specific and immediate problems should be dealt with through problem-solving approaches. The counselor may also use a structured life review to help the client put the past and future in perspective.

Alfred Adler's concept of birth order

Alfred Adler believed that birth order creates a different psychological situation for each child and that a person's place in the family influences adult interactions and family dynamics. The oldest child tends to be achievement oriented, dependable, and hard working. He or she needs attention and fears the loss of the parents' love when a second child comes into the family. They are likely to be given responsibility and be expected to be a role model for younger siblings. The second child is competitive with his or her older sibling. A middle child may feel left out and that life is unfair, but may develop an even temperament. The youngest child is likely to be pampered and may become dependent and selfish. An only child may be overprotected and spoiled, tend to like being the center of attention, and is likely to prefer adult company.

Life cycle of a family

Culture and class influence the details of family development; however, the most common pattern in the United States consists of five stages:

1. Independence –Young adults leave home and establish themselves as emotionally and economically independent from their parents.
2. Coupling – The young adults form new long-term emotional relationships such as a legal marriage.
3. Parenting – Children add to the family and create new dynamics along with new responsibilities.
4. Launching adult children – The children grow up and start cycles of their own.
5. Retirement or senior years – Generational roles shift as the parents age.

Culture or ethnicity and alternative families

Definitions of family vary depending on the cultural and ethnic groups concerned. The definition may be quite narrow as in a "nuclear family" which includes only father, mother, and their children, or it can be rather broad as in the societies where the family is expected to be multigenerational and expanded. Child rearing practices vary widely as do the transitions from childhood to adolescence and from adolescence to adulthood, which may involve traditional transitional rituals. Counselors must be aware of the client's cultural background and its influence on his or her development.

Alternative families in the United States include any family that is not a nuclear family. Among them are: single-parent families, consisting of one parent and one or more children; remarried families, which involve stepparents and may include children from several former marriages; childless couples, and gay and lesbian families which are single-sex relationships that may or may not include children. All the alternative family patterns include multigenerational dynamics and other problems that may beset a nuclear family.

Theoretical concepts of the family systems theory

To Murray Bowen, the family is an emotional unit and multigenerational family history must be considered in family counseling. His eight theoretical concepts are:

1. Differentiation of self – the ability of a person to separate his own thinking and emotions from those of his family.
2. Nuclear family emotional system – four basic relationship patterns govern where problems develop in a family. They are marital conflict, dysfunction in one spouse, impairment of one or more children, and emotional distance.
3. Triangulation – when two people have a problem with each other, one or both of them will turn to a third person.
4. Family projection process – the primary way parents transmit their emotional problems to a child.
5. Multigenerational transmission process – small differences in differentiation levels between parent and child become marked differences after several generations in a multigenerational family.

6. Emotional cutoff – family members reduce anxiety or stress with other family members by such mechanisms as moving away, diverting the conversation, or maintaining silence.
7. Sibling position – birth order affects the characteristics of a person.
8. Societal emotional process – Each concept in Bowen's theory can be applied to such non-family groups as coworkers and social organizations.

Important terms

- *Disability* - a physical or mental limitation or incapacity.
- *Extrinsic motivation* - motivation for a behavior based on the expectation of a reward or punishment.
- *Handicap* - a physical or mental deficiency that limits or prevents an activity.
- *Intrinsic motivation* - an internal motivation for a behavior such as a hobby. The motivation is based on the enjoyment of the behavior instead of a need or an external influence.
- *QUOID* - an acronym for quiet, ugly, old, indigent, dissimilar culturally – the most-undesirable client traits.
- *YAVIS* - an acronym for young, attractive, verbal, intelligent and successful – the most desirable client traits.

Helping Relationships

Building counselor and client relationships

- A relationship built on empathy, respect, and a lack of artificiality is the basic component of a successful counselor/client relationship.
- Social influence involving competence, power, intimacy, expertise, and trustworthiness are also important.
- The counselor must possess communications skills.
- Theory helps the counselor to understand the client's problems and choose the most appropriate way of dealing with them.

Robert Carkhuff

Robert Carkhuff, a student of Carl Rogers, conducted studies which revealed that therapy does not always have a positive outcome. He has been quoted as saying that "therapy may be for better or for worse." He developed a five-point scale for measuring empathy, genuineness, concreteness and respect in counseling.

- Level 1 – The therapist is defensive and may exhibit discrepancies between voice and non-verbal cues.
- Level 2 – The therapist exhibits a professional and impersonal demeanor.
- Level 3 - The therapist is implicitly defensive or professional.
- Level 4 – The therapist demonstrates neither defensiveness nor a façade.
- Level 5 – The therapist is significantly involved in the relationship with the client, and is open to experiences and feelings both pleasant and unpleasant without being defensive or resorting to professionalism. The therapist's verbalizations match his or her inner feelings.

Additional counseling skills

Restatement is rephrasing what the client has said with emphasis on the cognitive message.

Reflection is rephrasing what the client has said with emphasis on the feeling (affective) part of the message.

Paraphrasing is using different words to restate what the client has said in order to gain better understanding of the message.

Summarizing is a concise statement of the main points or ideas discussed in a session.

Silence may mean that a person is thinking, bored, hostile, or waiting for the other person to take the lead.

Confrontation is the technique in which the counselor identifies discrepancies and presents them to the client. It may also refer to a difference in perception between the counselor and the client.

Structuring is the process of defining the nature, limits and goals of counseling as well as the roles of the client and counselor.

Five tasks of healthy individuals

Part of the helping relationship is to assist persons who need help to become healthy. Witmer and Sweeney identified five tasks associated with healthy individuals who perform them through various interactions such as at their jobs, in relationships with peers and families, achieving educational goals, or attending church. The five tasks are spirituality, or the concept of having ethical or moral guidelines; self-regulation, in which the person has a positive sense of identity and self-esteem; work, which includes physical tasks and economic stability; friendship, including those close relationships with others besides family members; and love, which involves intimacy, trust, and giving of oneself to another.

Motives for helping others through counseling

A counselor may enter into a helping relationship to assist another person with finding personal fulfillment. While this is valid, the counselor must examine his or her own motives for entering the relationship as well since the affiliation also meets some needs of the counselor. Many counselors enter into these relationships as the helper in order to feel as if they are making a contribution to society. The action of serving others shifts the focus away from oneself and current problems or distractions. Counselors may decide to become helpers, because the people they serve have similar problems to their own. Some counselors choose to work specifically with others who struggle with the same issues so as to maintain their own sense of purpose and decision. Finally, many counselors choose to be helpers to establish credibility and to support growth of their own careers and experiences.

Coping skills

Part of the helping relationship involves the counselor assisting the client to make positive decisions that will improve his or her life. Counselors teach coping skills that will help clients to make positive choices, manage conflicting situations, and solve their own problems. Some types of coping skills that may need to be developed include: expressing feelings about the situation in order to identify and cope with emotions; utilizing problem-solving skills for issues that may arise which have no immediate answers; managing stress to support wellness and avoid illness or injury; changing thinking patterns to include positive thought processes and avoid self-defeating thought patterns; rearranging how certain events are perceived so that problems are identified as challenges rather than insurmountable obstacles; and finding support through networking and reaching out to others.

Empathy

Empathy is the process of understanding another person by identifying with his or her situation rather than seeing it from an outside perspective. Empathy involves putting oneself into another's shoes and seeing the situation as the affected person does. When used in a helping relationship, the counselor can utilize empathy by trying to see the client's viewpoint and consider the situation from the client's perspective rather than the counselor's. Empathy comprises two stages. The first stage is experiencing the same emotions as the affected person. An example of this might be when a counselor cries with a client who is experiencing significant emotional pain. Stage two of empathy involves realistically looking at the situation from the other person's point of view. An example of this situation might be when a counselor listens to the client and examines his own reaction by considering how he might feel in the same situation.

Cultural awareness

Cultural awareness is an essential aspect of the helping relationship. Being aware of cultural differences between the counselor and the client can provide open lines of communication and avoid misunderstandings related to perceived ideas about another person's background. Depending on the area of work, the counselor may be a helper to various people of different backgrounds and should have a basic working knowledge of expectations associated with some cultures. When cultural differences exist between the counselor and the client, the counselor should make every effort to remove barriers that may affect communication and the overall goals of the helping relationship. Counselors may do this by learning more about their clients' backgrounds and cultures; asking clients about their expectations for the relationship; and managing feelings of fear or anxiety related to unknown cultural practices or preconceived cultural stereotypes.

Initial phase of relationship building

The stage of building the relationship between the counselor and the client consists of four phases that will ultimately support a positive connection between both parties involved.
- Phase one is the entry phase, in which the reasons for the relationship are established. This phase is the initial preparation for how the relationship will ultimately develop.
- Phase two is the clarification phase, in which the counselor and the client determine the reasons for why the relationship is occurring. During this phase, the client asks for assistance or identifies why he or she is seeking help.
- Phase three is the structure phase, in which the counselor outlines the manner in which the relationship will proceed and what tasks will need to be performed in order to meet positive outcomes.
- Phase four is the relationship phase, when the counselor and the client work to build a helping relationship, moving forward in communication to meet the established goals.

Stages of positive interaction

During the helping relationship, the counselor must maintain a positive interaction with the client in order to achieve goals and to ultimately help the client. To facilitate positive action means to maintain a working relationship between the counselor and the client, so that the client is helped by the counselor and the relationship is positive and beneficial.
- Stage one involves exploring feelings, problems, and facts and then outlining a structure for problem solving as well as setting appropriate goals.
- Stage two is consolidation, in which alternative solutions to problems are identified and the client practices coping skills and other positive interventions taught by the counselor.
- Stage three involves planning for how to respond to further problems by using the recommended techniques.
- Stage four is termination or ending of the relationship when the client has successfully shown readiness to face challenges on his or her own.

Silence

Silence is used as a listening tool to convey understanding from the counselor. Silence should be used carefully in order to imply respect and thought without making the client uncomfortable. Therapeutic listening techniques utilize silence in order to allow the client to fully explain feelings or thoughts. When a client is talking or sharing important information, the counselor uses silence to avoid interrupting which can alienate the client and prevent further sharing. A brief silence, used as a pause, may be implemented after a client finishes speaking. The counselor can use this pause to show the client that he or she is listening and thinking about what was just said. During the early stages of counseling, silence must be used carefully until the client trusts that the counselor is pondering the discussion rather than being distracted, bored, or unsure.

Transference

Transference is the act of projecting thoughts or feelings about someone or something onto a new object or person. In the counseling relationship, transference may occur when a client transfers feelings for someone or something and directs them toward the counselor. An example of this might be former feelings from a parent-child relationship. If the client had a negative relationship with his father when he was young and he participates in transference of some of those feelings toward the counselor, the client may start to see the counselor as a negative paternal figure. This may result in feelings of distrust or anger depending on the client's relationship with his father. When transference results in negative transfer of emotions, the client-counselor relationship may be strained until the client can work through transference issues and recognize the inaccuracy of this practice.

Attending

Attending is a form of behavior that demonstrates interest and respect for what another person has to say. Counselors can use attending as part of listening skills by modeling certain behaviors that tell clients they understand and are genuinely interested in them. Eye contact, posture and distance are examples of attending behaviors. Eye contact supports the development of trust by showing listening; eye contact also communicates a message of caring and attentiveness. The helper may lean toward the client or show an open and friendly appearance to convey interest. Maintaining a sense of personal space that is of appropriate distance may allow the client to feel more comfortable without having the counselor too close. Too much personal space could imply disinterest. Finally, the counselor can demonstrate attending behavior by communication such as repeating what the client says, avoiding interruptions, and maintaining an expression of empathy while the client is speaking.

Client resistance

Resistance occurs when a client declines or avoids seeking help when needed. A client may consciously resist seeking help by deciding not to follow through with helping relationships or with seeking treatment through a therapist. For some people, seeking help through counseling is a sign of weakness, and they may resist developing a new relationship for that reason wanting instead to do it all on their own. Some clients resist seeking help on an unconscious level as well. This may be demonstrated in such ways as sabotaging efforts to make it to appointments or signing up for meetings and then finding reasons not to go. Unconscious resistance may be the result of fear. A helping relationship often requires change on the part of the client and it may be difficult to give up certain habits or ways of relating to self and others.

Questions

The counselor may use some types of questions in order to draw out more information from the client, to clarify feelings or data that have been shared, and to deepen the relationship to promote further feelings of trust and support. This is especially powerful when the counselor asks open-ended questions which involve a clarification or explanatory response. Asking questions that involve yes or no answers may lead to a curt conversation with limited ability to expand toward receiving further information.

<u>Disadvantages</u>
While asking questions implies a sense of interest from the viewpoint of the counselor, asking the wrong questions, offensive questions or asking too many questions may not be beneficial for the relationship. Although the counseling relationship often involves sharing of personal information, it may be difficult for the counselor to determine when a question crosses one of these boundaries. The client may begin to feel interrogated with too many questions. Additionally, the client may believe that the counselor is trying to lead him or her to feel or respond in a specific way which may produce answers that are no longer accurate. Finally, inappropriate or too many questions may elevate the client's dependence on the counselor during a time that should be spent exploring his or her own feelings and interpreting solutions.

Reflecting

Reflecting is a method used by a counselor that validates what the client is saying and tells the client that the counselor is listening. While the counselor may not agree with everything the client says, reflection affirms the client's feelings and emotions expressed toward the situation. Reflecting content is similar to paraphrasing in which the counselor repeats some of what the client is saying in fewer words or short phrases. Reflecting feelings involves describing how the counselor sees the client responding to a situation. For example, when a client is describing his mother's death, the counselor may use reflection by saying, "you felt sad about that." Reflecting experience involves analyzing both what the client is saying and his or her body language. The counselor then gives feedback to the client based on these observations.

<u>Errors</u>
While reflecting may be used as a positive tool from the counselor as a method to validate the client's feelings and concerns, there are some points of reflection that may be inappropriate or unhelpful for the client. If the counselor reflects on everything the client says, the client may feel that he or she is receiving the standard response from a counselor rather than helpful information or suggestions. Reflection may also be inappropriate in some cultural situations such as when a client has not fully developed trust of the counselor and sees the responses as phony. Counselors who truly listen and are sincere in making the client feel understood can offer reflection in a manner that is appropriate and ultimately helpful to the situation.

Guidelines for giving advice

Giving advice is often associated as an essential component of a counselor's job; however, counselors often must allow clients to help themselves by setting goals, utilizing coping mechanisms, and making their own decisions. There are some situations when giving advice is warranted, but the counselor must follow guidelines carefully in order to avoid blame from the client if the advice was followed incorrectly, was misinterpreted, or did not work out in its intended manner. The counselor should have a thorough understanding of the information and advice he or she is imparting to the client preferably as an area of expertise. Additionally, the counselor should avoid giving advice that is seen as the only correct way of handling the situation. Instead, advice should be offered more as a suggestion. In this way, the client may be more likely to feel that there is a choice in the matter and that the counselor is not dictating an answer.

Summarizing

A counselor may listen to a client talk during a session and then summarize what he believes the client is trying to say. This helps the counselor to verify that what he is hearing is correct and has not been misinterpreted. Additionally, the client may benefit by summarizing his own feelings and information for the counselor. Summarizing helps the client to see what points he is trying to make and to outline goals for himself.

Phases of a crisis period

A crisis is a situation in which a client's goals or intentions are interrupted in such a way that they cause an emotional response from the client. The person involved may feel fear, anger, shock, or anguish about the situation. A client often goes through four phases when dealing with a crisis:
1. The crisis occurs and the client responds, often in a negative manner that involves difficult feelings.
2. The client may then become more and more frustrated or stressed, depending on the continuation of the crisis situation.
3. Some clients may ease their own tension about the situation depending on how they handle it. Some examples include instituting coping mechanisms, acting out in fear or anger, giving up, or attempting to solve the problem.
4. Finally, the situation surrounding the crisis is somehow resolved, whether it is because the client successfully dealt with the situation, or repressed or avoided managing it.

Crisis intervention

Crisis intervention involves stepping into a potentially stressful or harmful situation to avoid escalation on the part of the client. The counselor who participates in crisis intervention must first assess the situation to determine if the client is a danger to self or anyone else. The counselor must then decide what type of help is most appropriate for the current situation. For example, a critical event such as a suicide threat requires swift and successful intervention to aid the client rather than trying to arrange a support group meeting. Following determination of the appropriate response to the situation, the counselor must then act to carry out the necessary treatment or help. The counselor may help the client to become calm in order to talk about feelings or identify coping mechanisms. Through action, the counselor stabilizes the situation and brings the client down from a state of crisis into a working relationship once again.

Critical incident stress debriefing

While many patients and clients are helped with processing their feelings surrounding critical events, counselors and professionals involved in the events also need guidance and an opportunity to share their feelings. A critical incident stress debriefing is designed as a meeting for involved professionals following a stressful event or crisis. The meeting is arranged to take place as soon as possible following the event and allows counselors or other professionals who witnessed or took part in the situation a chance to express their feelings about the event. This type of debriefing is designed to avoid the buildup of stressful emotions and negative feelings, rather than trying to repress them and move on without acknowledging the incident. An example of this might be when a team meeting is called for professionals who worked with a client who committed suicide in a very public manner. The feelings, fears, and concerns of those involved can be addressed at the debriefing.

Support

Support is the provision of feelings of comfort or understanding for a person, particularly when he or she is in a position of distress. Support helps to ease the psychological burden associated with stress and confusion. This gives a person a higher sense of well-being in knowing that there is someone else who understands, someone who will listen, or someone who can help in a time of need. Support, as provided by a counselor, may come from several sources. The actual helping relationship is one source of providing support. In this case, the client speaks with or relies on the counselor to discuss emotional needs and feelings. Support may also occur if the counselor provides help to the client through physical action rather than just listening. For example, a counselor may help a client arrange his bus schedule if he has difficulty getting to meetings on time. Finally, a counselor may support a client during a crisis situation. This type of emergency support not only helps the client to manage feelings but may prevent further harm.

Grief

Grief is a type of reaction typically associated with loss that may or may not be immediately recognized after an event. It is important for the counselor to understand certain characteristics of grief in order to identify these behaviors or activities and to better help the client. Grief may have physical characteristics such as weakness, increased pain, sleep disturbances, or loss of appetite. The client may also display emotional reactions including crying, anger, withdrawal, a lack of warmth toward others, or distracted behavior. Grief may also be manifested through restless behavior, irritability, or exaggerated responses to minor incidents. The client may report feelings of guilt, intense sadness, confusion, or despair.

For the counselor helping a client who experiences grief, working through the steps of the grief process may eventually lead to acceptance of the situation. The grief process may also be applied to other situations where the client is having difficulty such as during times of personal conflict or disappointment with a situation. Initially, the client should accept that working through grief will be a process and that resolution of grief is not instantaneous. Secondly, the counselor may help the client to express feelings associated with the grief through discussing emotions. If the client has difficult memories associated with the loss, the counselor may then help him or her to work through negative feelings to prevent continued pain through memories. The client must then learn how to live in the new environment following the loss through both practical experience and management of emotions. Finally, the client must learn how to forge ahead to new things such as developing new relationships, changing careers, or taking on hobbies.

Reassurance

Reassurance is the process of affirming or encouraging another person through verbal responses. These words validate the client and provide support through such times as managing confusion, making decisions, or experiencing setbacks. Reassurance is designed to remind the client of the strategies learned for coping with challenging situations; it also reduces the client's stress level through affirmation. Some goals that a counselor may strive for by providing reassurance are to increase the client's levels of confidence, to remind the client of the work and positive outcomes that have already been discussed during the helping relationship, to decrease the client's levels of anxiety in order to mobilize him or her to action, and to remind the client of strengths and positive attributes that will instill greater self-assurance for future decisions.

Promoting relaxation

Relaxation methods are effective tools for coping with stress. Because a distressed client may be unable to focus or use positive coping mechanisms for the current situation, employing relaxation techniques is a worthwhile measure to promote better concentration, increase comfort, and reduce tension, thereby allowing the client to face the situation at hand. Relaxation techniques may be employed within the helping setting and may involve concentrating on specific muscle groups and practicing relaxing these muscles. Taking deep breaths or focusing on breathing also helps to redirect a person's way of thinking; some counselors may invite their clients to repeat short phrases while focusing on breathing. Other examples that clients may learn to promote relaxation include meditation, sitting in a specific body position, utilizing massage, or enforcing positive imagery.

Making referrals

There are times when a counselor reaches limits for how much help can be provided to a particular client. In these cases, the counselor may offer referrals to other specialists who can provide sufficient help for client's needs that are beyond the scope of care of the counselor. When making a referral, the counselor should be aware of what community resources are available to assist the client, determine if the client is ready to receive a referral, and explain to the client why the referral is necessary. If possible, the counselor may need to contact the referral agency or person to notify them of the impending referral and to provide background information about the client. In many situations, the client must sign a release form for the cooperating agencies to share information before discussing his or her situation.

Goals

Goals are powerful tools used to measure a client's progress through therapy and to guide both the counselor and the client toward potential positive outcomes. Goals should be carefully considered to ensure they are attainable and reasonable, in order to promote success for the client. Setting goals that are too far out of reach may only promote a sense of failure for the client who is unable to achieve the desired outcomes. The client should take part in setting the goals to ensure they are outcomes that he or she wants to work toward; the goals should also be specific enough to be measurable. Using general terms may be helpful initially to help the client to identify goals, but specific terms are measurable and help the client to understand when the goals have been reached. For example, stating, "I will develop better self-esteem" is not as easy to recognize when achieved as stating "I will list four positive attributes about myself whenever I feel down."

Flaws in goal setting
Goals are helpful to guide clients to achieve outcomes and to change their thoughts and behaviors. However, there are some flaws associated with goal setting that may render the stated objectives as useless. Not setting goals to begin with whether because of distraction, disinterest, or an inability to understand personal desires may cause the helping relationship to flounder without any direction. Setting too many goals at once may also be unreasonable to expect the client to achieve. Too many goals could cause feelings of stress or pressure for the client, or may be confusing regarding which particular goal he or she is trying to meet at any given time. Finally, some goals are unclear and should be specific for the client's situation. The client can create a goal that is applicable, achievable, and that can be determined clearly to have been met or not.

Rational problem solving process

The rational problem solving process is simply a normal method of approaching a problem and devising a solution. The client first identifies a problem and then sets a goal for solving it. Together with the counselor, the client can determine if any alternatives exist that might reveal other obvious solutions. The client should also consider the effects of not solving the problem as well as possible consequences of different solutions. Once a list of solutions has been made, the client then decides on the best choice for the situation and then implements it. Finally, the client evaluates the effectiveness of the solution and determines whether it may be used to solve other similar problems.

Intuitive problem solving

Many clients use intuitive problem solving as a method of finding solutions for problems by using their own consciences, feelings, or intuitions. These decisions may prove to be appropriate and useful, but in some situations making decisions based on feeling can lead to disaster. For example, a client may feel good about choosing to spend time with a new friend based on a hunch that the other person is kind, likeable, moral, or has whatever qualities the client is looking for. Alternatively, making a major purchase such as a home or a car when only based on a hunch may be illogical without first researching the background of the purchase or analyzing financial matters. The counselor may help the client with intuitive problem solving by guiding them about what decisions may be made based on intuition and which ones require further thought and practical wisdom.

Modeling

Modeling involves demonstrating an appropriate behavior for the purpose of teaching another person. Modeling may be used for clients as a visual reminder of proper actions or responses to certain situations. A counselor may use modeling through verbal or body language toward the client and others. A counselor may also use modeling through role-playing when the client is faced with some situations that do not occur during the helping session. For example, a client who is struggling to end a dating relationship may engage in role-playing with the counselor who then models the appropriate behavior and responses to handling this situation.

Reinforcement when analyzing behavior

Reinforcement may be used to reward or support appropriate behavior as a method of teaching the client to continue making positive behavior choices. Reinforcement from the counselor may be used to encourage the client to continue discussion along a particular line of thought or to expand on feelings; it may help a client who is trying to change problem behaviors, such as negative or destructive habits that can be potentially damaging to a client's mental or physical health. A counselor may also use reinforcement to strengthen the process of forming new habits. For instance, a client may desire to stop using self-defeating phrases, and reinforcement provides a positive reminder.

Extinguishing

A person may extinguish a behavior or set of behaviors simply by discontinuing it. If a client has an addiction to shopping or spending money, extinguishing the addiction involves stopping the behavior. This is easier said than done in most situations although the rewards potentially involve positive outcomes when problem behaviors are extinguished. Extinguishing is performed by recognizing what behaviors need to be stopped and then ending the behaviors often through a plan of action for change. Additionally, the counselor may assist the client by coming up with alternative actions that reinforce the opposite of the behavior in order to support the original extinguishing decision.

Contract

A contract is a type of agreement drawn up between two people that is done to promote action and possible reward. A counselor may use a contract with a client who wants to change a behavior; for example, a client may express frustration about making rash decisions that significantly affect his personal life. As part of a contract, a counselor may require that the client agree to consult with a family member or professional before making any decisions that will affect his finances, family life, or health. The contract is drawn up with specific terms and signed by the client. Characteristics of a contract include feasibility—the contract should be written in such a way that the client can actually perform the terms. A contract should also be specific leaving little room for interpretation. Finally, the contract should be retractable, in that the client can decide that he or she does not want to perform the terms.

In-life desensitization

In-life desensitization is performed as a process to reduce a fearful situation and replace negative feelings with positive ones. For example, a client who is afraid of speaking to others in social situations may undergo in-life desensitization with the help of a counselor in order to overcome this fear and replace it with confidence. The counselor may initially expose the client to small social situations in which he or she must make conversation. As the client's confidence improves through successful small talk, the situations become more and more challenging. During the desensitization process, the counselor provides helpful feedback, reinforcement, and support to increase the client's confidence and self-esteem.

Symptoms of burnout

Counselors who work with clients as part of helping relationships may need to recognize that not every client will respond completely to suggestions and work. In particularly trying situations or those that are ongoing with few results, the counselor may begin to experience burnout in which case a re-evaluation of the necessity of the relationship is required. The counselor may experience symptoms such as fatigue, lethargy, headaches, back pain, difficulties with concentration, changes in sleep patterns, decreased appetite, depression, an overall negative attitude, increased symptoms of illness, or feelings of hopelessness.

Warning signs to consider before expressing personal feelings

A counselor may use self-disclosure to encourage a client to verbalize more of his or her own feelings or to reinforce some of the expressions a client has already manifested. Expressing personal feelings should be done carefully to avoid giving too much information or crossing the boundaries of the professional relationship. Additionally, the counselor should avoid expressing personal feelings when the client shows certain warning signs which could lead to further negative behavior, a breakdown in communication, or even legal action against the counselor. Warning signs to look for include a client with a volatile temper or explosive personality, a client who shows discomfort with the expression of feelings, a client who has a history of significant emotional reactions as a response to perceived feelings of rejection, or situations in which the counselor does not have control over his or her own emotions.

Support system

A support system is an essential component in a client's healing process. A support system may consist of individuals or groups of people who are available to provide support and encouragement to the client which may continue after the helping relationship has been discontinued. Establishing a support system involves assessing for persons who may already be involved in the client's life and who can provide support, determining the client's expectations for the roles members of the support system will play, gathering names of potential individuals or groups who may be available to serve as support members, and determining if those persons are realistic candidates. Finally, the counselor may help the client to make steps to develop new relationships and increase the network of contacts of those who will act in a supportive manner.

Characteristics of willingness to change

Counselors may work with some clients for great lengths of time only to discover that the relationship is not facilitating any change. Some clients are habitual seekers of help for emotional issues. Other clients make efforts at change but give up due to discouragement. Some people seek only the relationship from the counselor without truly wanting to change. Clients who actively participate in the relationship by attending meetings, deciding on goals, and expressing feelings are more likely to want to change. Clients who recognize their own responsibilities to take steps for change are also typically more compliant. Finally, clients who show rational thinking and are able to honestly express their emotions may be more receptive to the work involved with change.

Group work

While helping often takes place in one-to-one relationships, group work can also be an effective tool for change. Helping groups typically require the work of more than one counselor to act as a leader and to keep the group focused. There are various types of groups that serve as part of helping relationships. These groups may meet based on varying characteristics, such as client needs or demographic information. Some examples include groups of young men or women; groups of families; groups that share common health concerns, such as depression or arthritis; and groups of people who have similar struggles, such as overeating, or having some types of addictions.

Spirituality

Since spirituality may play a major role in a client's background, ignoring this concept in the counseling relationship is typically not a wise decision. The counselor must recognize the importance of spirituality within the client's life whether or not he or she agrees with the client's particular belief system. In some counseling situations, the helper may offer services designed to help some clients seek deeper meaning in their faith. Depending on the client's beliefs, examining how spirituality affects his or her own self-image, emotions, and feelings can lead the client to experience a deeper sense of peace or understanding of self.

Maslow's hierarchy of needs

Maslow's hierarchy of needs describes a theory of basic needs for each person set up in the style of a pyramid. In order to move upward, a person's basic needs must first be met. The lowest portion of the pyramid is physiological needs, including needs for food, sleep, and clothing. Unless these basic needs are met, trying to meet other needs, such as a sense of belonging, is irrelevant. The next level is safety, in which a person must feel secure psychologically; this may involve feelings of security for the future or freedom from uncertainty. Love and belonging is the next level, which involves feelings of being accepted and cared for by others and establishing rewarding relationships. Self-esteem makes up the next level, in which a person feels good about himself and his choices. Finally, self-actualization crowns the top of the pyramid, which involves a secure individual allowing himself to be challenged in new ways and finding satisfaction in new pursuits.

Wellness

The World Health Organization (WHO) defines wellness as a state of physical, social, spiritual, and mental well-being. A person does not merely reach a state of wellness at which to arrive and stay there. Rather, wellness is more of a process of regular decision-making that promotes well-being. A counselor works with a client to promote wellness by helping him or her learn how to make positive decisions that will reinforce well-being in these areas. For example, a counselor in a helping situation may help a client develop a plan for exercise to experience greater physical well-being and may counsel the client on how to make positive affirmations to promote emotional well-being. Much of the work of the helping relationship may serve to support the concept of wellness.

Finding happiness

Many people seek help through counseling in order to find happiness which is actually a vague term that implies different meanings for different people. Happiness is subjective well-being in that it is defined by the person seeking it. When reached, continued decisions can be made to maintain such a state. A counselor can recognize that happiness as a goal may not be specific enough to attain. Rather, the client may have more success in seeking this type of well-being by setting specific parameters for activities that lead to positive feelings or meet the client's needs. For example, a client who wants to be happy in a job may set smaller goals such as being thankful for each paycheck received or attempting to form new relationships with co-workers.

Structured and unstructured helping relationships

Helping relationships may occur as structured, regular meetings or as unstructured activities. Each type is designed to provide help to clients; however, there may be some types of relationships that are more successful in actually helping than others. Structured relationships are set up with the goal of providing help. Examples of structured helpers include counselors, therapists, social workers, teachers, mental health professionals, or nurses. Unstructured helping situations may also provide help in a more relaxed setting, but this may be less beneficial. Examples of unstructured helping scenarios include friendships, relationships with family members, church services, self-help books, or one-time seminars designed to promote good feelings.

Models of a helper

A helper may establish a role to facilitate growth from the client following certain types of patterns that are more common approaches. The behavioral engineer model involves the counselor helping the client to change behavior and responses for the surrounding environment. For example, the counselor may help the client to come up with positive thoughts as reactions to perceived negative interactions from others. In the priest model, the counselor may assist the client through spiritual activities that provide support. For example, a counselor may pray with a client or read through sacred texts to look for meaning that will apply to the client's situation. The medical approach uses diagnosis to describe the client's particular situation and to provide treatment. In this model, the therapist may diagnose a client with a type of mental illness and then work on activities that provide healing and management of the disease.

Congruence

Congruence in the helping relationship describes the counselor's ability to maintain agreement between words and actions. If a counselor expresses empathy or caring toward a client, he or she must maintain congruence by acting in an empathic or caring manner as well. A counselor who is congruent in behavior is more trustworthy in the eyes of the client because the actions back up the words. A counselor who does not establish congruence between behavior and words may be less likely to form a healthy helping relationship because a client may perceive conflicting messages. An example of not displaying congruence might be when a counselor tells a client that he is important and that what he has to say deserves the same respect as everyone else but then appears distracted or bored while the client is speaking.

Touch

Touch can be a powerful tool used by therapists to convey warmth, empathy, and acceptance toward clients. Some clients respond well to touch as a source of comfort. Among relationships that are close, touch promotes bonding as well as approval. Touch may be as simple as a pat on the back, a hand on the shoulder, or a hug. Alternatively, touch may be controversial when used in some situations. There are some people who are averse to touch from professionals, others whom they do not know very well, or even their own families. Some cultures find touching between different sexes or age groups to be quite offensive, and the counselor could risk alienating the client. Touch may also be a means for potential legal action if the client misinterprets the situation.

Imagery

Imagery is the act of using mental pictures or scenarios as a tool to solve problems. A client may use imagery by focusing on positive states of what he wants to occur. Counselors who use imagery approach this method as a way of utilizing the client's own inner power to solve problems. For example, a client who complains of feeling hopeless about not finding a job can use imagery to imagine looking for a job, asking for an interview, preparing answers to questions, and handing out his resume. Through the process of imagery, the client may not find a job immediately. The method of imagining the process may help him to visualize aspects of the scenario that he may not have considered before thus potentially promoting his success.

External stress, internal distress, and transitional state

Situations that cause crisis for clients may occur in a variety of forms and may be categorized according to the cause of the stress. Some conditions are beyond the client's control while other situations occur as a result of choices. External stress factors are those that can cause a crisis and are beyond the power of the client to control. Examples of external factors are crimes committed against the client, unemployment, natural disasters, illness, loss and bereavement. Internal distress often occurs as a result of external factors, and this may be based on how the client responds to stress or crisis. Examples of internal distress include feelings of depression, hopelessness, or suicidal ideation. Transitional states may cause stress for a client and may or may not be related to personal choice. Examples of these are job changes, divorce, relocation, or having a baby.

Group Work

Classification of groups designed by Gerald Caplan

Caplan divided counseling groups into three types – primary or guidance, secondary or counseling, and tertiary or therapy. Primary groups address living a healthy lifestyle and the reduction of problems. Secondary groups deal with problems that are not severe. Tertiary groups deal with problems that are long-standing, pathological, and may require a personality change or rehabilitation. Participants in tertiary groups may also be involved in individual counseling.

Group dynamics and cohesion

The dynamics of the group is the way the participants interact with each other and with the counselor or leader. The goals of the group, the content of the discussion, the process of the session, and the development of trust among the group members all contribute to the dynamics. Cohesion is the development of a sense of belonging and inclusion among the members. This usually results from self-disclosure by the members along with the lowering of defenses and commitments to each other. The group develops cohesion more quickly when the members have some characteristics in common.

Types of groups and their primary goals

The following are types of groups and their primary goals:
- Guidance –educational and may be led by someone without formal psychological training. These groups are often used by schools and other youth organizations in an effort to prevent behaviors such as teen pregnancy or drinking. "Affective education group" or "psychological education group" are other names for this type.
- Counseling – led by a trained counselor, this type of group has the goals of preventing problems while helping participants to grow and develop.
- Psychotherapy – led by a professional with advanced training, these groups address severe problems involving remediation and treatment.
- Psychoeducation – used by social services, mental health agencies, and universities, these groups provide education and skill building for growth and the prevention, management, and remediation of problems.
- Structured – deals with a single problem such as anger management or drinking.
- Self-help – leader is not usually a professionally trained counselor; these groups help participants deal with such stress-inducing issues as weight control.
- T-group (training group) – these groups are often used to help employees build and improve interpersonal skills.

Leadership styles

Three main styles of leadership have been identified.
- *Autocratic* or authoritarian leaders may accomplish goals quickly but may generate resentment because of their exercise of control and power.
- *Democratic* leadership is inclusive of all members of the group, allowing all to contribute, and helping to generate feelings of belonging. However, this style is not the best for all situations.
- Leaders who practice *laissez faire* set few rules or structures and allow members to do as they wish. This style can be quite effective with groups committed to a common goal such as a workgroup.

Roles of group members

Each member of a group assumes a role. Some roles advance the work of the group, some promote social interaction, but others hinder the functioning of the group. Among the work-related roles are the information seeker, the opinion-seeker, the opinion giver, the energizer, the initiator, and the elaborator. Social roles include the encourager, the compromiser, the standard setter, and the follower. Hindering roles include the aggressor, the blocker, the recognition seeker, the dominator, and the special interest pleader.

Core skills needed by group counselors

According to the Association for Specialists in Group Work, counselors must be able to:
- manage the group by opening and closing sessions
- keep the session on track
- connect common issues
- insure that each member works on his or her issue
- confront the behavior of members
- stop unproductive behavior
- encourage participation by all members
- be supportive of the group members
- be attentive to and acknowledge the behavior of each member.
- give and receive feedback
- clarify and summarize statements
- practice self-disclosure
- ask questions including open-ended ones
- provide empathy
- observe and identify group process events
- assist members in integrating and applying experience and learning
- listen actively and set goals.
- have an understanding of counseling theories and group dynamics
- adhere to the ethical and professional standards of group practice

Positive aspects of working with a co-leader

Having more than one leader for a group gives the members a wider range of experiences and insights especially when the leaders are of different genders, races, cultural backgrounds, etc. Co-leaders facilitate interaction within the group, provide a safer environment, reduce burnout, and insure that the group can continue when one leader must be absent. For the co-leadership to be successful, the leaders must be cohesive, share theoretical orientations, trust each other's competence, and not indulge in behavior that might fragment the group. While all co-leaders benefit from the situation through regular exchanges of information, feedback and the shared responsibility, such an arrangement is especially helpful for new leaders when they are teamed with more experienced persons.

Stages of a group

Groups develop through stages as the participants get acquainted and learn to work together. *Formation or Trust/Orientation* is the period when each member decides if he or she can fit into the group, if he or she can be comfortable with the leader and the other members, and to what extent he or she will participate. *Work/Productivity or Transition* is the stage during which the group members show caring and empathy for each other, give feedback, encourage each other, and confront each other when needed. Participants began to see how they can accomplish their goals and positive changes take place. *Closure or Consolidation and Termination* is the period during which the group reviews what has been accomplished and if some goals were not met. The leader encourages members to continue to use the skills they have gained through the group.

Purpose of family counseling

Family counseling is a type of group counseling. The group involved may be a single family or consist of members from several families. The goal of these groups is to identify problems in the family and resolve the problems by improving communications, changing behaviors and creating different interaction patterns. The counselor may work with parents and children together or in group couples counseling with just the adult couples. In group couples counseling, the group may deal with problems between the couple or problems the couple has with their children.

Psychoanalytic theory and group work

Since psychoanalytic counseling involves dealing with today's problems by exposing and understanding the past, such a group will concentrate on family history, early relationships, and suppressed emotions. These factors will be discussed, analyzed, and interpreted. Such open handling of personal information and the exposure of emotions may be unpleasant or even impossible for persons from cultures that put a high value on reticence and reserve. Persons from some cultures will want the counselor to be authoritarian and may not like the long-term commitment usually required by psychoanalysis.

Gestalt theory and group work

Gestalt therapy is based on the idea that mature people determine their own path in life and accept responsibility for their decisions and actions. Gestalt counseling groups have the goal of helping group members become more aware of their thoughts and emotions in present time so that they may translate that awareness into changes toward maturity. Techniques such as guided fantasy, role-playing, and confrontation are used. In a multicultural group, techniques can be chosen and adapted to accommodate the different cultural backgrounds of the group members.

Person-centered theory and group work

The goals of a person-centered group are to help the members better understand themselves and to bring each one closer to self-actualization. The counselor will establish an atmosphere that encourages the members to be open and to express their opinions and emotions as they work toward changing their self-concept. There will be few structured techniques, and the counselor will practice active listening and reflection. In such a group multicultural values will be respected, but some clients may prefer a more structured and less open approach.

Behavioral counseling groups

The counselor for a behavioral group is a teacher and expert. The goal of the group is to modify problem behaviors and improve each member's coping skills. Techniques may include such activities as contracts, reinforcement, modeling and analysis of the learning process and the situations that produce the troublesome behaviors. Behavioral counseling may appeal to multicultural clients because the emphasis is not on expressing emotion, goals are specific, and the duration of the counseling is short-term. One consideration for clients from some cultures is fitting the changed behaviors into their cultural context.

Transactional analysis theory and group work

The counselor in a transactional analysis group serves as a teacher. The goal of the group is to change the life pattern of each member through increasing self-awareness and awareness of others, the understanding of past life scripts and the games in one's life, and freeing oneself from them. The counselor may use such techniques as role-playing, contracts, interrogation, and confrontation. Transactional analysis is appropriate for clients from many different cultures since its emphasis on the past can allow for cultural values.

Reality theory and group work

In a reality counseling group, the counselor guides the members as they examine their behavior, develop plans for change, and carry out their plans. He or she must tailor activities and goals so that the individual concerns of the members are considered. The aim of the therapy is for the group members to improve their life situation through gaining better control of and more responsibility for their behavior. People from cultures that do not like to reveal emotions may find this type of group a good fit.

Rational emotive behavior counseling groups

The counselor for a rational emotive behavior group must balance process and outcome oriented activities. Among the techniques he or she may use are role-playing, self-discipline exercises, homework, and modeling. The goals of a group involved in this type of cognitive therapy include changes in thought and behavior patterns that promote greater self-acceptance and eliminating self-defeating behaviors and illogical thinking. The counseling is based more on thought and action instead of on the expression of emotions. This type of group appeals to clients from cultures that place a high value on strong leaders as well as those that discourage the display of emotion.

Structured vs. unstructured group sessions

Some structure is required at the start of any group in order to take care of the necessary chores of getting the group organized, setting goals, etc. The leader of an unstructured group will take a laissez faire approach to the later sessions and there will be few rules and guidelines for how the sessions will progress. A structured group will have a leader who is either authoritarian or democratic. Group activities will be planned and techniques chosen to follow the particular type of counseling used.

Adlerian theory and group work

Adlerian theory is based on the ideas that human behavior is purposeful and goal-oriented and that feelings of inferiority and a lack of social connectedness create emotional problems. In a group using Adlerian theory, the counselor guides the group members as they examine their early history, the roles of their families in their lives, their birth order, their lifestyles, and their belief systems. The group activities help the members to become aware of their strengths, improve their self-esteem, and accept responsibility for their behavior. This type of counseling may not be the best fit for clients from cultures that discourage sharing personal information.

Important terms

- *Group work grid* – developed by R. K. Coyne – a model that shows four levels of intervention (individual, interpersonal, organization, and community population).
- *Horizontal interventions* - the counselor works with the group as a whole.
- *Karpman's drama triangle* – in transactional analysis, a psychological and social model of interactions that shows the roles of victim, persecutor, and rescuer.
- *Risky shift phenomenon* – a person is likely to make a riskier decision as part of a group than he or she would alone.
- *Self-help group* – a group of people who share a common problem such as weight control or drinking where members share knowledge and encourage each other.
- *Sociometry* – a method developed by Jacob Moreno for measuring social relationships in groups.
- *T-group* – training group that can be for improving human relations such as a sensitivity training group.
- *Vertical intervention* - the counselor works with individuals within the group.

Career Development

History of career development

Before 1900, there was little literature or other information available to young people about careers and vocational choices. Jessie B. Davis, a school guidance counselor in Detroit between 1898 and 1907, is credited with starting the first systematic school guidance program. In 1908, Frank Parsons, who is known as the "Father of Vocational Guidance," established the Boston Vocational Bureau. In 1913, the National Vocational Guidance Association was formed. The progressive education movement during the 1920s and 1930s contributed to the growth of school counseling which included vocational guidance. Testing to determine the interests and aptitudes of students grew out of the tests used by the military during the 1940s. Further growth in vocational guidance was encouraged by the space race of the 1950s and 1960s. In 1985, the National Vocational Guidance Association became part of the American Counseling Association as the National Career Development Association. In addition to Parsons and Davis, important people in the field include Eli Ginzberg, Sol Ginsburg, Sidney Axelrad, John Herma, Donald Super, John Holland, Linda Gottfredson, and John Krumboltz.

Developmental approach
The developmental approach is based on the theory that career development occurs through stages over a period of time. The approach is holistic and recognizes the interaction of the person with his or her environment. Vocation guidance in this mode helps to educate the student and increase skills and competence. Self-concept, need, and life-span changes are part of the process.

Actuarial approach
The actuarial or trait-based approach to vocational guidance was developed by Frank Parsons. This approach assumes people are rational and capable of making intelligent vocational decisions when they are aware of which careers are best suited to their interests and aptitudes. Psychometric testing is used to discover the traits that determine in which employment fields a person is likely to succeed. The *Minnesota Occupational Rating Scales* is one such test and was used by Edmund G. Williamson to expand Parson's model.

Decision approach
Proponents of this approach think that vocational education should be an integral part of all students' education. H. B. Gelatt identified two types of decisions: terminal or final decisions and investigatory decisions. A person makes investigatory decisions with added information until he or she reaches a terminal decision. Gelatt devised a model that illustrates the decision-making process and shows information divided into predictive, value, and decision systems.

Donald Super's vocational development stages and vocational development tasks

The stages are:
- Growth – birth to 14 or 15 – self-concept, attitudes, interests, and needs develop, child develops a general understanding of the world of work.
- Exploratory – 15 to 24 – person explores choices through classes, work, and hobbies, makes tentative choice and develops related skills.
- Establishment – 25 to 44 – builds skills and stabilizes in a work situation.

- Maintenance – 45 to 64 – adjustments are made to improve job situation.
- Decline – 65+ person prepares for retirement, retires.

The development tasks are:
- Crystallization – 14 to 18 –develops and plans a possible occupational goal.
- Specification – 18 to 21 – chooses a specific vocation.
- Implementation – 21 to 24 – completes training and enters the job market.
- Stabilization – 24 to 35 – works at chosen career.
- Consolidation – 35+ - establishes self in career. According to Super these tasks can be repeated as a person adapts to changes in himself or herself or the work environment changes. They are also somewhat outdated since they were based on middle class white males with college educations during the 1950s and 1960s.

Super's Archway Model, Life Career Rainbow, and Career Pattern Study

The Archway Model delineates the changing diversity of life roles a person experiences over his or her life span and illustrates how biographical, psychological, and socioeconomic elements influence the development of a career. The name for the model came from the fact that it was modeled on the doorway of his favorite Cambridge college. The Life Career Rainbow is a graphic illustration in which each colored band represents a life role and numbers around the outer edge indicate age. The amount of time a person typically spends in each role is indicated by dots of varying sizes within the bands. The Rainbow can be used to help a person find a balance of work and life that is suited to himself or herself. The Career Pattern Study followed the vocational behavior of a group from the ninth grade to thirty years of age. The study revealed that a person who was mature and an achiever while in high school would likely be a successful young adult.

Life roles defined by Donald Super

Super identified eight life roles that describe the ways people spend time and energy:
- The *child* is the time spent relating to parents and lasts throughout the life of the parents.
- The *student* is time spent in education, starts in early childhood and may last into older adulthood.
- The *leisurite* is Super's coined word for time spent in leisure activities.
- The *citizen* is time spent volunteering or in other work for the community.
- The *worker* is the time one spends working for pay.
- The *parent* is time spent caring for a child; lasts throughout the child's dependent years and in many cases well beyond.
- The *spouse* is the time spent in a committed relationship.
- The *homemaker* is the time spent in maintaining a home – housework, yard work, repairs, shopping, etc.

John Holland's theory and hexagon

Holland's hexagon is a graphic illustration of the correlation between his six personality types and six occupational environments or categories that he called themes. The themes are positioned on the hexagon so that those with the most similarity are closest together and those with the most differences farther apart. A person's scores on the *Vocational Preference Inventory* and the *Self-Directed Search* determine which work environment is the best fit for his or her personality.

Holland believed that most people are not clearly of a single personality type, but will have characteristics from two or three types.

John Holland's modal personality types

Using an actuarial approach, Holland developed a theory that the choice of career is an outgrowth of personality that is influenced by the stereotypes people hold of different types of employment. He identified six modal personal orientations that he believed all people have in varying degrees.

- The *realistic* personality type is active and aggressive, prefers explicit tasks, and may not relate very well to others. Career choices would be mechanical or technical work.
- The *investigative* personality is intellectual, prefers creative activities, and may have poor social skills. Typical career choices would be in the sciences or the computer field.
- *Artistic* personalities are imaginative and expressive, with a preference for activities that are not rigidly ordered or systematic. Typical career choices would be something in the arts or some other creative field.
- *Social* personality types enjoy interaction with others and imparting information and have little interest in tools or mechanical devices. Teaching or counseling would be typical careers for them.
- *Enterprising* people are extroverted leaders who are willing to take chances and have little use for abstract thinking. Politics and business are possible careers.
- *Conventional* personality types are practical with a dislike for unorganized or ambiguous activities. Possible careers include office work and accounting.

John Krumboltz's Learning Theory of Career Counseling (LTCC)

Influenced by Bandura, Krumboltz identified four important factors in career related decision making.

- *Genetic endowments and special abilities* that could limit a person's occupational choices.
- *Environmental conditions and events* in a person's life such as education, activities, economic conditions and personal resources.
- *Instrumental and associative learning* about careers including the reactions and reinforcement from others.
- *Task approach skills* which include problem-solving ability, working and thinking patterns, and emotions. He saw learning as a life-long process and thought a person's beliefs could be changed through career counseling. He also believed that chance events could influence a person's career development. In working with clients he made use of the *Career Beliefs Inventory.*

Circumscription and Compromise theory of career development

Developed in the 1980s by Linda Gottfredson, the circumscription and compromise theory explains how vocational choice develops in children and teenagers. Vocational choices are narrowed (circumscribed) and inappropriate choices discarded (compromise) as the person develops and learns about career possibilities. Gottfredson described four stages of development.

1. *Orientation to size and power* is the period from ages 3-5.
2. *Orientation to sex roles* is the years from ages 6-8 when the child learns that many vocations are considered appropriate for one sex or the either.

3. *Orientation to social valuation* occurs from ages 9-13 during which time the child learns that society, including their peers and family, place values on particular occupations.
4. *Orientation to internal unique self* begins at about the age of 14 as the child's interests and ambitions influence his or her vocational choice. A person's self-concept determines a range of acceptable choices.

Roe's career development theory

Anne Roe's theory of career development was a needs approach in which genetics, childhood experiences, and the relationship with parents were contributing factors to the choice of a career. She believed that the parenting style would determine whether or not a person would be people-oriented. She also subscribed to Maslow's theory that careers are chosen to meet needs; a people-oriented person chooses a career that involves working with people while a non-people-oriented person will chose a career with less involvement with others. Roe pioneered the use of a two-dimensional occupational classification using fields and levels. The eight occupational fields she identified are: service, business contact, organization or managerial, technology, outdoor, science, general cultural, and arts and entertainment. Technology, outdoor, and science are non-person oriented careers. She also identified six levels of occupational skill: high level professional and managerial or p&m1; regular level professional and managerial or p&m2; semi-professional and managerial or semi-professional and small business; skilled, semi-skilled; and unskilled.

Theory of Ginzberg, Ginsburg, Axelrad and Herma

As developmentalists, Ginzberg, Ginsburg, Axelrad and Herma accepted the idea that occupational choice can be divided into three periods:
- *Fantasy* – up to the age of 11, during which period the child may use any occupation in play.
- *Tentative* – age 11-17, during which time the child examines careers in light of interests and values and his or her own capabilities.
- *Realistic* –age 17 to young adulthood, when the person makes a choice. The third period is subdivided into three stages:
  - o *Exploration* – during which the person limits vocational choices to personal interests and abilities.
  - o *Crystallization* – during which a definite choice is made.
  - o *Specification* – during which the person is educated for his or her choice of vocation. This theory was based on a study of a small group of young men from the middle-class in the 1950s and rather ignored the fact that gender, race and social standing were important factors in occupation choice at that time.

Cognitive information processing (CIP) career development theory

In 2001, the CIP career development theory was formulated by Sampson, Reardon, Peterson and Lenz. It is a method of dealing with career problems by using a series of sequential steps.
- Step 1 – communication, which identifies the person's career needs.
- Step 2 – analysis – identifies the components of the problem and sets up a conceptual framework.
- Step 3 – synthesis, which defines possible actions.

- Step 4 – valuing, which prioritizes the possibilities according to their likelihood of success.
- Step 5 – execution, in which the person implements the solution. Career counseling using this theory has the goal of identifying the needs of the client and helping him or her gain the skill and knowledge that will fulfill the needs.

Tiedeman and Miller-Tiedeman's decision-making model

Tiedeman & O'Hara saw career development as parallel to Erikson's psychosocial stages and believed that career decisions were made as ego related problems were solved. They believed that career decisions were related to other decisions one made about other areas of one's life and that each person can choose his or her career. They saw career decisions as a two-phase continuing process and identified the phases as *anticipation/preoccupation,* during which a person imagines himself working at a particular job and *implementation/adjustment*, when the person actually works at that job. Tiedeman and Miller-Tiedeman emphasized the key role an individual plays in making career decisions.

Constructivism and contextualism approaches to career development

Both constructivism and contextualism are postmodern approaches to career development. The main idea of constructivism is that each person builds his or her own reality. The counselor helps the clients to understand the meaning of their life stories and the life roles each plays as well as the relationship between those roles and their values and beliefs. Contextualism acknowledges a close relationship between a person's inner forces and that person's environment. Contextualism counselors believe each client's reality is drawn from his or her perception of an event and that each client has a personal way of organizing information. In counseling, the clients are encouraged to draw meaning from a situation and to consider the situation in its entirety rather than giving attention to a detail of the situation. Clients are also encouraged to regard their behavior from a cognitive and social context viewpoint.

Social Cognitive Theory of career development

Using concepts from Bandura's social learning theory, the social cognitive theory is based on self-efficacy. Self-efficacy is a person's belief or knowledge about what he or she is able to do and is a critical factor in choosing a career. Another key factor is personal agency, which is the person's ability to actually accomplish a goal. Performance, education, social environment and physical condition can strengthen a person's self-efficacy. Career counseling would be aimed toward increasing the client's self-efficacy.

Sociological model of career development

The sociological model of career development can also be called a situational model. This approach posits that a person chooses a career because of sociological reasons. In order to choose an occupation, the person must have some knowledge about that occupation. A person's choice is also influenced by such factors as ethnicity and cultural background, which can lead a person to choose a certain type of work or keep him from doing so. Other factors that may influence career decisions include the availability of jobs locally, the requirement for relocation, risks involved in the work, necessary education or training and its availability, and the image of workers in a particular field.

Career development theory of John Crites

Crites formulated his theory of career counseling after reviewing and writing about the major approaches to the subject. His theory is a comprehensive synthesis of those approaches plus some of his own ideas. He dealt with issues of diagnosis, the counseling process, and outcomes. His work reflects the influence of trait-and-factor and developmental career counseling. He believes that the diagnosis determines the outcome of the counseling. He identified three types of diagnosis: differential, which determines what the problem is; dynamic, which identifies the reasons for the problem; and decisional, which establishes how the problem is dealt with. He developed, used, and recommended that other counselors use the *Career Maturity Inventory.*

Limitations of career theories

Although career theories are still evolving and new ones are being developed, many of the classic theories grew out of studies done in the 1950s and 1960s. The subjects of the studies were usually young, middle-class white males, either college-bound, in college, or with college educations. Little work was done with females, with persons of color, or with people from the lower socioeconomic levels, although some attempts were made to apply the theories to these groups. The growing employment of women and socioeconomic gains by the non-white segments of the workforce has created a need for new theories. The occupations are changing also as the predominance of manufacturing is giving way to a more technical and highly skilled range of career choices.

Considerations when providing counseling services

Adults who have disabilities
Not all disabilities are visible or limit a person's ability to perform a job. During the intake interview and assessment the counselor should determine if the client has a disability and to what extent the disability will limit the choice of career. The client's self-concept, how well he or she has adjusted to the disability, social skills, how he or she copes with daily life, and any past employment must be assessed and considered in the counseling. The counselor should be knowledgeable about the *Americans with Disabilities Act,* state and local laws, and aid, including rehabilitation opportunities and assistance. It is helpful if the counselor is aware of local businesses that are especially accepting of persons with disabilities as well as those that are likely to be less welcoming.

Adults who have sexual orientation issues
Since many gay, lesbian, bisexual and transgendered (LGBT) persons conceal the fact that they are members of a sexual minority, it is very likely that most counselors work with them without ever realizing they do so. When the counselor is aware that the client has a LGBT sexual orientation, then such issues as self-concept as it relates to sexual identification, whether or not the client is "out" and to what extent, whether or not he or she prefers to be out at work, and how he or she handles discrimination must be dealt with. While many major companies are known to be gay/trans friendly, small local businesses may be very discriminatory. In order to work successfully with LGBT persons, the counselor must be accepting or at least able to keep his or her personal prejudices from affecting how he or she works with the client.

World-of-Work Map

The World-of-Work Map is a graphic illustration of how occupations are related via primary tasks. The primary tasks are working with data, ideas, people or things. The map was developed by ACT. It is a circle divided into six segments, each representing a cluster of occupations that correspond to

John Holland's six occupational types. The types are Administration & Sales, Business Operations, Technical, Science & Technology, Arts, and Social Service. Each cluster is divided into two regions and has from three to seven career areas. Two versions exist; one for counselors to use and the other for students.

Internet resources available

The internet has much to offer job seekers and career counselors. Counselors must be familiar with this tool, competent in its use, willing to use it, and familiar with major sites that can be useful to himself and the clients. Information available on the Internet includes educational resources, financial aid information, government and military information, information about particular businesses and corporations, job listings, job search sites, and help with resumes, interview skills, etc. Among the sites with which counselors should be familiar are US Department of Education, the Bureau of Labor Statistics, Military Career Guide, America's Job Bank, Monster.com, CareerBuilder, America's Career InfoNet, and Imdiversity, which offers information for minorities and women.

OOH, GOE, Workforce Investment Act of 1998, and 1994 School-to-Work Opportunities Act, and the definition of hidden job market

The *Occupational Outlook Handbook (OOH)* - a compilation of data concerning employment trends and outlooks, salaries, required training and education etc., published every other year by the U.S. Department of Labor.

The *Guide for Occupational Exploration (GOE)* – a compilation of data concerning occupations, skills and abilities, work environments, salaries, etc., divided into areas of interest.

Workforce Investment Act of 1998 – federal program that establishes a "one-stop" delivery system for workforce investment and educational services – includes Youth Opportunity, Migrant and Seasonal Farmworker and Native American programs, Job Corps, Adult Literacy Programs and incorporates the Rehabilitation Act of 1973.

1994 School-to-Work Opportunities Act – federally funded program to provide money for work-based learning, school-based learning and connecting activities that encourage collaboration between educational institutions and employers.

Hidden job market - employment opportunities that are not advertised and new employees are recruited by networking – approximately 80% of jobs.

DOT and O*NET

The *Dictionary of Occupational Titles (DOT)*, published by the U.S. Department of Labor, contains descriptions of 12,000 types of occupations and more than 28,000 job titles. It details tasks and gives educational and skill requirements for each job. It is available in print form or as a download from the Information Technology Associates web page. The DOT and O*Net can be downloaded together or both are available on a CD-ROM.

O*Net is the Occupational Information Network, a comprehensive database of occupational information and employee requirements. It features assessment and other occupation exploration tools. Eventually it will replace the DOT and become America's primary source of employment information.

Counseling dual-career/dual-earner couples

In an increasing number of families both partners are wage earners or are pursuing careers. Among the conflicts that can arise are the inequity of wages when one earns more (especially if it is much more) than the other, sex-role stereotypes and expectations, inequity of home maintenance and child care responsibilities, and questions of how money is handled and spent. Career advancement can cause conflict if one advances faster than the other or advancement for one partner requires relocation.

Women in the U.S. workforce in recent years

In the past ten years the number of women working full time has doubled and almost 50% of the labor force is now female. On average women earn only about 75% of male wages. Minority women earn even less with Hispanic-American women earning only 48% and African-American women earning 58%, while the earning level of Asian-American women is at 67%. Several social issues relating to children and family have developed from the increased numbers of women in the workforce. Since many of them are of childbearing age, pregnancy problems and childbirth insurance is needed. Childbirth leave is a concern for many. Childcare is of great concern and many companies have added in-house daycare facilities.

Outsourcing

Outsourcing is the shifting of activities to an agency outside a company or organization or the moving of operations to a non-U.S. location. Some companies use independent contractors for certain types of jobs rather than using employees since contractors do not receive benefits and taxes and social security do not have to be deducted. In recent years, many companies have closed factories and other operations in the United States and moved all or part of their production, technical support, and information services to countries where wages are lower and benefits less or nonexistent.

SDS

Developed by John Holland, the *Self-Directed Search* (SDS) is an assessment tool that lets a person match his or her interests and personality type to careers of the same type. The SDS is based on the theory that all people fall into one of six categories – realistic, investigative, artistic, social, enterprising, and conventional – and that occupations can be categorized the same way. People are more likely to experience job satisfaction and success when their career matches their type. The SDS determines the three-letter Holland Code that can then be used to explore careers that match a person's interests and skills.

Theories of Mark Savickas and H.B. Gelatt

Savickas's view of career counseling fits into the postmodern social constructivism approach. He sees the counselor as a catalyst who helps clients make sense of their lives and occupations. He uses a narrative method to guide a client in the building of a reality that fits with their social and cultural environment. Gelatt developed a five-step method for making decisions.
- Step 1 – recognize that a decision is needed.
- Step 2 – collect information and examine possible actions.

- Step 3 – examine the probability of possible outcomes.
- Step 4 – remember your value system.
- Step 5 – make a decision which can be either temporary or permanent.

His later, whole-brained approach is called "Positive Uncertainty" and considers both rational and intuitive components. He also developed a 2X4 process that designates two attitudes and four factors. "The attitudes are:
- accept the past, present and future as uncertain
- be positive about the uncertainty.

The factors are:
- what you want
- what you know
- what you believe
- what you do."

(From *Positive Uncertainty: A Paradoxical Philosophy of Counseling Whose Time Has Come* by H. B. Gelatt in ERIC Educational Reports.)

Self-efficacy theory

According to the self-efficacy theory, what a person expects influences what she or he does, how much effort is used, and if she or he will persist if there are difficulties. In career development, the expectations are choice, performance and persistence. Nancy Betz and Gail Hackett, among other theorists, believe gender variation in career decisions can be accounted for by self-efficacy, since a person's environment is an important element of his or her self-efficacy.

Undecided vs. indecisive

Undecided – the condition of a person who needs additional information in order to make a decision.
Indecisive – is descriptive of a person who has trouble reaching a decision even with full information.

Compensatory vs. spillover theories of leisure

Compensatory leisure theory – a person's occupation is the most important component of his or her life, and leisure is compensation for either job boredom or job excitement. *Spillover leisure theory* – a person's occupation has an effect on his or her personality, and leisure activities will be similar to occupational ones.

Career guidance vs. career counseling

Career guidance – helps a person develop skills for making decisions and to acquire information about opportunities in occupations and education.
Career counseling – works within the contest of a person's values and attitudes to help him or her acquire self-understanding as well as information about careers.

Competencies expected

Professional counselors should possess the following competencies:
- Extensive knowledge of counseling theories, techniques, and models, especially those specific to career counseling.
- Skill in working with both individuals and groups.
- The ability to use assessment techniques for both individuals and groups.
- Knowledge of resources and trends, especially those relevant to the locality.
- Management and leadership skills.
- Ability to coach.
- Respect for and ability to work with persons from various ethnic, religious, sexual, and socioeconomic backgrounds.
- Supervisory skills.
- An understanding of ethics and legal issues, and the ability to abide by them.
- Research and evaluation skills.
- An understanding of and ability to use current technology.

Career counseling process

First, the counselor establishes a rapport with the client, giving the client pertinent information about himself and learning basic facts about the client. Assessment comes next and may recur throughout the counseling. Both standard instruments and informal means may be used to ascertain the client's needs, goals, aptitudes, etc. The counselor gives information to the client concerning career opportunities and resources. He may direct the client to resources the client can use to find information for himself. The client makes a decision once he has resolved the problem and has the information he needs. The client implements his decision.

Counseling adults in career transition

Both mature adults and persons from minority cultures will need attention to details that do not apply to young people from the majority. For adults who have lost their jobs or want to change careers, such factors as obsolete skills and knowledge, physical and family limitations, life-style expectations and changes, and approaching retirement must be identified and addressed. In dealing with minorities, the counselor will need to learn about their cultural values and address issues arising from the culture including discrimination and prejudice, stereotypes, and the relationship of career to family and community. Both groups may be unacquainted with current technology and may need assistance with resume writing, interview skills and how to locate employment opportunities.

Area of assessment

Assessment and testing tools can be divided into five types: aptitude, achievement, interest, personality, and values. O*Net Resource Center has developed a set of exploration/assessment tools called profilers which includes *Interest Profiler* and *Ability Profiler* (aptitude). They have also produced the *Work Importance Profiler* which is a values measure. Other aptitude tests include *ASVAB (Armed Services Vocational Aptitude Battery)*, and the *General Aptitude Test Battery (GATB)*. Achievement measurement instruments include the *SAT (Scholastic Assessment Tests)*, *ACT (American College Test)*, *GRE (Graduate Record Exam)*, and the *Iowa Tests of Basic Skills (ITBS)*. Some of the interest tests available are *Career Assessment Inventory (CAI)*, *Campbell Interest and*

Skills Survey, Kuder Career Search with Person Match, and the *Self Directed Search (SDS).* Myers-Briggs Type Indicator is a personality assessment tool. Values assessment tools include *Super's Work Values Inventory-Revised* and the *Minnesota Importance Questionnaire.*

Computer-assisted career guidance systems

Modern technology has added a tool to the resources available to the career counselor in the form of computer-assisted career guidance systems. The *System of Interactive Guidance and Information (SIGI Plus), produced* by Valpar International, and *Discover,* produced by American College Testing, have the ability to determine interests, skills and values. They also offer some guidance through activities and provide extensive information. *Choices,* produced by Bridges Transitions Inc., *Focus II*, a production of Career Dimensions, and *Coordinated Occupational Information Network (COIN),* produced by Coin Educational Products, offer information about careers and educational institutions, but have more limited assessment capability. Software is available to assist people in writing resumes, developing interview skills, and job searching. Career Information Delivery Systems (CIDS), offered through many state employment offices, includes assessment, employment searching, and information about occupations and education.

Important terms

- *Career Education* - Programs intended to create career awareness in the elementary grades, explore careers in middle school and junior high school and prepare for a career in high school.
- *Dislocated worker* – A person unemployed because of job elimination, downsizing, company relocation or company closing.
- *Displaced homemaker* – A parent reentering the workforce or entering it for the first time after raising a family as a stay-at-home parent; often applied to a divorced or widowed woman who must support herself and may or may not have dependent children.
- *Expressed interest* - An interest that a person openly says he or she has.
- *FMLA* - Family and Medical Leave Act (FMLA) requires companies that employ fifty or more people to provide up to twelve weeks of leave without pay during any twelve months for childbirth or because of the illness of a member of the employee's immediate family.
- *Glass ceiling* - By unwritten agreement among the decision makers, the highest level in an organization that a person (a woman or a minority) is allowed to reach.
- *Leisure* – Time away from work during which a person can decide what to do; also refers to pleasure activities.
- *Lifestyle* – The overall pattern of a person's life including such factors as career, home life, romantic partner, interests, hobbies, and recreation.
- *Lifting requirement work classifications* – The level of lifting ability required for a particular occupation; sedentary work requires a ten pound maximum, light work requires a maximum of twenty pounds, medium work requires a maximum of fifty pounds, up to one hundred pounds is required for heavy work, and very heavy work is rated at one hundred pounds or more.
- *Manifested interest* - An interest that is revealed by what a person does.
- *Occupational Sex Segregation* – Occupations commonly thought of as female jobs usually have less pay and lower status than occupations regarded as work for men.
- *Outplacement counseling* - Career counseling for employees whose jobs are ending; may include job placement services.

- *PEC* – person environment correspondence; the relationship between job satisfaction and an increase in productivity.
- *Retirement counseling* - Helps people prepare for retirement by providing information on expectations including financial; home, social, and family life; medical and health issues; and legal matters.
- *SCCT* –social-cognitive career theory; posits that self-efficacy or a person's belief in what he is capable of doing influences career choice.
- *Tested interest* – determination of a person's interests through testing.
- *TWA* – the theory of work adjustment as developed by Renee V. Dawis and Lloyd Lofquist; the idea that the job must fill the needs of the person and the person must fit the job; correspondence or congruence between person and work.
- *Underemployment* - An employee whose education and/or experience exceed the requirements for the position.

Assessment

Types of reliability

Test reliability is a measurement of the consistency with which a test yields similar results in repeated uses.

- Stability – also called test-retest reliability; giving the same test to the same group twice with no more than two weeks between, so that the two sets of results can be correlated without intervening experiences affecting the outcome.
- Equivalence – the correlation of the results of using different tests covering the same content with the same group of test takers. Time between the tests and the formats used can affect the outcome.
- Internal consistency – measures the consistency of results from items in a test; do the responses from similar and opposing questions yield consistent information.

Validity

The validity of a test is the degree to which it measures what it is designed to measure. The content of the test must accurately measure the skills or information learned. The validity of a test is specific to a situation, including why and to whom it is administered. A testing instrument that is valid for one situation or population may not be valid for another. A valid test must always be reliable.

Face validity is obvious validity. For example, the questions on a math test will deal with math.

Content validity, which can also be called rational or logical validity, is the reflection of the subject matter in the content of the test. For example, a math test will contain material covered in the specific math course.

Predictive validity, which can also be called empirical validity, is the capability of a testing instrument to predict future behavior; for example. the ability of the SAT or GRE to predict a person's grade point average.

Concurrent validity is the immediate comparison of test results with the results from other sources that measure the same factors in the same short time span.

Construct validity is the extent to which a testing instrument measures an abstract psychological trait such as anxiety.

Administering tests to clients

Tests are used for many purposes in many different situations. In educational institutions, they measure academic achievement, and in job placement can help guide people to careers for which they are best suited. They can also be used to predict future performance and success in both education and work. Tests are also used to ensure the qualifications of persons who apply for licenses or certification in a field of employment. Counselors use various tests to evaluate clients and to help the clients learn about themselves. Among the reasons a counselor may administer a test to a client are:

- to determine if the client's needs are within the scope of the counselor's practice
- to help the client understand himself or herself
- to help the counselor better understand the client
- to determine which methods and techniques are most appropriate for a particular client
- to aid the client in decision making
- to identify interests
- to evaluate the counseling

Interpreting test scores with a client

- The counselor should be trained in test theory, and before administering the test should study the technical manual for the test.
- The counselor should understand the scores, profiles, and implications of the test.
- Using non-technical language, the counselor should explain the test to the client including the reason for the test and what it measures.
- When reviewing the scores with the client, the counselor should explain percentiles and other technical terms.
- The results of the test should be presented to the client in an organized manner and in layman's terms. The interrelationship of the multiple tests should be explained if more than one was used.
- The counselor should help the client to integrate the results of the test with other factors, and encourage the client to express reactions and emotions.
- The counselor should assure the client that test scores are just tools to help with decision making and not infallible limits placed on him or her.
- The interpretation session should not be rushed; time should be available for the client to ask questions and discuss the results.

Major types of tests and inventories

Intelligence exams are used to measure a person's mental ability. *Stanford-Binet Intelligence Scales, Wechsler Adult Intelligence Scale (WAIS-III),* and *Kaufman Assessment Battery for Children* are examples of this type.

Achievement tests measure learning and are often given in schools at particular grade levels or as "end of year" tests. They can also be used as diagnostic tools. Some examples are: the *California Achievement Test* and the *General Education Development (GED).*

Aptitude tests, which can also be called ability tests, are used to measure a person's ability to master skills or acquire knowledge.
Differential Aptitude Tests (DAT) and *Career Ability Placement Survey (CAPS)* are examples.

Personality tests are used to determine a person's personality traits and may be projective, inventories or specialized. Examples are: projective – *Rorschach,* and *Thematic Apperception Test (TAT);* inventory – *Minnesota Multiphasic Personality Inventory (MMPI-2)* and *Myers-Briggs Type Indicator;* specialized – *Tennessee Self-concept Scale* and *Luria-Nebraska Neuropsychological Battery.*

Interest inventories are used to determine a person's likes and dislikes. *Strong Interest Inventory, Career Assessment Inventory,* and *O*Net Interest Profiler* are examples.

Ethical issues in testing

Confidentiality of test results is of primary importance since some test results can label or stereotype the test taker, and in some instances may be an invasion of privacy. Confidentiality is especially important if test records are placed on a computer. The counselor must maintain security measures, both physical and on the computer, to ensure that the records are not accessible to unauthorized persons. Another issue concerns the tests themselves since most were developed to test white, middle-class males and may not accurately test females, non-white males, or persons from minority cultures. The counselor should make every effort to see that the tests he or she uses are as unbiased as possible. Some issues of validity, interpretation, and confidentiality concern computer administered tests which can include self-testing.

WAIS-III and adults

David Wechsler wanted to create a test that did not rely solely on verbal skills. The Wechsler Adult Intelligence Scale (WAIS-III) is one of the IQ tests developed by David Wechsler and administered on an individual basis. The WAIS-III provides a verbal IQ, performance IQ, and a full-scale IQ. There are a total of 7 verbal plus 7 performance scales. Wechsler also developed the WPPSI-R, Wechsler Preschool and Primary Scale of Intelligence, for children ages 3 years to 7 years/3 months. For children 6 years to 16 years/11 months, he developed the Wechsler Intelligence Scale for Children Revised, WISC-III.

Key contributors in the field of intelligence testing

Sir Francis Galton is recognized as the leading pioneer in the study of individual differences. He concluded that intelligence was primarily genetic and had a normal distribution similar to height and weight.

J.P. Gilford used factor analysis and isolated 120 factors that added up to intelligence. He also defined convergent and divergent thinking. Convergent thinking is when different thoughts and ideas are combined into a single concept. Divergent thinking is the ability to create a novel idea.

Alfred Binet, along with Theodore Simon, is credited with creating the first intelligence test. Conceived in 1905, the test consisted of 30 items of increasing difficulty, administered to discriminate normal from intellectually disabled Parisian children. It was adapted for America by M. Terman of Stanford University and became the Stanford-Binet IQ test. The original Stanford-Binet produced the intelligence quotient or ratio IQ (mental age divided by chronological age times 100: MA/CA x 100). Today the IQ formula is SAS, standard age score, with a mean of 100 and a standard deviation of 16.

John Ertl advanced the theory that the rate at which a person processes information is an indication of his or her level of intelligence - the faster the processing, the more intelligent the person. He also invented an intelligence-testing machine that uses an electrode helmet in conjunction with a computer and an EEG.

Raymond Cattell developed the theories of fluid and crystallized intelligence. Fluid intelligence is inborn, deals with abstract reasoning, is unrelated to experience, and decreases with age. Crystallized intelligence develops from acquired knowledge and skills. He is also the creator of the *16 Personality Factor Questionnaire.*

Arthur Jensen applied the theory that intelligence is genetic to adopted children, expecting them to have IQ scores closer to their biological parents than to their adoptive parents. He believed that 80% of intelligence is inherited and only 20% is environmental.

Robert Williams, an African-American psychologist, created the Black Intelligence Test of Cultural Homogeneity (BITCH) as proof that African-Americans can excel on intelligence tests when the cultural bias is toward their own experience rather than toward white culture.

Important terms

- Appraisal - A variety of assessment tools including tests and surveys used to evaluate traits and behaviors.
- Bell curve - A graphic illustration of the normal distribution of a data set.
- Coefficient of determination – The square of the correlation coefficient which shows the common variation between the two variables.
- Correlation coefficient – A measurement of the linear relationship between two variables.
- Cyclical test – Test has multiple sections and the questions in each section progress in difficulty.
- Dichotomous items - Questions such as true/false that give the test taker opposing choices.
- Difficulty index – In testing the percentage of test takers who respond correctly to an item.
- Forced choice items – Items such as true/false questions for which the test taker must recall information
- Free choice test – Short answer questions that elicit subjective information.
- Halo effect – A favorable evaluation of a personality based on the perception of a single trait.
- Horizontal test – A test procedure that covers material from different subjects.
- Intrusive measurement – Questionnaires, interviews, and other situations in which a person is aware he or she is being observed – that awareness can affect the results of the observation. Measurement can also be called reactive.
- Ipsative format - Allows a person to compare two or more examples of his or her own performance – does not allow for comparison with others.
- Mean – The average score from a group of tests.
- Measure – A score assigned to a person's traits or behavior.
- Median – The middle score from a group of tests.
- Mode – The score that occurs most frequently in a set of scores.
- Normative item format - Unlinked items on a test.
- Normative test - A person's test results can be compared to the scores of others; a percentile rank can be created.
- Objective test items – Based on a universal standard such as multiple choice and requires little or no judgment in scoring.
- Obtrusive measurement – (Nonreactive) subject is unaware of observation or investigation such as when records are reviewed or subject is observed through a one-way window.
- Percentile – On a scale of 100, the number that shows the percent of a data distribution equal to or below it.
- Power test – Untimed test that determines mastery level.
- Projective tests – Unstructured tests that may reveal basic personality, concealed feelings, and internal conflicts.
- Psychometric - refers to any form of mental testing.

- Q-Sort – A tool for measuring self-esteem by choosing statement-bearing cards that are "most like me" or "least like me."
- Range – The lowest score subtracted from the highest.
- Rating scale - a cart used to indicate the degree to which an attribute or characteristic exists.
- Regression to the mean - a statistical concept where earning a low score or a high score on a pretest means the individual will probably score close to the mean on the posttest. The error is due to chance, personal and environment factors that will be different on the posttest.
- Reliability – The consistency with which a test yields similar results measured by the use of a correlation coefficient. Reliable does not equate to validity.
- Skew – The amount a score deviates from the norm.
- Sociometry - coined by Joseph Levy Moreno, a method of tracking the relationship of individuals within a group. A sociogram is a map or diagram showing the structure of the group or relationships of the members.
- Speed tests – Timed test; difficulty is more in how quickly questions can be answered than in the content.
- Spiral test – Starts with easier questions and progresses to the harder ones.
- Standard deviation – A measure of statistical dispersion; how widely spread the scores are from the mean.
- Standard error of measurement (SEM) – A statistical range that will include a test taker's score; calculated by the multiplication of the test's standard deviation by the square root of 1, then the subtraction of the reliability coefficient.
- Standardized score - Same as z-score
- Stanine, or Standard Nine – A way of scaling test scores - nine divisions, five of them in the middle with a standard deviation of 2. The lowest scores comprise the first group and the highest scores the last.
- Subjective test items – Items such as essay questions; scoring of these items requires judgment and may reflect the scorer's bias.
- Test - A systematic method of measuring or evaluating.
- Test battery – A collection of tests given to the same group of people and scored against the same standard.
- T-score – A score within a normal distribution with a mean of 50 and a standard deviation of 10.
- Variance – The square of the standard deviation.
- Vertical tests – tests on the same subject given at different levels or ages.
- Z-score – A method for determining a standardized score; subtract the mean from an individual score then divide by the standard deviation.

Research and Program Evaluation

Research

Research is the collecting and analyzing of information about a particular subject. It may involve searching through written material, experiments, observation of a phenomenon or of people. Research can be divided into deductive and inductive types. Deductive research sets out to prove or disprove a theory by collecting data and testing hypotheses. Inductive research works from known information to develop a theory by establishing relationships or patterns in the data.

Non-experimental quantitative research

Quantitative research is systematic and usually uses scientific methods. Non-experimental types are survey, descriptive, comparative, correlational, and *ex post facto*. *Surveys* can be questionnaires or interviews and can be used to ascertain attitudes, beliefs, and opinions. Surveys sent out through the mail often have a poor response rate which may invalidate generalizations make from them. *Descriptive* or statistical research can be used to document such factors as frequencies, averages, etc., showing the who, what, when, where, and how of the data. An example is a ratings chart. *Comparative research* compares two or more groups without changing any of the experiences of the groups. A comparative survey would ask, "Which are more alike?" In correlational research, the degree of relationship between variables is determined by the use of the correlation coefficient. *Ex post facto*, or causal-comparative, research discovers the relationships between pre-existing variables. The t-test and variance statistics may be used.

Qualitative research

Qualitative research is an in-depth investigation of the subject which often is a group of people, but may be an individual. The group may be a family, a community, or even an ethnic or cultural minority. The motivation for the research usually involves learning the reasons why the subject practices certain behaviors. Research methods include observation, case studies, and participant observation. One type of qualitative research is ethnographic research which is the foundation of anthropology. Interactive qualitative research includes case studies and ethnography. Non-interactive qualitative research includes a study and analysis of the literature about a particular subject.

Experimental and quasi-experimental quantitative research

The cause and effect relationship between variables can be discovered by experimental quantitative research. In such research, there will be a control factor, a dependent variable, and an independent variable while random and confounding variables will be eliminated. The hypothesis is tested by the measurement of the changes in the independent variable as compared with the control. An example would be a foreign-language class in which half the students (the control) receive only the classroom lessons, and the other half watch a film with subtitles in the language they are learning. Quasi-experimental research is much like experimental but may not use a control. The results from quasi-experimental research may not be unequivocal.

External validity

External validity is the accuracy with which the results of a study can be generalized to a larger population. Loss of external validity can come from such factors as too small a sample or from differing circumstances. For example, a study using only high school students cannot be generalized to all students. Nor can a study of factory workers be generalized to all employed people. Changing circumstances during the study can also affect external validity. Generalization can also be affected by the Hawthorne effect, the Rosenthal effect, and demand characteristics. The Hawthorne effect is caused by the study subjects knowing they are involved in a study or by the attention paid to the subjects. The Rosenthal effect, also called experimenter bias and the Pygmalion effect, happens when the study subjects change their behavior because of the attitudes, expectations, or behavior of the researcher. Demand characteristics are caused by information received by the subjects including rumors they heard before the start of the study.

Internal validity

Internal validity is the extent to which the results of an experiment can be attributed to the variable under study because extraneous or confounding variables have been controlled. Confounding variables can include the selection of subjects, the testing instruments, the maturation and experiences of the subjects during the study, and the researchers themselves. *Subject selection* becomes a confounding variable unless the control and experimental groups are identical in age, gender, ethnicity, and socioeconomic background. Identical *testing and recording instruments* must be used with both groups and must remain reliable and consistent. If the study endures for more than a few weeks, then the *maturation and/or experiences of the subjects* become confounding variables. If group members drop out of the study or die during it, their loss will affect the outcome. The *researcher* becomes a confounding variable if he allows his biases to influence his reporting of the study and the results, or if such factors as health and fatigue affect it.

Sampling

Random sampling is choosing the subjects for a study entirely by chance. Such sampling reduces the likelihood of bias.

Stratified sampling divides the population into subgroups according to some criteria – such as age, ethnicity, gender, or socioeconomic level, and then selects subjects from each subgroup. This increases the validity of generalizing the findings to the entire population.

Proportional stratified sampling is the selection of the number of subjects from each subgroup that corresponds to the percentage of the population that fits into that subgroup.

Cluster sampling divides the population into subdivisions or clusters, and then selects a random sample from the clusters.

Purposeful sampling is the selection of subjects for in-depth study. Generalizations are not derived from these studies.

Studies based on convenience or volunteer samples do not produce normal score distributions, but may provide useful information.

Levels of measurement

Nominal measurements are categorical variables such as gender, race, marital status, and religion. In a study nominal measurements are used to describe the demographics of the subjects.

Ordinal measurements are used to describe variables that can be arranged in some type of order or ranking. Opinion and attitude scales are examples.

Interval level of measurement is used to describe variables with similar or equal distances between the ranks. Generations and crime rates are examples.

Ratio level of measurement applies to variables that have equal intervals and a zero reference point. This type of measurement is infrequently used in the social sciences since attitudes are usually not measured at the zero level.

Independent and dependent variables and Type I and Type II errors

The independent variable is the factor in an experiment or study that is changed by the researcher. The dependent variable is what is being measured by the study and is changed in response to the changes in the independent variable.

In a type I error (alpha error), the null hypothesis is rejected as false or unproven when it is actually true. A researcher makes a type II error (beta error) when he or she does not reject the null hypothesis when it is actually false. Type II errors are often the result of a sample size that is too small.

t-test

The t-test compares the mean of two independent data sets to determine if there is a significant statistical difference between them. The test makes reference to an established *table of t-values*. It can establish the existence or non-existence of relationships between data sets before a full standard deviation value is determined. This test can be especially useful for small sample groups.

Forms of hypothesis

A *hypothesis* is a statement or prediction of what will be shown by a study. It may be a hunch, an educated guess, or derived from a theory. A *null hypothesis* assumes no difference or no association between variables. A *directional hypothesis* predicts how the independent variable will affect the dependent variable. A *non-directional hypothesis* predicts an effect, but does not state how the dependent variable will be affected.

The significance level indicates the probability of making a type I error in a hypothesis test. It is usually set as low as possible with a level of .05 or 5% being a commonly used level.

Analyses of variance

Factorial analysis of variance (ANOVA) is used in the study of two or more variables. The 2X2 design, in which there are two independent variables each with two distinct values, is the most common, although multi-level designs can be used.

One-way analysis of variance is a test for differences when the study involves three or more independent groups or levels.

Multivariate analysis of variance (MANOVA) is used in studies involving several dependent variables and at least two independent variables.

Analysis of covariance (ANCOVA) is used in studies where the dependent variables are controlled. Possible techniques of controlling the variables are to use non-random samples or to statistically adjust variables that affect the dependent variable.

Chi-square and bivariate tabular analysis

Chi-squared is used to determine if there are significant differences in the distribution of two data sets. This test is used to determine whether the data fits a known type of distribution or whether different attributes or factors in a single data set are related or independent of each other. Another use for the test is to determine if two data sets or populations are homogeneous when compared to each other.

Bivariate tabular analysis is a method of graphically illustrating the relationship or non-relationship of two variables by the use of an X/Y graph. Traditionally the independent variable is shown on the horizontal axis and the dependent variable on the vertical axis.

Post hoc and nonparametric tests

Post hoc tests, which are multiple comparison tests, can be done after the data sets in a study are determined to have similar *F* values. Popular tests, listed in order from most conservative to most liberal include: Scheffe's, *Tukey's Honesty Significant Difference (HSD),* Newman-Keuls, *Duncan's New Multiple Range Test,* and *Fisher's LSD.* Nonparametric tests are validation tests used when a study yields values that are not distributed normally or the sample variance is close to that of the population. When two samples are independent of each other and have significantly differing means, the *Mann-Whitney U Test* is appropriate. The *Wilcoxon Signed-Rank Test* is useful in situation where each individual has two or more scores or two data sets have the same values. A nonparametric one-way analysis of variance is the *Kruskal-Wallis Test* used when there are multiple values for a single variable or factor.

Accountability

Accountability is primarily concerned with the effectiveness of the treatment and with justification of the cost. Both formative evaluation which analyzes the effectiveness of a treatment, process, or technique, and summative evaluation which measures how well a program meets its goals are used to determine if a program is worthwhile. Justification of the cost of a program is related to its effectiveness and must answer the question "Is the results worth the cost?" Whether it is an insurance company, an individual, a government agency, or a business providing a service to its employees, whoever is paying for the program wants an explanation for the cost as well as information about the effectiveness of the program. Specific measurable objectives must be established and the level of achievement measured and documented.

Writing issues faced in doing research

In addition to the ethical issues of accurate reporting and giving credit where it is deserved, the researcher must write his or her report in an acceptable style. The *Publication Manual of the American Psychological Association* is the standard style manual for most counseling and psychological publications as well as for many college and university dissertations. Reports should be free of sexist, racist, and any other inappropriate language. Reports may be written for a sponsoring agency, for publication, or both. If the report is submitted for publication, it should only be submitted to one journal at a time.

Ethical issues faced in doing research

Primary ethical issues in research involve informed consent, confidentiality, credit, and truthfulness in reporting. Research subjects should always be aware that they are participating in a research project and should have given their consent to participate only after being fully informed about the research and any risks involved. The informed consent is especially important in any research where there may be harm to the subjects such as in drug testing where the control group receives a placebo or the new drug may produce harmful side effects. All personal information should be held in strict confidence and raw data should be accessible only to the research team. In reporting the results of the research it is imperative that the report be accurate even when the results disprove the researcher's theory and that proper credit be given to all involved.

ERIC

ERIC is the acronym for the Educational Resources Information Center, an electronic library of educational research and information. Sponsored by the Institute of Education Sciences, a part of the U.S. Department of Education, ERIC provides access to bibliographic records of journals and other literature from 1966 to the present. The database also has a growing number of full text materials. Currently, ERIC indexes more than 650 journals and offers free, full-text access to over 100,000 other materials.

Important terms

- Biserial correlation coefficient - A measure of the relationship between one variable with multiple values and another that is dichotomous.
- Correlation - The relationship between variables. Positive correlation – both variables have the same directional change.
- Cross-sectional - A study of the characteristics of multiple groups. The study of one group's characteristics over a period of time is a longitudinal study.
- Degrees of freedom - How many observations the researcher may make after he or she has made the minimum number needed for the study.
- Double-blind technique - Neither the subjects nor the researchers know at least one variable. For example, in a drug test neither would know which subjects had received the actual drug or which had received the placebo.
- Factor analysis - Examines the relationships among a group of variables for the purpose of determining the simplest explanation for those relationships which is usually the smallest number of factors involved.
- Heteroscedasticity - Unequal variance of the data.
- Homoscedasticity - Statistical variances are assumed to be equal

- Likert scale – A rating scale on which study participants agree or disagree with statements that measure attitudes or opinions.
- Meta-analysis – Answering a research question through the comparison of results from multiple studies.
- Multiple regression - A procedure in which the researcher uses a correlation coefficient to learn about the relationship between multiple independent variables and a dependent variable. The procedure can be used to determine the best predictor of a particular event or outcome. An example would be which personality trait best predicts social adjustment.
- Negative correlation – the variables change in opposite directions.
- Parameter - A value used to represent a characteristic of the population.
- Parsimony - The researcher interprets the results of a study in the simplest and least complex manner; sometimes called Occam's razor.
- Probability - The quantitative description of the likelihood of a particular event occurring.
- Sample size – The number of samples included in a study.
- Scatterplot – A graphic using horizontal and vertical lines to illustrate the relationship between two variables.
- Semantic differential - A method for measuring a subject's reactions to words or concepts through the use of a bipolar scale using contrasting adjectives.
- Solomon four-group design - A study of whether or not a pretest affects the subjects of a study by sensitizing or influencing them before the start of the research. Such effects must be considered in the comparison of the results with the control group.
- SPSS (Statistical Package for the Social Sciences) - A software package for use statistical analysis.
- Statistic - A value calculated from a data sample.
- Table of random numbers – A list of random numbers (usually computer-generated) that can be assigned to potential study samples, and used to randomly select those who will participate in the study.
- Zero correlation – the variables have no relationship.

Professional Orientation and Ethical Practice

History of counseling through the 1950's

In the years after the Civil War, the first American counselors were deans and advisors who were responsible for female college students.

- 1879 – First psychological laboratory established by Wilhelm Wundt.
- 1890 – Freud began psychoanalysis treatments.
- 1898 – Jesse Davis started work as a counselor in a high school in Detroit.
- 1908 – Frank Parson was director of the Vocation Bureau in Boston and Clifford Beers published <u>A Mind That Found Itself</u>, a book about conditions in mental health institutions.
- 1909 – Parson's <u>Choosing a Vocation</u> established the trait-factor approach in guidance.
- 1913 – The first professional counseling association, the National Vocational Guidance Association, was established.
- 1917 – The Smith-Hughes Act was passed, establishing the first federal funding for guidance and vocational education.
- 1931 – The <u>Workbook in Vocations</u> by Proctor, Benefield, and Wrenn changed popular usage from "guidance" to "counseling."
- 1939 – Williamson published <u>How to Counsel Students</u> modifying Parson's trait-factor approach.
- 1941 – Rogers published <u>Counseling and Psychotherapy</u>
- After 1945 – counseling services were expanded by the Veteran's Administration.

History of counseling from 1960 to the present

- 1960s – Behavioral, Gestalt, rational emotive, and reality approaches to counseling were developed.
- 1962 – Wrenn's <u>The Counselor in a Changing World</u> was published. California became the first state to pass a law licensing marriage, family and child counselors.
- 1976 – Virginia passed the first law to license general practice counselors.
- 1981 – The Council for the Accreditation of Counseling and Related Educational Programs was established.
- 1983 – The APGA became the American Association for Counseling and Development.
- 1992 – The AACD became the American Counseling Association.
- 1990s – Specialty counseling areas developed and laws regarding the profession were passed at the federal level.

Current and continuing trends

Counseling deals with a wide variety of human conditions, activities, and characteristics including personal growth, mental health, career development, wellness, social and interpersonal relationships, and pathological psychology. Changes in society and growing social awareness are increasing the influence of multiculturalism, spirituality, justice, oppression and violence. Technology has brought about several changes and will continue to be a major influence in the field with the Internet and computer-assisted counseling (CAC) as important trends. As the involvement of electronic resources increases, there will be a need for research into the positive and negative effects of the trend. Currently, there is little or no research on the subject although some counselors feel that CAC is having a depersonalizing effect on counseling. Counselors are currently licensed by the states and not all states have reciprocity with all others. The question of credentialing will become even more important as Internet counseling grows since an Internet cliental could spread far beyond a geographical location. Efforts by the American Association of State Counseling Boards may lead to portability for licensed counselors. The establishment of the National Credentials Registry in 2005 was a step in that direction.

Principles of ethical decision-making and the purpose of the *ACA Code of Ethics*

While each counselor has his or her own ethical standards, some general principles underlie many of the ethical decisions counselors make. These principles include: beneficence, not causing harm, respect for freedom of choice and self-determination, fairness, and honoring commitments. The *ACA Code of Ethics and Standards of Practice* is a document produced by the ACA that establishes principles of ethical behavior to which all ACA members must adhere.

Ethical issues

Ethical issues that must be addressed in group counseling
The ethical issues such as informed consent that pertain to individual counseling are valid for group counseling. One issue that expands for a group is confidentiality. Confidentiality must be maintained by all members of the group so that no identities or other information is revealed to anyone outside the group. There should be a clear understanding of when confidentiality must be waived. Members should not engage in social relationships with each other or discuss the sessions outside of the meetings. The counselor should maintain an environment that discourages cliques and subgroups, but encourages respect for all group members regardless of such factors as race, gender, religion, sexual orientation, or socioeconomic level.

Ethical issues that must be addressed in family counseling
In family counseling both the counselor and the family involved must be very clear as to whether the family as a whole or an individual family member is actually the client. The identity of the client will determine how the counselor deals with diverse issues (family vs. family member) and where the counselor focuses attention. Confidentiality is another issue that will arise since there is a distinction between information shared with the counselor in an individual session and in discussions when the entire family is present. If the counselor learns of child abuse or incest, that information must be reported to the authorities. Confidentiality may be waived if the counselor is required to testify in court in cases of abuse, involuntary commitment, or child custody. The counselor must be aware of his or her own biases and prejudices, and able to set them aside when dealing with an alternative family or with a family from a different cultural background.

ICD, PL94-142, and 1958 National Defense Education Act

ICD – the Manual of the International Statistical Classification of Diseases, Injuries and Causes of Death – a publication of the World Health Organization that can be used as an alternative to the DSM in coding client diagnoses for insurance purposes.

PL94-142 – *The Education Act for All Handicapped Children*, passed in 1975, is a federal law mandating that states provide a free education for all disabled children between the ages of 6 and 17 (potentially also ages 3-5 and 18-21 if the state also provides education to non-disabled children in those age groups); that placement for handicapped persons will be in the least restrictive environment; and that an Individualized Education Plan (IEP) will be provided for every child.

1958 National Defense Education Act – (NDEA) - a federal law passed in reaction to the launch of Sputnik that provided student loans in areas of science and technology and also in such fields as counseling, librarianship and foreign language.

ACA Code of Ethics

Section A: The Counseling Relationship describes the counselor's obligation to respect the dignity of the client and promote his or her welfare. This section requires that the counselor receive informed consent for the counseling, that he or she communicates important information such as the client's rights and responsibilities both verbally and in writing. Also in this section is a review of the relationship of the counselor with the client as an individual, as part of a group and at the institutional and societal levels. Sexual contact with clients is expressly forbidden. The quality of care for terminally ill clients, the collection of fees and receiving gifts are also covered in this section, as is the ethical use of technology.

Section B: Confidentiality, Privileged Communication and Privacy covers how information about clients must be handled and deals with the issue of trust. This section delineates the circumstances under which confidential information may be disclosed. Confidentiality in group work is discussed as is the storage and disposal of records. Prior consent from the client is required for the recording of a counseling session and for the transfer of information to third parties unless specific exceptions permit the transfer. This section also states that counselors must disguise the identity of a client when information is used in training, research, or publication. Information must be handled in a culturally sensitive manner.

Section C: Professional Responsibility states the requirements that counselors practice within their competence levels, continue their education, avoid working with clients who might be harmed by the counselor's problems, and truthfully represent their credentials and services in advertising and at other times. The section also prohibits the recruitment of clients through a counselor's other employment or social contacts, sexual harassment, exploitative relationships with subordinates, and unjustified compensation. Relationships with other professionals serving the clients and employment conditions that might negatively impact the counselor's work are also covered. Techniques and procedures must be based in accepted theories or the client must be told they are unproven.

Section D: Relationships with Other Professionals stresses that counselors must respect different approaches to treatment and develop good working relationships and communications with colleagues so that services to the clients are enhanced. This section also addresses working with an interdisciplinary team, informing employers if inappropriate practices are observed, the selection and treatment of employees, and the provision and use of consultation services.

Section E: Evaluation, Assessment and Interpretation addresses the reasons for assessment and states that the assessment method must be appropriate for the client and within the competence of the counselor. The client must give informed consent for the assessment. This section also discusses the release of assessment data. Assessment techniques used to diagnose mental disorders must be carefully selected and used appropriately, and the client's cultural and socioeconomic background must be considered in the diagnosis. Forensic evaluation is also covered in this section.

Section F: Supervision, Training and Teaching deals with the role and responsibilities of the counseling supervisor who has the obligation to secure training in supervision. The section also addresses the issues of competence; multiculturalism and diversity; and relationships between supervisors and supervisees, including sexual relationships and sexual harassment. Also delineated in this section are the responsibilities of counselor educators, who develop, implement, and supervise programs of education that include clinical experience for future counselors. Student welfare and responsibilities, student evaluation and remediation, and the relationship between educators and students are covered in this section.

Section G: Research and Publication encourages researching counselors to contribute to the profession's knowledge base. This section describes the parameters for research using human participants and requires that counselors observe stringent safeguards to protect the rights and welfare of the participants. Among the rights of the participants are informed consent, limits on the use of deception, confidentiality of the collected information, and clarification of the nature of the study. The section also covers disposal of research documents and the relationships between the researcher and the participants. Publication guidelines are also included.

Section H: Resolving Ethical Issues addresses the necessity of commitment to a high ethical standard, as exemplified by the <u>ACA Code of Ethics.</u> Conflicts between the ethical standards and the law should be resolved, if at all possible, without violation of the standards, but if such resolution is not possible, the counselor must abide by the law. This section also deals with the reporting of ethical violations, organizational conflicts, and cooperation with ethics committees.

Important terms

- Aspirational ethics - Ideal practices.
- Differentiation - The ability of each member of a family to maintain his or her own sense of self.
- Morphogenesis - An adaptability skill a family may use in handling change.
- Morphostasis - An adaptability skill a family may use in balancing stability.
- Paradox - Prescribing the problem but with an exaggeration or some sort of twist; should not be used with addictive behaviors that harm the client or others.
- Quid pro quo - Something for something; an exchange in which each person does something for the other

Fundamentals of Counseling

Difference between emotion and mood, ego-dystonic and ego-syntonic, and clinical assessment and diagnosis

Emotion is a mental state arising spontaneously as a reaction to some stimulus and is usually accompanied by physiological changes in the person's body. Mood is a state of mind which can be caused by emotions, events or a combination of the two.

Ego-dystonic pertains to behaviors, values, and feelings which are inconsistent with the person's basic concept of his self (ego) and can lead to a psychological disorder. Ego-syntonic pertains to behaviors, values, or feelings that are consistent with the person's ego.

Clinical assessment uses tests and tools to determine the psychological, biological, and social factors that are the cause of a psychological disorder. Diagnosis determines whether or not the problems meet the DSM criteria for a psychological disorder.

Neuropsychological assessment

Used at first to determine the extent of the loss of a particular skill and the area of the brain that might have been damaged by injury or neurological illness, neuropsychological assessment has become a measurement of brain dysfunction relating to language, attention, concentration, memory, perceptual and motor skills. Examples of neuropsychological assessment instruments are the Luria-Nebraska Neuropsychological Battery which is used to measure organic brain damage and the location of injury and the Bender® Visual-Motor Gestalt Test which measures brain dysfunction.

Formal mental status exam

A formal mental status exam is an assessment of a person's appearance, behavior, thought processes, mood, emotions, intelligence, awareness of surroundings, time, location and identity. Some factors such as thoughts, feelings and behavior may be assessed by direct observation while psychological assessment tests are used to evaluate intelligence and personality characteristics. Some of the assessment instruments are unstructured projective tests in which the person's responses reflect his personality including hidden emotions and internal conflicts. These instruments include Rorschach, Thematic Apperception Test and Incomplete Sentences Blank. Personality tests such as the Minnesota Multiphasic Personality Inventory (MMPI) can be used to ascertain stable aspects of a person's character. Intelligence tests include the Wechsler Intelligence Scale for Children (WISC-III-R) and the Stanford-Binet (SB:IV). They are used to determine the level of a person's intellectual ability.

DSM

The Diagnosis and Statistical Manual is the standard classification of mental disorders used by mental health professionals in the United States. It is used by practitioners in clinical, research, administrative, and educational fields. The information consists of three major components: the diagnostic classification, the diagnostic criteria, and the descriptive text. The DSM assigns each disorder a code consisting of five digits with a decimal point after the third digit. The manual does not include treatment information. It is also a classification system with periodic revisions. The DSM also takes cultural context, cultural belief systems, and cultural differences between client/worker into account and includes Culture-Bound Syndromes.

DSM-5 Classifications:

- Neurodevelopmental disorders
- Schizophrenia spectrum and other psychotic disorders
- Bipolar and related disorders
- Depressive disorders
- Anxiety disorders
- Obsessive-compulsive and related disorders
- Trauma- and stressor-related disorders
- Dissociative disorders
- Somatic symptom and related disorders
- Feeding and eating disorders
- Elimination disorders
- Sleep-wake disorders
- Sexual dysfunctions
- Gender dysphoria
- Disruptive, impulse-control, and conduct disorders
- Substance-related and addictive disorders
- Neurocognitive disorders
- Personality disorders
- Paraphilic disorders
- Other mental disorders
- Medication-induced movement disorders

Anxiety disorders
Panic disorder—recurrent brief but intense fear in the form of panic attacks with physiological or psychological symptoms.
Specific Phobia—fear of specific situations or objects
Generalized anxiety disorder—chronic physiological and cognitive symptoms of distress, excessive worry lasting at least 6 months of duration.
Separation anxiety disorder- excessive anxiety related to being separated from someone the client is attached to
Selective mutism- unable to speak in social settings (when it would seem appropriate) though normally able to speak
Social anxiety disorder- anxiety about social situations
Agoraphobia- anxiety of being outside of the home or in open places

Treatments include:
- Short-acting anti-anxiety medications for episodic symptoms (panic attacks) and antidepressants for longer term use (ex. Social/general anxiety)
- Psychotherapy such as supportive therapy, cognitive-behavioral therapy (systematic desensitization), DBT (Dialectical Behavioral Therapy),

- Group therapy
- Inpatient hospitalization (when a threat to self or others)
- Exposure exercises

Dissociative disorders

These are all characterized by a disturbance in the normally integrative functions of identity, memory, consciousness, or environmental perception.

- Dissociative identity disorder (previously multiple personality disorder): Two or more personalities exist within one person. Each personality is dominant at a particular time.
- Dissociative amnesia: Inability to recall important personal data, more than forgetfulness. Is not due to organic causes and comes on suddenly.
- Depersonalization/Derealization disorder: Feeling detached from one's mental processes or body, as if one is an observer.

Treatment is primarily done via psychotherapy, with the goals of working through unconscious conflict or recovering traumatic memories, and integrating feeling states with memories or events.

Somatic symptom and related disorders

All somatoform disorders are marked by multiple physical/somatic symptoms that cannot be explained medically. Symptoms impair social or work functioning and cause distress.

- Somatic symptom disorder – Somatic symptoms (including pain) that are persistent and distressing about which feelings regarding these symptoms take up an extremely large amount of time and energy.
- Illness anxiety disorder – Preoccupation with getting or currently having an illness
- Factitious disorder – Falsely presenting oneself or someone else as ill, even when there are no obvious gains in doing so.
- Conversion disorder (functional neurological symptom disorder): Motor or perceptual symptoms suggesting physical disorder, but actually reflect emotional conflicts.
- Psychological factors affecting other medical conditions – the client has a medical condition that is adversely affected by psychological behavior.

No definitive treatment, but goal is early diagnosis in order to circumvent unnecessary medical/surgical intervention. Attempt to move attention from symptoms to problems of living. Supportive Therapy to help individual cope with symptoms. Long-term relationship with single physician. No medication.

Depressive disorders

Depressive disorders include

- Disruptive mood dysregulation disorder
- Major depressive disorder
- Persistent depressive disorder (dysthymia)
- Premenstrual dysphoric disorder
- Substance/Medication induced depressive disorder

Major depressive disorder criteria includes: The client experiences 5 or more of the following symptoms during 2 consecutive weeks. These symptoms are associated with a change in the client's normal functioning. (Note: Of the presenting symptoms, either depressed mood or loss of ability to feel pleasure must be included to make this diagnosis).

- Depressed mood
- Loss of ability to feel pleasure or have interest in normal activities

- Decreased aptitude for thinking
- Thoughts of death
- Fatigue (daily)
- Inappropriate guilt/worthlessness
- Observable motor agitation or psychomotor retardation
- Weight change of more than or less than 5% in one month
- Hypersomnia or Insomnia (almost daily)

The episode causes distress or social/functional impairment. The symptoms cannot be attributed to a substance or another condition/disease. The episode does not meet the criteria for schizophrenia spectrum or other psychotic disorder or for manic episode or a hypomanic episode.

- Antidepressants for major depressive disorder and dysthymia. Anti-psychotics if accompanied by psychotic features. Mood stabilizers if bipolar I, bipolar II, or cyclothymia. Consistent administration and monitoring for effectiveness and side effects required.
- Interpersonal/psychodynamic therapy.
- Behavioral therapy
- Cognitive therapy
- Group psychotherapy
- Self-help groups

Bipolar and related disorders and depressive disorders are called mood disorders. The mood disorders are the most common psychological illnesses and are increasing worldwide in both the adult and child populations.

Schizophrenia spectrum and other psychotic disorders
The schizophrenia spectrum and other psychotic disorders classification includes:
- delusional disorder
- brief psychotic disorder
- schizophreniform disorder
- schizophrenia
- schizoaffective disorder
- substance/medication-induced psychotic disorder
- psychotic disorder due to another medical condition
- catatonia

To have schizophrenia, schizophreniform, or schizoaffective disorder, the client must have at least 2 of the following symptoms:
- Hallucinations (known as a core positive symptom)
- Delusions (known as a core positive symptom)
- Disorganized speech (known as a core positive symptom)
- Severely disorganized or catatonic behavior
- Negative Symptoms (such as avolition or diminished expression)

For diagnosis the client must have at least one of the 3 core positive symptoms listed above.

Neurodevelopmental disorders

Intellectual disabilities are neurodevelopmental disorders that include a cognitive capacity deficit and an adaptive functioning deficit. The onset of an intellectual disability must be during the developmental years. The severity of the disability ranges are mild, moderate, severe, and profound. The severity is determined by the client's adaptive functioning level, rather that the client's cognitive capacity. The DSM-5 has changed the wording of "intellectual disability" to intellectual disability to align more closely with other medical, educational, and advocacy groups.

Communication disorders are a neurodevelopmental disorder with subcategories including language disorder, speech sound disorder, chldhood-onset fluency disorder (stuttering), and social communications disorder.

Autism spectrum disorder (ASD) has two components in its diagnosis: delays or abnormal functioning in social interaction/language for social communication and restricted repetitive behaviors, interests, and activities. Both of these pieces will be present in the ASD diagnosis. Severity levels are: Level 1 (requires support), Level 2 (requiring substantial support), and Level 3 (requiring very substantial support). Of note, ASD now encompasses four disorders that were previously separate under DSM-IV autistic disorder, Asperger's disorder, childhood integrative disorder, and pervasive developmental disorder.

ADHD is characterized by two symptom domains, inattentiveness and or/hyperactivity and impulsivity. Requires symptoms persisting for at least six months, and symptoms not motivated by anger or wish to displease or spite others.

Inattentiveness symptoms: Forgetful in everyday activity ● Easily distracted (often) ● Makes careless mistakes and doesn't give attention to detail ● Difficulty focusing attention ● Does not appear to listen, even when directly spoken to ● Starts tasks but does not follow through ● Frequently loses essential items ● Finds organizing difficult ● Avoids activities that require prolonged mental exertion

Impulsivity/Hyperactivity symptoms: Frequently gets out of chair ● Runs/climbs at inappropriate times ● Frequently talks more than peers ● Often moves hands and feet, or shifts position in seat ● Frequently interrupts others ● Frequently has difficulty waiting on turn ● Frequently unable to enjoy leisure activities silently ● Frequently "on the go" and seen by others as restless ● Often finishes other's sentences

Motor disorders are a type of neurodevelopmental disorder and they can be classified as developmental coordination disorders, stereotypic movement disorders, and tic disorders. Tic disorders are further classified as Tourette's disorder, persistent motor or vocal tic disorder and provisional tic disorder.

Feeding and Eating Disorders
- Pica
- Rumination disorder
- Anorexia nervosa
- Avoidant/restrictive food intake disorder
- Bulimia nervosa
- Binge eating disorder

Anorexia nervosa: Criteria A: Extreme restriction of food, lower then requirements, leading to low body weight. Criteria B: An irrational fear of gaining weight or behaviors that prevent weight gain, though at low weight. Criteria C: Distorted body image or a lack of acknowledgement of gravit of current weight.

Bulimia nervosa: Criteria A: Cyclical periods of binge eating: 1. Discretely consuming an amount of food that is larger than most individuals would eat eat in the same time period and situation. 2. The client feels a lack of control over the eating. Criteria B: Characterized by binge eating followed by purging via self-induced vomiting/laxatives/fasting /vigorous exercise in order to prevent weight gain. Criteria C: At least one binge eating episodes per week for three months. Criteria D: It is marked by a persistent over-concern with body shape and weight. Criteria E: The eating and compensatory behaviors do not only occur during periods of anorexia nervosa.

Substance related disorders
Substance related disorders may be caused by abusing a drug, by medication side-effects, or by exposure to a toxin.
Substance intoxication or withdrawal—the behavioral, psychological, and physiological symptoms due to effects of the substance. It will vary depending on type of substance.
Substance related disorders includes the following classes: caffiene; hallucinogens; alcohol; cannabis; stimulants; tobacco; inhalants; opioids; other; and sedatives, hypnotics and anxiolytics. The severity of the particular substance use disorder can be determined by the presence of the number of symptoms.
Also present may be substance induced delirium, dementia, psychosis, mood disorders, anxiety disorder, sexual dysfunction, or sleep dysfunction.
Treatment should focus first on the substance. Treatment options include outpatient or inpatient; residential or day care; group, individual, and/or family counseling; methadone maintenance (for opiates); detoxification; self-help groups; or a combination of therapies and medication.
Substance-related and addictive disorders now includes gambling disorder, as evidence shows that the behaviors of gambling trigger simliar reward systems as drugs.

The type of remission is based on whether any of the criteria for abuse/dependence have been met and over what time frame:
Early Remission: After the criteria for a substance use disorder have been met, none of those criteria are fulfilled (except for the criteria for craving) for at least three months but not more than 1 year.
Sustained Remission: After the criteria for a substance use disorder have been met, none of those criteria are fulfilled (except for the criteria for craving) for 1 year or longer.
If the client is in remission in a controlled environment, this should be specified.
Maintenance Therapy- a replacement medication that can be taken to avoid withdrawal symptoms. The client could still be considered in remission from a substance use disorder if while using maintanance therapy, they do no meet any criteria for that substance use disorder except for craving. For tobacco use disorder this would include using nicotine replacement systems. For opioid use disorder this could include medications such as methadone.

Personality disorders

- **Paranoid personality disorder:** pervasive and inappropriate interpretation of others' actions as threatening or demeaning. Does not cause psychotic symptoms.
- **Schizoid personality disorder:** lack of concern for social relationships and a restricted range of emotional experience and expression. Incapacity to form intimate social relationships/experience affection for others, and lack of caring about others' responses.
- **Schizotypal personality disorder:** characterized by deficits in interpersonal connectedness; peculiarities in various thought, perception, speech and behavior patterns (i.e. magical thinking, ideas of reference, recurrent illusions).
- **Antisocial personality disorder:** a history of chronic irresponsible and antisocial behavior, beginning in childhood or adolescence. Violations of others' rights and occupational failure over several years. Early lying/stealing can lead to acting out sexual behavior, drinking, drugs, and later failure at work and home and adult violations of social norms.
- **Borderline personality disorder:** instability in relationships, mood, and self-image. Unpredictable and impulsive acting-out, which can be self-destructive. Strong mood shifts from normal state to rage. Chronic fear of being alone, dread of feeling emptiness. May have short-lived paranoid or dissociative symptoms.
- **Histrionic personality disorder:** excessive emotionality and attention seeking. Constant seeking of reassurance, approval, or praise. Overly dramatic and intense behavior.
- **Narcissistic personality disorder:** grandiose sense of self-importance, fantasies of unlimited success, chronic exhibitionism, difficulty dealing with criticism, indifference to others. Relationship difficulties—feeling entitled, taking advantage of/exploiting others, polarizing others by idealizing or devaluing.
- **Avoidant personality disorder:** characterized by social discomfort, fear of criticism, timidity, extreme sensitivity to possibility of social rejection, fear of social relationships, desire for closeness but withdrawing socially, low self-esteem.
- **Dependent personality disorder:** characterized by a persistent pattern of dependent and submissive behavior, a lack of self-confidence, and an inability to function independently.
- **Obsessive-compulsive personality disorder:** characterized by a persistent pattern of perfectionism /inflexibility. Limited ability to demonstrate positive emotions. Perfectionism for trivial detail. Demand others comply. Preoccupied with work; tight with money.

Obsessive-Compulsive and related disorders

Body dysmorphic disorder, hoarding disorder, trichotillomania (hair-pulling disorder), excoriation (skin-picking disorder) and OCD.
OCD Criteria: The client exhibits obsessions, compulsions, or both.
Obsession- continuous, repetitive thoughts, compulsions, or things imagined that are unwanted. Compulsion- recurrent behavior the client feels obliged to perform after an obsession. The compulsion is usually not connected in an understandable way to an observer. The obsessions /compulsions take at least 1 hr/day, cause distress, are not caused by a substance, and are not explained by another mental disorder.

Trauma- and stressor-related disorders

Reactive attachment disorder – child rarely seeks or responds to comfort when upset, usually due to neglect of emotional needs by caregiver
Disinhibited social engagement disorder – child has decreased hesitations regarding interacting with unfamiliar adults.

Posttraumatic stress disorder - persistently re-experiencing a severe trauma for > 1 month. Individual exhibits arousal-anxiety symptoms, and avoidance of things associated with the trauma or numbness.

Acute stress disorder – anxiety and dissociative symptoms develop within 1 month of experiencing a trauma.

Adjustment disorder – the client has distressing and disproportional behavior/emotional changes occurring within 3 months of a stressor.

Neurocognitive disorders

Major or minor neurocognitive disorders (NCD) which may be due to:

- Alzheimer's disease
- Frontotemporal lobar degeneration
- Lewy body disease
- Vascular disease
- Traumatic brain injury
- Substance/Medication use
- HIV infection
- Prion disease
- Parkinson's disease
- Huntington's disease
- Another medical condition
- Multiple etiologies

Criteria A: A change in cognitive ability from baseline. This information can be determined by the client, a well-informed significant other, family member, or caretaker, or it can be determined by neuropsychology testing.

Criteria B: For a major neurocognitive disorder, the cognitive change interferes with ADLs and independence. For a minor neurocognitive disorder, the cognitive change doesn't interfere with normal ADLS and independence, if accommodations are used.

Criteria C: The cognitive change cannot be defined as delirium only.

Criteria D: The cognitive change is not better described as another mental disorder.

Sleep-wake disorders

Insomnia disorders – Difficulty falling asleep, staying asleep, or early rising without being able to go back to sleep.

Hypersomnolence disorder – sleepiness despite getting at least 7 hours with difficulty feeling awake when suddenly awoke, lapses of sleep in the day, feeling unrested after long periods of sleep.

Narcolepsy – uncontrollable lapses into sleep, occurring at least three times each week for at least 3 months.

Obstructive sleep apnea hypopnea – Breathing related sleep disorder with obstructive apneas or hypopneas.

Central sleep apnea – Breathing related sleep disorder w/central apnea.

Sleep-related hypoventilation – Breathing related sleep disorder with evidence of decreased respiratory rate and increased CO_2 level.

Circadian rhythm sleep-wake disorder – sleep wake disorder w/primary cause a mismatch between circadian rhythm and sleep required.

Non-rapid eye movement sleep arousal disorder- awakening during the first third of the night associated w/ sleep walking/sleep terrors.

Nightmare disorder- Recurring dreams that are well remembered and cause distress.

Rapid eye movement sleep behavior disorder- arousal during REM sleep associated with motor movements and vocalizing.

Restless legs syndrome- the need to move the legs due to uncomfortable sensations, usually relieved by activity.

Suicide

Suicide is among the ten most frequent causes of death in the United States with approximately 30,000 recorded each year. The actual number is estimated to be closer to 75,000. The suicide rate increases with age. Among 15-24 year olds, suicide is the third most frequent cause of death with about 4,000 each year. Males are more likely to commit suicide than females, but the attempt rate is higher among females. Groups at greatest risk include Native American and Alaska Native adolescents and homosexual youth. No differences in the profiles of suicidal and non-suicidal individuals are revealed by such standard personality tests as the MMPI and Rorschach. Indications that a person may make a suicide attempt include depression and anger, experiencing loss or rejection, talking about suicide, planning and securing the means to commit suicide, and giving away possessions. Counselors should be aware of support groups, have a crisis plan, and involve the community when working with at-risk clients.

Theories of Leon Festinger, Kubler-Ross and Masters and Johnson

Leon Festinger developed the concept of cognitive dissonance. Cognitive dissonance is the mental discomfort that arises when a person does something that conflicts with his beliefs or normal behavior or when he holds conflicting opinions. Festinger presented his theory in his 1957 book *A Theory of Cognitive Dissonance.*

On Death and Dying by Elisabeth Kübler-Ross described five stages people go through when faced with death or other catastrophic changes. The five stages are denial, anger, bargaining for time, depression, and acceptance.

William Howell Masters and Virginia Eshelman Johnson, pioneers in the field of research into human sexuality, advanced the ideas that sexuality is a healthy human trait and that pleasure and intimacy during sex are socially acceptable goals. They made several discoveries about human sexual response and wrote several books on the subject.

Differences between diagnosis, prognosis, intervention, recommendation, statistical norm and cultural norm

Diagnosis is the identification of a disease based on the symptoms or through laboratory tests. Prognosis is the prospect of recovery from a disease based on its usual course or the particularities of the specific case.

Intervention is the introduction of services, activities, or products in an effort to cause change or improvement.

A *recommendation* is a counselor's statement of the recommended course of treatment.

The *statistical norm* is a mathematical distribution that can be used to measure the average expectation of how a group of people will act.

A *cultural (or social) norm* is the expectation of how a population will or should behave as opposed to what they actually do.

Theories

Social exchange theory links behavioral psychology and economics. According to the theory, positive relationships are characterized by profit. As long as the rewards of the relationship exceed the cost, the relationship will continue.

Complementarity theory states that relationships strengthen when the personality needs of each member of the couple enhance those of the other. The theory advances the idea that the couple together makes up for what each member lacks.

Assimilation-contrast theory is the idea that when there are similarities between the client and the counselor, the similarities will be viewed as being more like the client's own (assimilation), and dissimilar attitudes will be exaggerated. The more respect the client has for the counselor and the more trustworthy he or she believes the counselor to be, the more the client will accept the counselor's statements.

Basic tenets of Durkheim, McDougall, Berne and Parsons

Emile Durkheim is considered to be the founder of French sociology and is credited with making sociology into a science. He studied social values and alienation, and believed technology and mechanization were threats to ethical and social structures.

William McDougall, an opponent of behaviorism, advocated the idea that behavior is goal oriented and purposive. His term for this theory was "hormic psychology."

In his book *Games People Play,* Eric Berne introduced the concept that games are ritualistic behaviors that can indicate hidden feelings. He developed transactional analysis (TA) as an alternative to the psychoanalytic techniques in use in the 1950's.

Frank Parsons, known as the father of vocational guidance, advanced the theory that personality traits should be matched to job factors.

Traits of active-directive and person-centered counseling models and the predictions of the Osgood and Tannenbaum's Congruity theory

The active-directive counseling model is especially appropriate for clients from cultures that value authority figures. This model involves the counselor providing advice while speaking with authority and exhibiting a strong attitude. A teacher and student atmosphere complete with homework may be used. Created by Carl Rogers, the humanistic person-centered counseling approach is appropriate for use in multicultural and multiracial situations. The method is non-judgmental, assumes the client already had the solution to his or her problems, and uses active listening and paraphrasing. Rather than interpreting unconscious thoughts, the counselor helps the client to accept and understand his or her feelings.

Based on Heider's theory of balanced relationships, Osgood and Tannenbaum's Congruity Theory advances the idea that the more similar the client and counselor are, the more readily the client will accept suggestions from the counselor.

Tenets of the psychoanalytic counseling theory

The psychoanalytic theory developed by Sigmund Freud is based on his theory of personality involving the id, ego, and superego. The id is the unconscious motivation ruled by the pleasure principle. The ego id ruled by the reality principle and the superego provides internalized ethics. Psychoanalysis makes use of the concepts of transference and countertransference. Transference is the projection of the emotions of the client onto the counselor and countertransference is the reverse. The object of the therapy is to help the client work through to his unconscious and uncover the source of conflicts and motivations. Among the techniques used are free association and the interpretation of dreams.

Object relations theory

Object relations theory is based on psychoanalytic concepts and posits that interpersonal relationships shape a person's current interactions with people. The relationships in question can be real or fantasized.

Four broad stages occur during the first three years of life. They are:
- Fusion with the mother during the first 3-4 weeks
- Symbiosis during the third to the eighth month
- Separation/individuation starting in the fourth or fifth month,
- Constancy of self and object occurring by the thirty-sixth month.

Progress through these stages helps the child develop trust that his or her needs will be met. Otherwise, the child may develop attachment, borderline or narcissistic disorders. The work of Margaret Mahler, Heinz Kohut and Otto Kernberg has been important in the development of this theory.

Karen Horney, Erich Fromm and Harry Stack Sullivan

Ad Neo-Freudian psychoanalysts, Horney, Fromm, and Sullivan placed emphasis on the ego as the driving psychological force in development. Horney identified the major motivational factor as security. She found that a lack of security caused anxiety and that irrational ways of mending disrupted relationships may cause neurotic needs to develop. According to Fromm, society offers opportunities for mutual love and respect. He found that people need to join with others in order to develop self-fulfillment. Otherwise they become lonely and nonproductive. Sullivan's studies of the social systems used an interpersonal approach and were an effort to understand human behavior. He believed behavior must be examined in respect to social interactions rather than as mechanistic and linear.

Counseling skills in relationship to the counseling setting

- Empathic understanding is the counselor's awareness of the client's feelings and knowledge
- Congruence is the counselor's ability to be genuinely involved in the counseling session. Congruence is also harmony between a client's behavior and his or her values and beliefs.
- Unconditional positive regard or acceptance is the counselor caring about the client without imposing conditions or being judgmental.

- Concreteness is the extent to which the counselor and client confront issues in specific terms.
- Immediacy is the counseling process dealing with the client's current issues.
- Interpretation is a therapeutic technique that uncovers or suggests meanings, significance or relationships.
- Self-disclosure is the counselor sharing personal experiences with the client.
- Attending refers to such behaviors as listening, engaging in eye contact, and being psychologically present during a counseling session.

Theory of Carl Jung

Carl Jung regarded the psyche as having three parts: the ego, the personal unconscious, and the collective unconscious. The ego is the conscious mind and the personal unconscious includes things that are not presently conscious such as memories that can be brought to mind and those that have been suppressed. The collective unconscious he regarded as a reservoir of our experiences as a species. Jung applied several terms to the contents of the collective unconscious, but the term that has gained widespread use is "archetypes." An archetype can be compared to instinct in Freud's theory, but are more spiritual than biological. Two of the archetypes are the anima and the animus. The anima is the female traits in a man while animus is the male traits in a woman. The goal of Jungian therapy is to help the client develop self-realization.

Gordon Allport, Kurt Lewin, Aaron Beck, Joseph Wolpe, and Donald Meichenbaum

Allport emphasized the uniqueness of the individual. He defined personality as "the dynamic organization within the individual of those psychophysical systems that determine his characteristic behavior and thought."

Lewin is called the "father of social psychology.' He studied group dynamics and organizational development. His work toward combating racial and religious prejudices laid the foundation for sensitivity training.

Beck is known as the "father of cognitive therapy." He believed that people become depressed because they have unrealistic negative views of themselves, the world, and their future.

Wolpe believed that behavior therapy is as much an applied science as any other area of medicine. He developed the concept of desensitization, and his work led to assertiveness training.

Meichenbaum, a proponent of the constructivist perspective, is one of the founders of cognitive-behavior therapy.

Alcohol and substance abuse and associated counseling techniques

Substance abuse, which includes the abuse of alcohol, prescription drugs, and illegal drugs, is a major problem in the United States. More than three million teenagers have a problem with alcohol. There is a strong connection between drinking and such teenage problems as suicide, early sexual activity, and driving accidents. Abuse of alcohol and drugs affects not just the abuser, but family members, friends, and coworkers as well. Characteristics of substance abusers include low self-esteem, anxiety, sexual problems, suicidal impulses, fear of failure, and social isolation. Since addictions are both physical and mental, successful treatment must involve both. The Substance

Abuse Subtle Screening Inventory (SASSI) can be used to detect indicators of addiction. One effective treatment method is a Twelve-Step Program coupled with individual, group, and family counseling. It is especially important that counseling involve the family. Behavior modification and social learning theory can be used effectively in a residential program.

Important terms

- ACA (The American Counseling Association) - A not-for-profit organization that promotes the educational and professional growth of counselors and establishes professional and ethical standards. Since the passage of the Civil Rights Act of 1964, the organization has encouraged cross-cultural counseling.
- Accountability - Being responsible or accountable for ones actions. For a counselor, accountability means being able to explain or justify treatment decisions and activities used with a client.
- Adaptive functioning - Coping with stressful situations through defense mechanisms such as anticipation, humor, and sublimation. Persons who fail to adapt can develop a breach with reality.
- Androgyny - Defined as having both male and female characteristics.
- Archetype - An ideal model of a person, thing, or concept; a stereotype or a defining example.
- Assertiveness training - A psychotherapy method that helps a person to learn to state both negative and positive feelings directly. The method does not encourage aggressive behavior.
- Balance theory - As proposed by Fritz Heider, it is a motivational theory of attitude change. It explains relationships in terms of people striving for cognitive balance in their likes and dislikes.
- Chaining - Behaviors that occur because of a cue from an earlier behavior.
- Circular causality - Called "systems theory" by Ludwig von Bertalanffy and expresses the idea of many forces from different directions acting upon each other at the same time. The situation has no clear cause, and the focus is on the process that is taking place.
- Co-dependents - People in relationships with addicted or troubled persons. The addiction can be to drugs, alcohol, or self-destructive behavior. Some form of psychological dysfunction may also be involved. The relationship may be that of lovers, spouses, family members, friends, or co-workers. The codependent becomes an enabler or rescuer for the other person. He or she makes excuses for the person or may deny that there is a problem.
- Comorbidity - The coexistence of two or more diseases or disorders such as alcoholism and depression. The conditions may have a causal relationship with each other, or there may be an underlying predisposition for both or all of them.
- Contextualism - The concept that behavior, decisions and actions must be understood in context.
- Culture - The shared norms, values, arts, beliefs, and institutions of a community or population.
- Displacement - A defense mechanism in which a person does not display anger at the time of the anger-inducing incident, but displays it later and directs it toward a different person.
- Eidetic imagery - The ability to recall minute details of something a person has observed.
- Equifinality - Can be defined as multiple paths leading to the same outcome. An example of equifinalilty in abnormal human behavior would be physical injury or illness, the loss of a loved one or alcoholism leading to depression.

- Etiology - The study of the causes of disease or abnormal conditions, whether the cause is biological, psychological, or arises from the patient's social environment.
- Extinction - The withholding of reinforcement for a behavior as a means of eliminating the behavior.
- Introjection - The process by which a child adopts the values of another person.
- Linear causality - Expresses the idea that a particular thing cannot happen unless another particular thing happens first. This idea can also be expressed as "one thing leads to another."
- Mandalas - Drawings Carl Jung called protective circles representing self-unification that he used to analyze himself and clients.
- Mediation - The resolution of a conflict between two or more parties by the intervention of a neutral party.
- Paralanguage - The use of nonphonemic properties of speech such as intonation, pitch, tempo, and gestures to convey attitude or meaning.
- Projection - Attributing a person's own characteristics to others.
- Psychological dysfunction - A breakdown in a person's thought processes, emotional functions or behavior. A diagnosis of psychological dysfunction must consider the patient's cultural context, his personal distress and the extent to which his ability to function is impaired.
- REBT (Rational-emotive behavior therapy) - Based on the concept that people adopt irrational behaviors and beliefs that hinder the achievement of their goals. The therapy aims to change the "must, should, ought" behavior into "wish, prefer, want." The therapy puts less emphasis on mental illness, and sees the counselor as a teacher.
- Reciprocal determinism - Albert Bandura's term for the idea that each person is influenced by his or her environment, and at the same time exerts influence on that environment. The idea expresses the dynamic, continuous process of the interaction between an individual and his or her home situation.
- Relational causality - A cause and effect situation in which the effect is caused by the relationship rather than a single factor of the relationship being the cause.
- Robber's Cave – A summer camp in Oklahoma was used in an experiment by psychologist Muzafer Sherif to demonstrate the importance of cooperation on shared goals in resolving conflict peacefully.
- Sleeper effect - The concept that the effect of communications increases after some time has passed. Communications between a counselor and the client may have little initial impact, but the effect may increase as time passes.
- Society - A population that occupies a defined territory and had shared interests and institutions. All members of a society may not share the same culture. An example would be a Native American culture inside the United States.
- Sour grapes rationalization - A defense mechanism by which people rationalize that they did not really want something they did not get.
- Stanley Milgram - Known for his research into obedience to authority. In his 1961-62 experiments, he found that 65% percent of his subjects would administer powerful electric shocks to others when told to do so by an authority figure.
- Sweet lemon rationalization - A defense mechanism by which a person rationalizes a distasteful event into an acceptable one.
- TAT (Thematic Apperception Test) - A projective test introduced by Henry Murray, in which a client tells stories about pictures the therapist shows him or her.

- Therapeutic surrender - Occurs when a client psychologically surrenders himself or herself to a counselor from a different culture or class. The relationship must involve trust and rapport resulting in the client becoming open with his thoughts and feelings.

Group Counseling

Johari Window

Devised by Joe Luft and Harry Ingham, the Johari window is a useful model for describing human interaction. The window, divided into four panes, represents four different types of personal awareness: open, blind, hidden, and unknown. The open quadrant (the arena) is information known by the person and by others. The blind quadrant (the blindspot) is information about himself that the person does not know but that others do know. The hidden quadrant (the façade) is information the person knows about himself, but that others do not know. The unknown quadrant (the unknown) is what the person does not know about himself and others also do not know. The window is used in self-help groups and in corporate settings. Group participants select adjectives from a list of fifty-five to describe themselves and other group members. The selected adjectives are then mapped onto a "window" for each individual. The goal of the exercise is to improve self-awareness and mutual understanding.

Group counseling

Group counseling is a situation in which a counselor works with several people who are all concerned with the same or a related problem or behavior. Psychodrama, which can be considered a precursor to group therapy, dates back to at least the early 1600s. In the United States, group therapy started in the late 1800s and early 1900s in such organizations as Hull House as an effort to help immigrants adjust to life in their new country. In 1931, Jacob Mareno invented the term "group therapy" as a description for the role-playing in psychodrama. The growth of group therapy was encouraged by the shortage of individual therapists following World War II. The first professional association for group therapists, The American Society for Group Psychotherapy and Psychodrama was formed in 1942 by Mareno. In 1943, S. R. Slavson founded the American Group Psychotherapy Association. In December 2003, the Association for Specialists in Group Work was established as a division of the American Counseling Association.

Advantages and goals

The goals of group counseling are for the clients to learn new behaviors in a social setting where they can experience peer confrontation and develop new skills in a non-threatening environment. The advantages of the group situation are the social setting and the dynamics of the group; the possibility for each client to experience a number of different roles; and a perspective to clarify goals and values. The group situation also acts to dissipate counselor bias, allows the counselor to deal with more clients, and may reduce the per-client cost of the therapy.

Counseling group considerations

The first issue is membership – will the group be homogeneous with members who have a similar problem or heterogeneous with members who have separate problems and may have trouble relating to each other? Will the group be open and welcoming to new members if some original members leave or closed with a set group of members? The second issue is the size of the group. Optimum size for an adult group is eight, but children's groups should be smaller with only three to four members for the very young. Duration of the group is the third issue. For how long will the group meet? The fourth issue is the duration of the meetings, which can run ninety minutes to two hours for adult outpatients, but should be no more than twenty or thirty minutes for young children.

Ethical considerations

Before the sessions begin the members should be fully informed of what to expect and what will be required of them. They should consent to participation unless their attendance is required for some reason. If a member is a juvenile, the informed consent would apply to a parent or guardian. The members should be informed if the sessions will be connected in any way to a research project. They should understand the rights they have – freedom from undue pressure, voluntary participation, and freedom to leave the group. Information concerning the skills and competencies of the group's leader(s) and the resources available to the participants should be given to each member. The importance and limits of confidentiality both as it applies to what the counselor learns about each member and what they learn about each other, should be carefully explained.

Screening process

Prospective members for a counseling group are usually screened through an interview with the group leader. Typically, the counselor will discuss the goals and purpose of the group, the rules, the appropriateness of the group for the prospect's needs, and confidentiality issues with the prospect. The counselor will also try to assess the attitude, motivation, and characteristics of the prospective member since successful groups need members who are of similar intellectual levels and who do not exhibit disruptive or dominating behavior. During the interview, the prospective member should have a chance to explore whether or not group counseling is appropriate for him or her.

Eleven curative factors of group counseling identified by Irvin Yalom

The eleven curative factors are:
- *instillation of hope* –encourages participants to continue with the group since it seems likely that needs will be met;
- *universality* –lets the group members know they are not alone with their problems;
- *imparting of information* – participants share information and resources and give advice to each other;
- *altruism* – raises self-esteem, helps the members feel needed and useful;
- *corrective emotional experience* – increases understanding of how one interacts with others;
- *development of socializing techniques* – members develop coping and conflict resolution skills;
- *imitative behavior* – members learn by seeing how others solve problems;
- *interpersonal behavior* – the group can provide positive interpersonal relationships;
- *group cohesiveness* – the group provides a safe environment with feedback;
- *catharsis* – emotions can be purged;
- *existential factors* – participants learn that they must take personal responsibility for their own behavior.

Leadership functions defined by Yalom

Among the functions necessary for leaders in group counseling is the creation of a caring environment that will encourage trust and self-disclosure among the group members. The leader must also manage the group, guide the activities, set the pace for the sessions, and stop any inappropriate interactions. He or she must interpret what takes place by clarifying, reviewing and explaining. The leader must encourage the members to express emotions, values, opinions, and beliefs, and to confront and challenge each other when such activity is appropriate.

Michael Waldo's theories

According to Michael Waldo, the problems of the group members should determine the type of leadership appropriate for that group. The problems should also determine whether the group is an inpatient or outpatient one and other such functions as time limits and the goals of the group. Other functions that should be determined by the type of client involved would include the level of emotional stimulation, how strictly the leader controls the content of the meeting and how he or she fits that content to the group members.

Jacob Moreno's theories

Moreno, who was associated in the 1920s with the "Theater of Spontaneity" in Vienna, became a leading figure in the use of psychodrama. He believed psychodrama could be used to help a troubled person reach insight and catharsis as well as for reality testing. In using psychodrama, the group leader serves as the director with members of the group taking the needed actor roles, while other members serve as the audience. A portion of the meeting room may serve as the stage or the action may move to a different location.

Multicultural issues

Before starting work with a group that will include multicultural members, the counselor needs to educate him or herself about those cultures. Attention to factors such as manners (greetings, whether or not it is polite to look directly at or touch a person, etc.), sharing personal information, and displaying emotion are especially important since different ethnic groups place different values on such factors. What is completely acceptable to a person from one background may be an unforgivable insult to a person from another. A discussion of such differences along with information about the purpose, goals, and techniques of the group plus a question and answer session may need to be a large portion of the first group meeting. For the group to develop cohesion, it is essential that cultural differences be respected.

Important terms

- Gatekeeper - A person in a group who wants to be in charge and tries to manage the group.
- Integrative psychotherapy - The integration of multiple therapy approaches; used by 30% to 50% of therapists.
- Intellectualization - Using reasoning to protect oneself from emotional stress or conflict.
- Isolate role - The person in a group who receives little or no attention; he or she may be afraid to participate or others in the group may actually ignore him or her.
- Mimesis - As defined by Minuchin, the copying of a family's style by a counselor.
- Norms – a group's standards of acceptable behaviors.
- Object - The person, thing, or concept to which a person relates; can also refer to a transition object such as a blanket or stuffed animal, which a child cuddles or holds as a comfort device when the mother is not present.
- Perverse triangle - As used by Hayley, the situation in which two members of a family team up against another member in an effort to reduce his or her authority.

- Projective system – Due to childhood events or relationships, a person has unrealistic expectations of someone with whom he or she has an adult relationship. The term was defined by Robin Skynner.
- Resistance - Behavior in a group that interferes with the work of the group.
- Scapegoating - Blaming someone who may not be responsible for the action or event.
- Skeleton keys - As used by Steve deShazer, a standard intervention that can be used in dealing with several problems.
- Splitting - The separation of contradictory or conflicting thoughts, so that they can be handled separately since the person cannot consider them together.
- Universality - Something that is true for all times and places, also the understanding that one is not alone in experiencing a particular problem or situation.
- XO - An abbreviation used by counselors. X means treatment and O indicates observation; can also indicate a measurement, score or dependent variable.

Programmatic and Clinical Intervention

Individual psychology as defined by Adler and Dreikurs

Alfred Adler and Rudolph Dreikurs advanced the idea that the uniqueness of each person is influenced by social factors. They believed that everyone strives for superiority. A person's lifestyle is made up of and given meaning by such factors as habits, family, work, and attitudes. Counselors use techniques such as life histories, homework assignments, and paradoxical intentions to help clients understand their lifestyles and identify appropriate social and community interests.

Rogerian and Gestalt theories

The Rogerian theory as advanced by Carl Rogers in the 1940s is person-centered. It deals with the trustworthiness of individuals, and the belief that people have an innate ability to move toward self-actualization which is the process of becoming. The theory also says that no two people perceive the world in exactly the same way. Counselors using the Rogerian theory focus on the present and the client's feelings, and work to promote conditions for change rather than doing things to bring about change. The counselor should have unconditional positive regard for the client and empathic understanding, so that he or she can help the client to understand the impact of the client's choices and actions.

Existential principles and a holistic systems viewpoint are aspects of the Gestalt approach. The goal of an individual is to become a whole being. In this approach, the past is considered less important than what is done, thought or felt in the present. Counselors can use role-playing, dream work, and confrontation to help a client relive experiences and bring closure to them. What happens is interpreted by the client rather than the counselor. The goal is to help the client learn more effective ways of coping, and for him or her to assume more responsibility for what happens in his or her life.

Phenomenology and existential therapy

Phenomenology is the study of conscious experiences from a first person viewpoint. It is the basis for existential therapy. Existential philosophy emphasizes freedom of choice and responsibility for one's own acts. Existential therapy is client-centered and emphasizes the ability to make choices not dictated by heredity or past experiences. The goals are for the client to understand who he is and who he is becoming, to make socially constructive choices, and achieve authentic relationships with others. Leading existential theorists include Rollo May, Viktor Frankl, and Irvin Yalom. Frankl developed "logotherapy," which assists clients to reappraise what is most meaningful in their lives.

Eric Berne's transactional analysis

Transactional analysis is a method of psychotherapy in which emotional problems are treated by helping clients analyze their relationships in social situations (transactions). The method was developed by Eric Berne in the 1960s. He identified three ego states: child, adult, and parent which are analogous to the id, ego, and superego of Freud's theory. Transactional analysis psychotherapy is oriented to the immediate present, and consists of identifying and analyzing the client's style of interaction. Useful techniques include the use of contracts, confrontation, and teaching the clients concepts they can use in their everyday lives.

Rational Emotive Behavior Therapy (REBT)

REBT, introduced by Albert Ellis in 1955, is a form of psychotherapy that can help clients change dysfunctional behaviors and emotions by becoming aware of and modifying the beliefs and attitudes that cause the problems. The central idea is that a person's emotional state is caused by the person's beliefs about an event rather than the event alone. According to an article by Ellis on the Albert Ellis Institute Website, "REBT helps restore the emotional balance in an individual's life by providing methods for thinking more realistically and level-headedly about ourselves, other people, and the world."

Cognitive and behavioral counseling

In cognitive and behavioral counseling, it is desirable that there be a strong personal relationship between the counselor and the client. The therapy identifies the origins of the undesirable behavior and uses learning techniques such as problem solving, social modeling, direct training, and reinforcement to change the attitudes, beliefs, and assumptions that cause the client's problems. Cognitive therapists concentrate on learning principles such as perception, reasoning, and judgment. Rational-emotive therapy (RET, later REBT) is an attempt to help the client understand his or her irrational thinking and its consequences. Behavior therapies include:

- Exposure therapy in which the client is placed in actual, stressful situations (in vivo) or in imagined situations (in vitro) in an effort to help him create new, non-anxiety associations.
- Contingency management in which desirable actions are reinforced or rewarded and undesirable behavior is ignored.
- Behavioral activation is a psychotherapy often used in treating depression. It focuses on getting clients more active in solving problems and engaging in meaningful and pleasurable activities.
- Modeling in which the client observes a desired behavior, sees that it has no negative repercussions, and learns to copy the behavior.
- Biofeedback in which the client learns to monitor and control a bodily function. This technique can be very effective in dealing with panic attacks.

Reality Therapy

Reality therapy, based on the choice theory, is a type of psychotherapy and counseling developed primarily by Dr. William Glasser in the mid-1960s. His view is that people who behave inappropriately need help in acknowledging their behavior as inappropriate and in learning to act in a more appropriate way. Five basic groups of needs are identified: survival, power, love and belonging, freedom, and fun. Everyone must learn to meet his needs in ways that do not create conflict with other people. The therapy focuses on the present and encourages the client to evaluate his behavior by asking the question, "Is what I'm doing getting me closer to what I need?" It also helps the client to create and follow through with workable plans for meeting his needs. Choice and responsibility are emphasized.

Multimodal therapy and Integrative counseling

The multimodel therapy approach to psychotherapy was founded by Arnold Lazarus. It is a comprehensive, holistic method based on the concept that as biological creatures, humans think, feel, act, sense, imagine, and interact. These functions are called "modalities" and each should be addressed in psychological treatment. Assessment and treatment are built on the framework of *BASIC ID* which is an acronym for behavior, affect, sensation, imagery, cognition, interpersonal, and drugs/biology").

Counseling techniques are drawn from a variety of theories and tailored to the individual client. They may include anxiety-management training, hypnosis, assertiveness training, modeling, relaxation training, and biofeedback.

Integrative counseling is an approach that draws from multiple theories and techniques. It deals with the whole person – body and spirit as well as mind and also considers cultural and social influences such as family and work. The treatment is tailored to the individual.

Solution-focused brief therapy (SFBT)

A post-modern therapy, solution-focused brief therapy is a short-term approach that focuses on solutions rather than problems. Treatment usually lasts six sessions or less. The focus of the counseling is the future not the past. The counselor leads the client to envision the desired future, and helps him or her to discover ways to make that future a reality. The client is helped to recognize what is working now and encouraged to continue or increase those behaviors. What does not work is also identified, and the client is encouraged to cease or decrease those behaviors.

Feminist therapy

Feminist therapy grew out of the feminist movement of the 1960s. It is a form of therapy that emphasizes the empowerment of women and the strengthening of such areas as self-esteem, assertiveness, and communications. Feminist therapy recognizes that our sexist society has harmful effects, but does not seek to blame males for the problems of women. The counselor may use a variety of techniques including gender-role analysis, assertiveness training, and bibliotherapy.

Postmodern approach and narrative therapy

Since there is no objective measurement for mental health, postmodern psychotherapists accept as fact that it is almost impossible to identify what is "psychologically healthy." A dominant aspect of the therapy is "deconstruction" in which common expectations or "givens" are examined to determine whether or not they are useful to the client.

Narrative therapy is based on the premise that people make sense of their lives through stories. The stories are subjective and influenced by the client's environment of family, culture, gender, etc. The therapist listens to the client, and encourages other perspectives and interpretations of the story which helps the client to view his or her life in alternative and preferred ways. Among the techniques the counselor may use are re-authoring the story to emphasize the client's strengths or positive characteristics, and helping the client to separate himself from the problem. Michael White and David Espton developed narrative therapy.

Behavioral techniques of token economy, paradoxical intention, implosive therapy and thought stopping

Token economy is a behavior modification technique that uses points, ratings, etc. to reinforce desirable behavior. Acceptable behavior is rewarded with a token. Tokens can then be exchanged for privileges or items.

Paradoxical intention is a therapy technique in which the client intentionally engages in the unwanted behavior in order to increase his or her awareness of it and of the consequences. This method is appropriate for curbing behaviors like smoking, anger, and flying anxiety.

Implosive therapy is a behavior modification technique in which the clients are given clues or shown vivid images in order to induce anxiety. The repeated exposure in a non-threatening environment is expected to reduce or eliminate the anxiety.

Thought stopping is consciously stopping thoughts that are bothersome or that lead to impulsive, compulsive, or addictive behavior.

Consultation and list the models of consultation

Consultation is voluntary and has the goal of building attitudes and skills that will help the client to function more effectively in interpersonal relationships. Counseling skills are used in consultation, but the role, function and context differ. In content-oriented consultation the consultant imparts information to the client. Process-oriented consultation uses communication theory, attribution, change or motivation theory. Bergan's behavioral model emphasized verbal interaction involving the identification and analysis of the problem plus plan implementation. Bandura's social learning model assesses the interplay of behaviors, cognitions, and environment in identifying problems with solutions involving modeling, rehearsing, and changing cognitions. Schein's doctor-patient model is a diagnostic process and identifies interventions. Caplan's mental health model is a consultation between two professionals in which the discussion may involve the client, the consultant and the client, the program, or the consultant and administration. A nine-stage consultation process was described by Splete.

Neurolinguistic Programming, Eye Movement Desensitization and Reprocessing, Kinesics, Proxemics, and Paradigm shift

Neuro-linguistic programming (NLP) – a communication theory developed in the 1970s that posits that mind, body and language interact to govern perception and behavior. Its use in therapy is somewhat controversial.

Eye movement desensitization and reprocessing (EMDR) – a counseling technique in which eye movements are used to help the client access memories of distressing experiences. This technique can be used in the treatment post-traumatic distress syndrome.

Kinesics – a type of non-verbal communication expressed by movement including gestures and expressions.

Proxemics - how people use space and how differences can affect whether a person feels relaxed or nervous. Physical territory is a person's physical environment while personal territory is the space a person maintains between himself and others.

Paradigm shift – a change in viewpoint or way of thinking.

Multi-cultural perspective and psychoanalytical, reality, and behavioral therapy

Psychoanalytical counseling may not be the best approach for clients who seek short-term, solution-oriented counseling, but may appeal to clients from cultures where the focus on family dynamics fits well.

Reality therapy identifies problems and suggests solutions within the cultural environment of the client and works with current situations instead of the past. Both these factors make it well suited for use with clients from many different cultures. However, unless the counselor understands the communication patterns, social and economic environment, and political realities of the different cultures, he or she may have difficulties in reaching the "real" issues with some clients.

Behavioral therapy, which is short term and downplays the role of feelings, is well suited to use with some multicultural clients. Counselors must assist clients in understanding how to fit their new behaviors and any consequences of the behaviors into their cultural environment.

Client-centered theory, which encourages open dialogue, eliminates cultural barriers, and adds respect for the values and differences of others, is more effective when used with clients from cultures that do not rely heavily on an authority figure.

Existential theory helps clients search for meaning and purpose in their lives. Free will and personal responsibility for one's decisions are key elements. The theory is not the best choice for clients who are not used to having personal choice.

Gestalt makes use of a range of techniques from which the counselor can choose the one that is the best fit for each client. Gestalt techniques that focus on nonverbal communications can be useful with clients from cultures that discourage the expression of emotions. It can also be helpful to address current situations rather than dealing with a client's past.

In cognitive-behavior therapy, the emphasis is on thinking rather than feeling as beliefs and premises are examined, which makes it appropriate for persons from cultures that refrain from displaying emotion. The counselor must respect the client's culture and understand how solutions will harmonize with the client's cultural background and religious beliefs.

Feminist therapy is concerned with the empowerment of women and the ways in which they can deal with societal and family issues. Feminism and multiculturalism are two good examples of the increasing attention to the role of the client's environment in problems and coping strategies. Again, it is important for the counselor to be aware of the client's cultural background and any potential consequences of the client's changed behaviors. The counselor must help the client to find an acceptable solution.

Family vs. individual counseling theories

Individual psychotherapy deals with the problems of a particular individual and may involve long-standing situations and require long-term treatment. Usually the counselor has only the information the client supplies about external influences since there is usually no contact with family members or others that may contribute to the situation. Family counseling places the focus on the family even when only one member is actually the client. The counseling may be extended to the client's social context rather than being restricted to the immediate family. It may involve sessions with individuals, but is intended to resolve family problems. The treatment is likely to be more short-term than individual therapy.

Psychodynamic theory of family counseling

Nathan Ackerman used an interactive style of family therapy that considered the psychological heritage of each family member. He coined the term "homeodynamic principle" to express the concept that each family has a basic dynamic and that following an interruption such as counseling, the family will return to that dynamic even if it is dysfunctional. In a healthy family this results in structure and stability. During counseling, Ackerman served as a catalyst to bring out defenses and neutralize imbalances. According to James Framo, a person's social environment helps to shape their behavior and each member of a relationship brings any conflicts from his or her birth family to the current relationship. Framo starts therapy with the entire family, then moves to couple and couple group therapy and finishes with intergenerational conferences involving the family of origin.

Experiential and humanistic family counseling

Experiential family therapy focuses on current experiences of the family and emphasizes experience rather than insight or cognitive knowledge as causes for change. Attention is on emotions and what they represent. The therapist's relationship with the client is important. A leading name in the field is Carl Whitaker. An important name in humanistic family counseling is Virginia Satir. Her view is that the counselor is a teacher and trainer, but that the self-concept of the person allows him or her to grow and develop. Believing that good communication within the family is necessary for the family to function in a healthy manner, she identified five styles of communication. They are placater, blamer, super-reasonable, irrelevant and congruent communicator. Congruent communicator is the healthiest style of communication.

Strategic family therapy

The focus of strategic family therapy is on changing behavior rather than insight. It is a practical approach that deals with family communication, interaction, and behavior patterns. Creative interventions are an important part of the therapy. The therapy relies on strategies to change behavior, achieve goals and focus is on the immediate problem. Strategies can be designed to expose games within the family's interactions and reframe members' motives.

The three main models of strategic family therapy are the MRI (Mental Research Institute), Haley and Madanes, and Milan.

Structural family therapy

Salvador Minuchin is a leader in the use of structural family therapy. He considers a family to be an organization for which the rules are transactional patterns among the members and with subsystems (parents, siblings, students, etc.) with boundaries and rules of membership. Boundaries may be permeable or diffuse. Alignments are the way family members work together or against each other, power is who has authority or responsibility, and coalitions are alliances among specific family members. A structural family map diagrams the current family structure with boundaries, alliances, etc. and shows possible dysfunction. The therapy challenges the transaction patterns of the family with the goal of establishing clearer boundaries or better defining a subsystem. Minuchim's role during the therapy session is an active one as he portrays aspects of the family and encourages the acting out of dysfunctional interactions. He also presents a constructive viewpoint.

Use of behavioral/cognitive therapeutic approaches in family therapy

Behavioral/cognitive therapy can be divided into four types: behavioral marital therapy, behavioral parent skills training, functional family therapy and conjoint sex therapy. Behavior marital therapy, which has not been found to be long-term effective, is an effort to teach couples better communication skills and healthy handling of conflict. Cognitive-behavioral marital therapy adds a consideration of how specific thoughts relate to feelings and moods and how moods affect behavior. Behavioral parent-skills training is an effort to improve child management by educating both parents and child in the use of such techniques as timeouts and contingency contracts. To functional family therapy, all behavior is adaptive and serves a function. Therapy involves intervention and prevention using everyday situations. Families discuss attainable goals without assigning blame. Conjoint sex therapy is the treatment of sexual dysfunctions through work with both partners in a couple. Some sessions may be with one individual, but others will involve the couple together.

Milan systemic family therapy

To Milan therapy, a family is a system of connections among the members. Acknowledging that the family "plays a game" in order to maintain the system, therapy often consists of family interactions while under observation by a team of therapists. The answers to circular questioning in which each family member is asked the same relationship questions reveal the connections among the members and the different ways they interpret an event. The therapist makes use of family patterns and rituals and makes suggestions for ways to alter beliefs and attitudes in an effort to change family rules and relationships.

Narrative family therapy

Narrative family therapy is a postmodern therapeutic approach that works through the tendency of human beings to create narratives or stories of their life experiences. Families bring these narratives to the counseling sessions where the narratives are deconstructed to reveal their underlying assumptions other interpretations are suggested. The process allows the family to re-author the narrative which empowers them. The therapist creates the structure for the new narrative. Narrative family therapy is appropriate for the entire family since it fits quite well with the developmental abilities of children.

Beliefs of social constructionists

Social constructionists subscribe to the idea that such widely accepted concepts as nationality, gender, religion, morality and language exist not as natural objects, but have been created by people. To them, a social construct is an institutionalized entity or artifact that has been invented or constructed by members of a particular culture or society. Counselors using a social constructionist approach include those who make use of such methods as narrative, collaborative language systems, and solution-focused therapy. Practitioners pay little attention to the history or underlying causes of a problem but focus on solutions. Important names in the field include Steve deShazer and William O'Hanlon.

Gender-sensitive issues in family therapy

Gender-sensitive issues are often feminist issues that affect both the females and the males in a family. They may grow out of the culture, especially in ethnic groups that regard females as being of little value or require that a woman be completely subject to the males in her family. Such issues also come from the long devaluing of the female's economic and political role in the United States. In therapy, these issues must be considered in the contest of the social, cultural and political environment of the family. The therapist must be aware of these issues as they relate to himself or herself, so that he or she does not demonstrate a prejudicial attitude in helping the family move beyond traditional sex roles.

Psychoeducational family therapy

Psychoeducation is a therapeutic technique that assists a family in dealing with their daily life and specific issues such as an illness in the family. Life coping skills, medication management, stress and time management and self-care issues can be included. Marriage enrichment and stepfamily issues may also be addressed. Psychoeducation can be especially helpful for families dealing with the mental illness of a family member, as well as for the patient who needs to understand what is happening, why certain medications are needed, the signs of relapse, etc. The process, in combination with medication, has been used successfully in the treatment of patients with schizophrenia, bipolar disorder, ADHA, and depression.

Play therapy

Play therapy is intended to create an atmosphere where the child feels free to show emotions. It allows the child to express feelings and lessen tensions by releasing emotions such as disappointment, fear, anger, and confusion. The child can also act out dreams and ambitions. By observing the child at play, the counselor can assess his reaction to his environment and how he communicates, then analyze his conflicts and help him develop ways to deal with the emotions or let them go.

Counseling styles and techniques

Counseling techniques associated with therapy styles are described below:
- Adlerian – the counselor exhibits empathy and support; techniques include modeling and education with homework and goal-setting assignments.
- Behavioral (& Cognitive Behavioral) Therapy – counselor is the expert, teaching and directing; techniques include positive and negative reinforcement, environment planning, desensitization, implosion, flooding, and stress inoculation.
- Existential – emphasis is on free will and personal responsibility for choices; techniques include the use of literature, modeling, and sharing of experiences; anxiety is used as a motivator.

- Gestalt – counselor exhibits authenticity; techniques include verbal and non-verbal messages, role-playing, fantasy, psychodrama and other exercises developing from the interaction between the counselor and client.
- Person-centered – counselor exhibits acceptance and empathy; techniques include open-ended questions and active/passive listening.
- Psychoanalysis – exploration of the unconscious through such techniques as free association, and the analysis and interpretation of dreams.
- Rational Emotive Behavior Therapy – sessions involve teaching and confrontation; techniques include homework assignments and bibliotherapy.
- Reality Therapy – after establishing a relationship with the client, the counselor acts as teacher and model; techniques promote responsibility, working in the present, and stress freedom without blame.
- Transactional Analysis - counselor acts as teacher; techniques include contracts for change, interrogation, confrontation, and illustration.

Definitions

- Alignment - The alliances, either short or long-term, formed among family members as they move toward homeostasis.
- Attending - The attention the counselor pays to the client during a session; includes listening to the client and both verbal and nonverbal interaction. In task-facilitative attending behavior, the counselor's attention is on the client. In distractive attending behavior, the counselor's attention is on his or her own concerns.
- Aversive conditioning - The application of an unpleasant stimulus in an effort to reduce or eliminate an unwanted behavior.
- Behavioral rehearsal - A role-playing strategy in which a client acts out a behavior he wants to change or acquire; can be quite useful in assertiveness training.
- Boundary - A limit or border. In family therapy, the term refers to membership in the subsystems (parents, siblings, students, etc.) within the family and can be summed up as "who does what with whom."
- Catharsis – the purging of emotions.
- Closed system - A system that is self-contained, has impermeable boundaries, and does not interact with other systems.
- Coalitions - Alliances, either short or long term, among family members against other family members.
- Collecting trading stamps - In transactional analysis, the saving up of enduring, non-genuine feelings, then "trading" them for a script milestone such as a drinking binge or an anger outburst.
- Conjoint - Therapy in which the counselor works with two or more family members at together.
- Counter transference - The projection of the therapist's feelings onto the client.
- Cybernetics - The study of the flow of information through feedback loops.
- EEG (electroencephalogram) - Used to measure brain waves.
- EKG (electrocardiogram) - An electrical recording that provides information about how the heart is beating.
- EMG (electromyogram)- Used in biofeedback training to measure muscle tension.
- Empathy - The ability to recognize, perceive, and understand the emotions of another.

- Enmeshment - A family organization pattern in which family members are over-concerned and over-involved in each other's lives thereby limiting each member's autonomy.
- Fixed role therapy - A treatment method created by George Kelly in which the client is instructed to read a script at least three times a day, then act, speak and think like the script's character.
- Flooding therapy - The exposure of the client to the actual anxiety stimulus in conjunction with response prevention. Care is necessary to insure that overexposure does not increase anxiety.
- Free association - A therapy strategy in which the client responds with whatever comes to mind to clues given by the therapist.
- Homeostasis - A dynamic state of equilibrium – a balanced system.
- Identified patient (IP) - The member of a family who is the primary focus of treatment.
- Implosive therapy - A method for decreasing anxiety by exposing the client to an imaginary anxiety stimulus. The method is risky because overexposure can actually increase anxiety.
- Joining - The strategy of the therapist entering a family system in order to explore and modify dysfunctions.
- Nuclear family - The basic family unit of father, mother, and child(ren) living together in one household.
- Open system – A system with permeable boundaries that allow interaction with other systems.
- Preconscious mind - The portion of awareness that includes information of which a person is aware but to which he is not currently paying attention.
- Racket - In Transactional Analysis a set of behaviors that originate from a childhood script.
- Reaction formation - A defense mechanism in which a person acts in the opposite manner from an impulse he or she cannot accept.
- Repression - The involuntary forgetting of an incident in order to protect oneself from anxiety.
- Retroflection - Doing to oneself what one would like to do to someone else.
- Sculpting - Creates a picture or representation of family relationships. The representation is often made by the family members' physical placement of each other.
- Sensate focus - A series of exercises for a couple in which they take turns paying attention to their own senses.
- Strategic - A therapeutic method in which the therapist devises strategies and interventions to resolve the problem.
- Stress inoculation - An effective technique for dealing with stress developed by Donald Meichenbaum as part of his "self-instructional therapy." It has three phases: educational, in which the problem is identified and the client is given information about what to expect; rehearsal, in which the client practices the stressful event or behavior while using relaxation techniques; and implementation, in which the client uses the new skills to deal with the stressful situation.
- Structural - A therapeutic method of realigning the family in order to change dysfunctional interactions.
- Sublimation - Defense mechanism in which a person uses a socially acceptable behavior to act out an unconscious impulse.
- Systematic desensitization - A type of behavioral therapy to help overcome anxiety and phobias. The client is taught relaxation techniques, and then uses those techniques to react to and overcome situations in a hierarchy of fears.

- Temperature trainer - A biofeedback-training thermometer; expensive and extremely accurate.
- Transference - The projection of a client's feelings for another onto the counselor.
- Triangulation - When two members of a family have a problem with each other, one or both may turn to a third person.

Professional Practice Issues

Tasks of a counselor as a consultant

A consultant is an expert who can use his or her expertise, proven methods, and advice to help a business, an organization, or an individual solve a problem or improve a situation. The tasks of the consultant may include gathering information about the client and/or outside research and the analysis of the information, conferences, workshops, or seminars that address a client's interests and concerns, participant observation programs, organizational or project assessment, and making recommendations for change or improvement.

Public Law 93-380

Public Law 93-380, commonly known as the Buckley Amendment provides for the confidentiality of school and college related information. An educational institution may not release private information even to parents without the student's consent unless the student is under 18 years old or listed as a dependent on the parents' federal tax return. Students and parents of dependent students have the right to inspect the student's record and correct errors.

Accreditation

Accreditation is the recognition that an educational program meets established criteria and standards. The Council for the Accreditation of Counseling and Related Educational Programs (CACREP) is the accrediting agency for counseling programs that offer the master's and doctoral degrees. More than 300 programs in the U. S. offer a master's degree and at least fifty offer a doctorate. Some degrees are specific to a particular discipline such as school, marital, career, or gerontological counseling. Other agencies that accredit programs include the Council on Rehabilitation Education, the American Association for Marriage and Family Therapists, and the American Psychological Association.

Licensure

Licenses are issued by the states and each state has its own laws and requirements for licensure. Most states require a master's degree in counseling with courses in eight content areas, student field experience, post-degree supervised experience, and a passing score on a state exam. Both the National Counselor Exam and the National Clinical Mental Health Counseling Exam are used. Some states have just a "title control" law, which allows non-licensed counselors but forbids their usage of the "Licensed Professional Counselor (LPC)" title. Other states have "title and practice control" laws. Some states limit the use of psychological tests and others are reducing the scope of counseling practice. Some psychologists object to the licensure of counselors.

Certification

National Certified Counselor (NCC) is a designation held by nearly 40,000 American counselors. The designation means that each has met the qualifications set by the National Board of Certified Counselors (CBCC). Those qualifications include an educational requirement of an advanced degree in counseling with coursework in eight content areas and that the candidate serves an internship, a supervised experience requirement of 3,000 hours in the counselor's specialty, and a passing score on the National Counselor Examination for Licensure and Certification. The CBCC was established in 1982 and has responsibility for certifying counseling professionals. After achieving the NCC, a counselor may qualify for a specialty credential in school counseling, mental health counseling, or working with addictions. A continuing education requirement of 100 clock hours per five years of certification must be met in order for the counselor to maintain certification. Graduate students in a CACREP program can be certified at graduation. Rehabilitation counselors are certified by a separate board. School and drug and alcohol counselors are also certified by the states in which they practice.

Tarasoff Case and the duty to protect

In 1976 the Tarasoff family sued the University of California Board of Regents after Prosenjit Poddar, a client of a university psychologist, murdered Tatiana Tarasoff. The psychologist, in maintaining confidentiality, had failed to warn Ms Tarasoff that Poddar was a danger to her. The outcome was that counselors are now required to warn their clients intended victims even when the warning violates both confidentiality and privileged information.

The duty to protect means that a counselor has a responsibility to protect clients from suicide. The counselor should have procedures and guidelines in place for handling such situations, be aware of referral possibilities, and be thoroughly familiar with signs that the client may be planning suicide.

Confidentiality and privileged communication

These two issues are related but are not identical. Confidentiality is an ethical issue that requires a counselor not to discuss a client, or even acknowledge that a particular person is a client, with anyone outside of the agency. Privileged information is a legal issue established by law that prohibits communications between counselors and clients from being revealed in court. There are some situations that require or permit the waiver of privileged information and confidentiality. These situations include child abuse allegations, involuntary hospitalization, the client is a threat to himself or others, or a court order requires the release of information.

Professional liability and malpractice

Professional liability is the counselor's responsibility to provide clients with services that meet the standards of the profession. Malpractice is the legal term for a situation in which the counselor fails to deliver services, the services are substandard, or harm results to the client because of the negligence or ineptitude of the counselor. Clients who feel they have not received proper services or have been harmed by the counselor's treatment may bring a malpractice suit against the counselor and/or the agency. Successful malpractice suits require that there was a client/counselor relationship, the counselor was negligent, the services were substandard, the client was physically or psychologically harmed, and the injury resulted from a breach of duty. Counselors can protect themselves by carrying liability insurance which is available through the ACA and other agencies.

Steps in establishing a counseling program

- Develop an understanding of the context in which the program will operate.
- Assess the need for the program and develop a mission statement.
- Set goals and objectives and establish criteria for measuring success.
- Set up feedback procedures.
- Check for problems by conducting a small-scale pilot program.
- Create a development plan that includes needed personnel, facilities, funding, and other resources.
- Create an implementation plan with a schedule for hiring and training personnel and other start-up activities.
- Start operations and fine-tune procedures and services.
- Evaluate the program and report to the responsible authorities.
- Review the program and make modifications as needed.

Skills needed in order to manage a counseling program

Counseling program managers need the same management skills as managers in any other field. Among the necessary abilities are planning, organizing, establishing goals, setting standards, creating and managing a budget, and the allocation of resources. Personnel management skills including hiring, training, supervision, scheduling, and evaluation are vital. It is quite likely that marketing, dissemination of information about the program, report writing, and fund raising may also be included in the manager's responsibilities.

Ethical standards of practice

- The counselor must adhere to a code of professional ethics.
- The profession defines ethical practice.
- Informed consent must be obtained before treatment is started.
- Clients must be informed if it is necessary to break confidentiality.
- Parental consent must be obtained when treating a minor.
- Clients must be informed if a session is to be recorded, a supervisor will observe, or if the counselor is still in training.
- The counselor must never engage in a sexual relationship with a client. Any such contact must be delayed for at least five years after the end of the counselor/client relationship.
- The counselor may inform the client's partner if the client has AIDS or is HIV positive.
- Counselors should not treat friends or family.
- Counselors should continue their education including the development of an awareness of other cultures.
- Confidentiality must be maintained except in the specific circumstances of danger to the client or others, consultations with other professionals, release of information at the request of the client, court orders, and release of information to such agencies as the client's insurance company.
- The counselor's primary responsibility is to the client.

Professional standards of practice

In some states, standards of practice are part of the laws that govern counselor licensure. At least twenty states require counselors to adhere to the ACA Code of Ethics. Among the major ethical and legal issues are:

- Counselors should be familiar with the standards of the state in which they practice and with the ACA Code of Ethics.
- Counselors should use diagnostic systems to assess clients' needs and fit the techniques and procedures used to each client.
- Methods and techniques should be justified by the theoretical basis of each program.
- The counselors should use methods, procedures, and techniques that are consistent with their training and experience.
- Each counselor should practice within his or her level of competence.
- Training and credentials must not be misrepresented.
- The relationship with a client must be terminated when the counselor's services are no longer helpful.

Legal aspects of counseling

Laws governing counseling practices are usually made at the state level and often overlap ethical principles. Among the issues addressed by law are the requirement that suspected child abuse be reported, that insurance claims not be fraudulent, and that counselors not engage in sexual contact with clients. In most cases, parents or guardians of minor children have access to the child's records although there are some circumstances under which a child can receive counseling with parental consent. In most states, licensure grants privileged communication between counselor and client.

Important terms

- Abandonment - A counselor closes a practice or is unavailable for some time without notifying the clients.
- Contempt of court - Disrespect or disobedience to the authority of a court. Counselors who refuse to testify in a court proceeding may be charged with contempt.
- CRC - Certified Rehabilitation Counselor – a person who has earned at least a master's degree in rehabilitation counseling and passed the certification exam.
- Defamation - An attack upon a person's reputation by slander (untrue verbal statement) or libel (untrue written statement).
- EPA (Employee Assistance Programs) - Programs provided by companies to assist employees in dealing with problems, either through an in-house counselor or referrals to outside agencies.
- HIPAA (Health Insurance Portability and Accountability Act) - A national law that sets the privacy standards for client information and the transfer of information.
- MAC - Master Additions Counselor – a specialty certified by the National Board for Certified Counselors.
- Managed health care - A system that controls the delivery of health care to members of the system and the payment for that care. Members of Health Maintenance Organizations (HMOs) and Preferred Provider Organizations (PPOs) must choose care providers from lists supplied by the organizations in order for insurance to pay for the services.

- Registry - A list of service providers. Some states allow counselors who are included in a registry to use the "registered professional counselor" title.
- Release of information - A document through which the client gives the counselor permission to share confidential information with another agency or professional; should specify what information may be given to whom at what time.
- Statement of disclosure - A legal document given to the client before the start of counseling that includes the counselor's credentials, office hours, billing information, privacy policy, and emergency and grievance procedures, as well as information about the counseling procedures and techniques the client can expect.
- Third party payment - Payment of the counselor's charges through an insurance company or through the employer if the counselor is employed by an agency or under the supervision of a psychologist.
- Title IX of the Educational Amendments of 1972 - A federal law that bans sexual discrimination in academic institutions from kindergarten to university. Although the law has been applied most often to sports, it applies to academic and all other activities at any educational institutional receiving federal funding.

Practice Test

Practice Questions

1. The sensorimotor period is part of whose developmental stage theory?
    a. Freud
    b. Piaget
    c. Erikson
    d. Kohlberg

2. Presenting stimuli in different sequences to reduce "order of presentation" influences in an experiment is called
    a. countertransference.
    b. counterculture.
    c. counterbalancing.
    d. countercounseling.

3. The Eskimo word "piblokto" refers to "arctic hysteria" characterized by uncontrolled screaming and crying that is often accompanied by running through the snow naked. This is an example of what kind of disorder?
    a. Culture-specific
    b. Culture shock
    c. Culture free
    d. Cross-cultural

4. Intervention performed with three or more clients at a time is known as
    a. group cohesion.
    b. group practice.
    c. group dynamics.
    d. group therapy.

5. Which of the following is known for person-centered counseling?
    a. Rollo May
    b. Carl Rogers
    c. Fritz Perls
    d. Aaron Beck

6. Which is NOT true of assigning diagnostic codes to clients solely for the purpose of insurance reimbursement?
    a. It is a legally mandated practice.
    b. It may constitute insurance fraud.
    c. It is unethical.
    d. It is illegal.

7. Research that compares findings across many studies is known as
   a. quasi-experiment.
   b. survey method.
   c. meta-analysis.
   d. comparative research.

8. If a therapist has a good ability to perceive and appreciate their client's subjective reality (i.e., emotions and cognitions), the therapist is said to have
   a. empathic understanding.
   b. congruence.
   c. unconditional positive regard.
   d. reflection.

9. Changes in human growth and development which are qualitative are
   a. changes in number, degree, or frequency.
   b. changes in structure or organization.
   c. changes which are sequential.
   d. changes which are discontinuous.

10. Jim's new therapist believes in the uniqueness of each individual. She talks about the importance of social influences on a person. She tells Jim that everybody has a sense of inferiority, and as a result is always striving to attain superiority. Her counseling goals are to help Jim understand his lifestyle, or unified life plan, which gives meaning to his experiences, and to help him identify social and community interests most appropriate for him. She also wants to help explain Jim to himself. The techniques she uses in her therapy include life histories, homework assignments, and paradoxical intentions. Describe the therapeutic modality that best describes this therapist's approach.
   a. Client-centered therapy
   b. Gestalt therapy
   c. Individual psychology
   d. Transactional analysis

11. Which of the following is NOT considered a specialty counseling certification from the National Board for Certified Counselors, Inc. (NBCC)?
   a. National Certified School Counselor (NCSC)
   b. Certified Clinical Mental Health Counselor (CCMHC)
   c. Master Addictions Counselor (MAC)
   d. National Certified Counselor (NCC)

12. Which of these is NOT a measure of central tendency?
   a. Norm
   b. Median
   c. Mean
   d. Mode

13. All of these are characteristics of test reliability EXCEPT:
   a. Stability
   b. Equivalence
   c. Internal consistency
   d. Predictive

14. According to Ginzberg, Ginsburg, Axelrad, and Herma's developmental theory, occupational choice passes through three periods. Which is NOT one of the main periods they identified?
    a. Fantasy
    b. Tentative
    c. Transition
    d. Realistic

15. Career counseling based on Bandura's social cognitive theory emphasizes all of these concepts EXCEPT:
    a. Personal agency
    b. Positive uncertainty
    c. Self-efficacy
    d. Vicarious learning

16. Managing a counseling program requires skills in which of these areas?
    a. Program design and development
    b. Marketing and public relations
    c. Budgeting
    d. All of these

17. Which of these is/are NOT considered underlying principles of ethical decision making?
    a. Beneficence and nonmaleficence
    b. Justice (fairness), fidelity (faithfulness)
    c. Informed consent and confidentiality
    d. Autonomy and self-determination

18. Sallie attends two different therapy groups in an attempt to find one that suits her. In group A, the leader uses high levels of emotional stimulation, frequently uses caring functions, and uses low amounts of executive direction. In group B, the leader uses low amounts of emotional stimulation, low amounts of caring functions, high use of executive behavior, and low amounts of meaning attribution. According to Yalom, which group leader is more effective?
    a. Group A's leader is more effective.
    b. Group B's leader is more effective.
    c. It depends which Sallie likes better.
    d. Neither leader is more effective.

19. Pat's therapist tells her that "self-talk" and "crooked thinking" cause emotional disturbances. He believes we all have the potential to think rationally. He uses techniques like role-playing and imagery to help Pat work through some of her issues. He also follows an A-B-C-D-E system. Pat's therapist believes that we are not influenced by the events we experience, but by our interpretation of them. Pat's therapist subscribes to which of these therapeutic approaches?
    a. Existential therapy (May, Frankl, Yalom)
    b. Rational Emotive Behavior Therapy (Ellis)
    c. Reality Therapy (Glasser)
    d. Multimodal Therapy (Lazarus)

20. How does consultation differ from counseling?
    a. It uses different skills than counseling does.
    b. It is for resolving, not preventing, problems.
    c. It is a voluntary, work-related process.
    d. It is process-oriented, not content-oriented.

21. Which of these is NOT a common role for a member of a therapy group?
    a. Facilitative
    b. Autocratic
    c. Maintenance
    d. Blocking

22. Jenny recently lost her job and fell behind in her mortgage payments, so now she is facing foreclosure. She is seeing a counselor to help her cope with the stress in her life. She feels like a failure and wants her self-esteem to be higher, and she feels that she is not living up to her potential. Her counselor tells her that her first priorities are to fulfill her more basic needs, such as applying for food stamps so she will not go hungry and getting help with her housing situation so that she meets her needs for safety and physical security. The counselor tells her that once she has addressed these basic needs, she can then address her higher-order needs for self-esteem and fulfilling her potential as a person. Which theorist has most influenced Jenny's counselor?
    a. Abraham Maslow
    b. Edward Thorndike
    c. Erik Erikson
    d. Harry Stack Sullivan

23. Elisabeth Kübler-Ross identified five stages that grieving people experience. Which of these accurately identifies these five stages?
    a. Shock, Panic, Sorrow, Depression, Acceptance
    b. Denial, Anger, Bargaining, Depression, Acceptance
    c. Depression, Fear, Bargaining, Stoicism, Acceptance
    d. Fear, Withdrawal, Bargaining, Resignation, Peace

24. Becky is an elementary school student who displays a number of attention-seeking behaviors which are disruptive in the classroom. Her teacher was approached by a local university researcher to refer students for an experiment. The teacher and her parents ask Becky if she would like to participate in the study and she agrees. The research team has collected baseline behavioral data on Becky from the teacher. Early in the study, they find that her behavior is much improved compared to the baseline. Which of these is the most likely explanation for Becky's better behavior during the experiment?
    a. The Rosenthal effect
    b. The Pygmalion effect
    c. The Hawthorne effect
    d. The Placebo effect

25. What is meant by the term "regression toward the mean?"
   a. It means that most individuals are more likely to score near the mean on most standardized tests.
   b. It means that most individuals' standardized test scores will go down from a pretest to a posttest.
   c. It means that those individuals scoring near the mean on a pretest will score lower on a posttest.
   d. It means that most scoring very high or low on a pretest will score nearer the mean on a posttest.

26. Which of the following are four core elements in building a helping relationship?
   a. Friendship, knowledge, cultural foundations, direction
   b. Leadership, skills, empathy, emotional influence
   c. Human relations, social influence, skills, theory
   d. Assertiveness, social influence, knowledge, theory

27. Which of the following neo-Freudian theorists most strongly believed that behavior can be understood best in terms of social interactions and interpersonal relationships?
   a. Erich Fromm
   b. Harry Stack Sullivan
   c. Wilhelm Reich
   d. Karen Horney

28. Four broad stages of development in the first three years of life are identified in object relations theory. Which of these represents the correct chronological order of these four stages?
   a. Fusion with mother; Symbiosis with mother; Separation/individuation; Constancy of self and object
   b. Symbiosis with mother; Fusion with mother; Separation/individuation; Constancy of self and object
   c. Constancy of self and object; Separation/individuation; Symbiosis with mother; Fusion with mother
   d. Separation/individuation; Constancy of self and object; Symbiosis with mother; Fusion with mother

29. Which of the following best represents the beliefs and practices of Carl Rogers?
   a. The psychoanalyst is directive and in charge of giving advice, teaching, and interpreting.
   b. The focus of counseling is based on the client's phenomenological world and feelings.
   c. The therapeutic process is holistic, focused in the present, and it is existentially based.
   d. The counseling process is focused upon helping clients to gain insights into themselves.

30. Which of these books was authored by Eric Berne?
   a. *I'm OK – You're OK*
   b. *In And Out of the Garbage Can*
   c. *Games People Play*
   d. *On Becoming a Person*

31. What is the difference between classical conditioning and operant conditioning?
   a. There is no real difference; they are simply different names for the same essential process.
   b. Classical conditioning involves a stimulus while operant conditioning involves a response.
   c. Classical conditioning is concrete operational while operant conditioning is formal operational.
   d. Classical conditioning evokes involuntary responses; operant evokes voluntary responses.

32. Which is the correct chronological order of the five stages of development identified by Sigmund Freud?
   a. Oral, anal, phallic, latency, genital
   b. Oral, phallic, anal, genital, latency
   c. Oral, latency, anal, genital, phallic
   d. Oral, anal, genital, latency, phallic

33. Which demographic is projected about the U.S. population by the year 2050?
   a. The numbers of Hispanic Americans will exceed the numbers of White Americans.
   b. The largest numbers of Americans in the U.S. population will be Non-Hispanic Whites.
   c. All of the minority groups combined will outnumber the Non-Hispanic White population.
   d. Non-Hispanic Whites will outnumber all the minority groups combined in the population.

34. People born after the year 1976 in America are commonly referred to as
   a. Baby Boomers.
   b. Baby Busters.
   c. Generation X.
   d. Millennials.

35. Which is most accurate regarding homogeneous vs. heterogeneous therapy groups?
   a. Homogeneous groups are too much alike to experience effective group dynamics.
   b. Heterogeneous groups may have more difficulty being able to relate to each other.
   c. Heterogeneous groups are not as similar to the real world as homogeneous groups.
   d. Homogeneous groups are more likely to simulate interactions among the members.

36. Which is NOT an example of resistive individual or group behavior that would impede progress in a therapy group?
   a. Being unable to set goals
   b. Talking too much or too little
   c. Discussing members' problems
   d. Arriving late to group meetings

37. Which is true of open vs. closed therapy groups?
   a. In an open group, anyone is allowed to join the group.
   b. In an open group, members who leave are replaced.
   c. In a closed group, only certain members may join.
   d. In a closed group, members who leave are replaced.

38. In Donald Super's developmental approach to careers, which vocational developmental task did Super associate with the period of ages 18 to 21?
    a. Crystallization
    b. Specification
    c. Implementation
    d. Stabilization

39. Which of the following pairs does NOT represent two of John Holland's six personality types?
    a. Realistic and investigative
    b. Artistic and social
    c. Enterprising and conventional
    d. Exploratory and directive

40. Which of the following does NOT use John Holland's typology for determining a person's career type?
    a. The Vocational Preference Inventory
    b. The Self-Directed Search
    c. The Career Pattern Study
    d. The Career Assessment Inventory

41. Which of the following is NOT true of standard deviation?
    a. Standard deviation describes the variability within a distribution of scores.
    b. Standard deviation is basically the mean of all the deviations from the mean.
    c. Standard deviation is a term of quantity which is equal to the term variance.
    d. Standard deviation is an excellent way to measure the dispersion of scores.

42. Counselors should be familiar with the distribution of test scores within the normal, bell shaped curve. Which of these correctly describes this distribution?
    a. 68% makes up one standard deviation from the mean, 13.5% makes up two, and 4% makes up three.
    b. 13.5% makes up one standard deviation from the mean, 68% makes up two, and 99% makes up three.
    c. 95% makes up one standard deviation from the mean, 68% makes up two, and 13.5% makes up three.
    d. 99% makes up one standard deviation from the mean, 95% makes up two, and 68% makes up three.

43. Which of the following is true about the correlation coefficient?
    a. A perfect correlation coefficient can be a positive one but cannot be negative.
    b. A correlation coefficient shows the relationship between two sets of numbers.
    c. A correlation coefficient shows a cause and effect relationship between variables.
    d. With a strong correlation, knowing one score will not help to predict another score.

44. Which of these is true of quantitative research?
    a. This kind of research tends to use naturalistic observation of individual behaviors.
    b. This kind of research tends to use impressions, feelings or judgments of researchers.
    c. This kind of research has as its primary goal the description of the nature of reality.
    d. This kind of research tends to investigate with a goal of finding causal relationships.

45. Which of these is true of qualitative research?
   a. This kind of research assumes social elements have a single objective reality.
   b. This kind of research tends to study groups, such as samples or populations.
   c. This kind of research assumes that different realities are socially constructed.
   d. This kind of research tries to avoid influencing its data collection instruments.

46. Which of the following is true of either inductive or deductive research?
   a. Deductive research is practical and begins with the real world.
   b. Inductive research originates from previously established theory.
   c. Deductive research is descriptive, correlational, and historical.
   d. Inductive research often tends to lead to the building of theory.

47. Which of the following tools/methods are characteristic of experimental research designs?
   a. Survey questionnaires and interviews
   b. Control groups and randomization
   c. Use of the correlation coefficient
   d. Use of numbers to describe groups

48. Who established the very first psychological laboratory in history?
   a. Wilhelm Wundt
   b. Sigmund Freud
   c. Jesse Davis
   d. Clifford Beers

49. When did the State of Virginia pass the first general practice counselor licensure law?
   a. 1954
   b. 1962
   c. 1976
   d. 1981

50. Which of these is true regarding the licensure of counselors?
   a. Licensure can be at the state level or at the national level.
   b. Licensure requirements are the same in every U.S. state.
   c. Licensure is possible in several different states at once.
   d. Licensure is portable from one U.S. state to another.

51. In the landmark 1976 Tarasoff case, the California court ruled that failure to warn an intended victim is professionally irresponsible. Out of what event did this ruling come?
   a. A university psychologist by the name of Tarasoff was murdered by one of his clients.
   b. A client named Tarasoff, under the care of a university psychologist, was murdered.
   c. A university psychologist murdered his client, Tatiana Tarasoff, and her family sued.
   d. A client of a university psychologist murdered Tatiana Tarasoff and her family sued.

52. Developmental changes occur in all BUT which of the following broad areas?
   a. Physical development
   b. Cognitive development
   c. Psychosocial development
   d. Sociocultural development

53. An infant first sucks on a nipple to nurse. Then the infant sucks on other things—a toy, Daddy's finger, etc. Later, this infant discovers other things to do with objects beyond sucking on them such as grasping them, shaking them, and otherwise manipulating them. These two behaviors were labeled by Jean Piaget with what terms, in order of their occurrence?
    a. Adaptation and assimilation
    b. Adaptation and organization
    c. Assimilation and accommodation
    d. Accommodation and assimilation

54. You meet a group of people that includes the following subgroups or categories: Members of racial, ethnic, and religious minorities; women; single parents; divorcé(s); elderly persons; people with disabilities; gay men; lesbian women; poor people; children; and young adults. Of all these categories, to which does the term cultural pluralism refer?
    a. Only the members of racial, ethnic, and religious minorities
    b. Racial, ethnic, and religious minorities and the gays and lesbians
    c. Racial, ethnic, and religious minorities and people with disabilities
    d. The term cultural pluralism refers to all of the individuals listed

55. People are said to be products of five different cultures. Two are inevitable culture sources (a culture of human biology and a culture of ecology, which refers to the climates in which people live). Which is NOT one of the other three?
    a. Racio-ethnic
    b. Linguistic
    c. Regional
    d. National

56. Which of the following is NOT a central concept in existential therapy?
    a. Guilt
    b. Anxiety
    c. Free association
    d. Search for meaning

57. How did Albert Ellis view "self-talk" in his theory?
    a. As the source of our emotional disturbances
    b. As the symptom of neurosis or even psychosis
    c. As a therapeutic technique for solving problems
    d. As a kind of mental chatter that is to be ignored

58. Which two psychologists most emphasize freedom of choice and responsibility in their theories?
    a. B.F. Skinner and Arnold Lazarus
    b. William Glasser and Rollo May
    c. Carl Rogers and Heinz Kohut
    d. Albert Ellis and Eric Berne

59. Which is NOT considered a weakness of Adlerian counseling?
    a. It is not firmly based in research.
    b. Its concepts and terms can be overly vague.
    c. It is a rigid and inflexible approach.
    d. Its approach is very narrow in nature.

60. Which of these psychologists' theories completely ignore the unconscious?
    a. Glasser's reality therapy, Rogerian counseling, and behaviorism
    b. Freudian psychoanalysis, Jungian, and Adlerian counseling
    c. Karen Horney, Erich Fromm, and object relations theory
    d. Rollo May, Victor Frankl, Abraham Maslow's existentialism

61. Who is best known for the terms "collective unconscious" and "archetypes?"
    a. Alfred Adler
    b. Sigmund Freud
    c. Carl Jung
    d. Aaron Beck

62. A group that is focused on a central theme such as anger management or learning job seeking skills is known as a
    a. structured group.
    b. self-help group.
    c. psychoeducation group.
    d. T-group.

63. What are two contrasting elements of group dynamics?
    a. Content and context
    b. Process and product
    c. Context and product
    d. Content and process

64. Styles of group leadership have been described as all BUT the following:
    a. Autocratic
    b. Effective
    c. Democratic
    d. Laissez faire

65. Who developed the archway model of self-concept determinants?
    a. John Holland
    b. Linda Gottfredson
    c. Donald Super
    d. John Krumboltz

66. Which of the following is the correct chronological order of the four career development stages identified by Linda Gottfredson?
    a. Orientation to size and power, orientation to sex roles, orientation to social valuation, orientation to the internal unique self
    b. Orientation to the internal unique self, orientation to sex roles, orientation to size and power, orientation to social valuation
    c. Orientation to sex roles, orientation to size and power, orientation to social valuation, orientation to the internal unique self
    d. Orientation to social valuation, orientation to the internal unique self, orientation to sex roles, orientation to size and power

67. Which of the following is NOT true about standardized scores?
  a. Standardized score scales allow comparison of different test scores for the same individual.
  b. Standardized scores enable comparisons of scores between or among different individuals.
  c. Standardized scores indicate the individual's distance from the mean in standard deviations.
  d. Standardized scores may be discontinuous and may employ units which are not equivalent.

68. Which of these is NOT correct regarding standard scores?
  a. We obtain a standard score by converting raw score distributions.
  b. A z-score is a type of standardized score which is commonly used.
  c. An n-score is a type of standardized score that is commonly used.
  d. A t-score is a type of standardized score which is commonly used.

69. Which of the following is true regarding validity and reliability of tests?
  a. Validity is how consistent the test is.
  b. A test may be reliable, but not valid.
  c. A test may be valid, but not reliable.
  d. Reliability is specific to the situation.

70. Which of these is an example of noninteractive research?
  a. Historical analysis
  b. Ethnography
  c. Case study
  d. None of these

71. There are many confounding variables that can threaten an experiment's validity, but which of the following is a threat to both internal validity and external validity?
  a. Attrition (mortality)
  b. Instrumentation
  c. Selection of subjects
  d. Experimenter bias

72. What are the four levels of data measurement used to determine the statistics used?
  a. Nominal, random, stratified, cluster
  b. Ordinal, purposeful, cluster, nominal
  c. Ratio, random, cluster, interval
  d. Nominal, ordinal, interval, ratio

73. Who first established the trait-factor guidance approach?
  a. Jesse Davis
  b. Frank Parsons
  c. E. G. Williamson
  d. Clifford Beers

74. What are some signs to look for in assessing the risk of suicide in a client?
  a. A lifting of depression due to the relief of having made a decision
  b. An unnatural sense of gaiety as all responsibilities are discarded
  c. Frequent explosions of hostility or rage directed at other people
  d. Establishment of a definite plan and having the means available

75. Which is NOT included in the conditions required for a successful malpractice claim against a therapist?
    a. A professional relationship was established.
    b. There was a breach of duty causing an injury.
    c. The client disliked the counselor's methods.
    d. A client was physically or psychically injured.

76. Arnold Gesell believed that:
    a. development was genetically pre-ordained and realized via maturation.
    b. development was differentially influenced via environmental conditions.
    c. development resulted from a combination of genetics and environment.
    d. development could be realized via nature or nurture, depending on the individual.

77. Robert Havighurst is identified with all BUT which of the following?
    a. Stages of growth, each of which must be completed to reach the next one
    b. Stages of growth resulting in successively higher levels of cognitive function
    c. Developmental tasks arising from maturation and environmental influences
    d. Developmental tasks that are acquired via maturation, social learning, and effort

78. Gilbert Wrenn's term "cultural encapsulation" refers to all EXCEPT:
    a. Replacement of reality with model stereotypes
    b. Ignoring cultural variations for a universal truth
    c. Technique-oriented use of the counseling process
    d. Remaining isolated within one cultural context

79. Which is correct regarding the notion of world views?
    a. An emic world view is the belief in a global view of all of humanity.
    b. An etic world view is the belief in taking each group's perspective.
    c. An etic world view is the belief we are more similar than different.
    d. An emic world view is the belief in transcending all our differences.

80. Which of the following would least relate to one of Lazarus' seven modalities?
    a. The act of standing up or of sitting down
    b. A perception of an odor that doesn't exist
    c. Having a conversation with an acquaintance
    d. Having an idea about how to solve a problem

81. In Ellis' rational-emotive behavior therapy (REBT), what do the A, B, and C stand for in his AB-C-D-E modalities' taxonomy?
    a. Action, belief, consequent affect
    b. Activity, behavior, consequences
    c. Alternatives, beginning, correction
    d. Avoidance, basis, conceptualizing

82. In Ellis' rational-emotive behavior therapy (REBT), what do the D and E stand for in his A-B-C-D-E modalities' classification?
    a. Decision, externals
    b. Doubt, engaging
    c. Disputing, effect
    d. Denial, excitement

83. What would G. L. Harrington or William Glasser most likely say regarding transference?
    a. It is a normal process in therapy that can be analyzed and resolved.
    b. It impedes progress and need not occur if the therapist is genuine.
    c. It is disregarded as an internal state without observable behaviors.
    d. It is encouraged, and it is used as an exploratory therapeutic tool.

84. What is NOT one of the strengths or benefits of Rogerian counseling?
    a. Acceptance
    b. Concreteness
    c. Openness
    d. Versatility

85. If a group has co-leaders, which of the following is true?
    a. Both co-leaders should always have the same amount of group experience.
    b. It is better if both co-leaders are the same sex (two males or two females).
    c. Co-leaders with different theoretical orientations create a better dynamic.
    d. Different reactions from co-leaders can help stimulate group energy and discussions.

86. Which of the following is the least supported technique for dealing with resistance in a group?
    a. Confrontation
    b. Modeling
    c. Discussion
    d. Extinction

87. In Frank Parsons' actuarial or trait-factor approach to career counseling, which step listed is NOT a part of the process?
    a. Study the individual
    b. Survey occupations
    c. Give a prognosis
    d. Make a match

88. When E. G. Williamson expanded the trait-factor approach, he included all EXCEPT which of these steps?
    a. Decision
    b. Synthesis
    c. Counseling
    d. Follow-up

89. John Crites' comprehensive model of career counseling includes three diagnoses of a career problem. Which of the following is NOT one of them?
    a. Differential diagnosis
    b. Maturational diagnosis
    c. Dynamic diagnosis
    d. Decisional diagnosis

90. Convergent validation and discriminant validation occur within what type of validity?
    a. Content validity
    b. Predictive validity
    c. Construct validity
    d. Concurrent validity

91. Which of the following is correct regarding either norm-referenced tests or criterion-referenced tests?
    a. Norm-referenced tests show what knowledge an individual has.
    b. Criterion-referenced tests show an individual's rank in the group.
    c. Criterion-referenced tests compare an individual's score to others.
    d. Norm-referenced tests compare an individual's score to others.

92. You are given the Wechsler Adult Intelligence Scales (WAIS-IV) by a psychologist. When showing you your results, the tester compares your score on the vocabulary subtest to your score on the digit span subtest and your score on the block design subtest, etc. This type of assessment is:
    a. Norm-referenced
    b. Criterion-referenced
    c. Ipsatively interpreted
    d. None of these

93. Which is NOT one of the types of Analysis of variance (ANOVA)?
    a. One-way
    b. Factorial
    c. Multivariate
    d. Covariate

94. Which of the following is NOT a reason to use nonparametric statistics?
    a. You have a homogeneous sample.
    b. You have a normal score distribution.
    c. You have two independent samples.
    d. You have nominal (categorical) data.

95. You give a questionnaire to a group of respondents to measure their opinions on certain topics. Each question has seven possible choices: Strongly Agree, Agree Somewhat, Agree, Neutral, Disagree, Disagree Somewhat, and Strongly Disagree. This measurement technique is known as
    a. a Likert scale.
    b. a scatterplot.
    c. a Kruskal-Wallis test.
    d. a Wilcoxen signed-rank test.

96. Gilbert Wrenn's book *The Counselor in a Changing World* (1962) stressed the role of the counseling profession as being focused on
    a. neurotic needs.
    b. collective (group) needs.
    c. developmental needs.
    d. individual needs.

97. What did passage of the Smith-Hughes Act accomplish?
    a. It provided money to fund the training of school counselors.
    b. It granted federal funds for vocational education and guidance.
    c. It required the licensure of marriage, family, and child counselors.
    d. It greatly expanded the counseling services to veterans in the VA.

98. Identify the first professional counseling association and its founding year.
    a. The National Vocational Guidance Association in 1913
    b. The Vocation Bureau in Boston in 1908
    c. The American Personnel and Guidance Association in 1951
    d. The Office of Vocational Rehabilitation in 1954

99. As of the 21st century, the number of certified and licensed counselors in the U.S. is close to
    a. 10,000.
    b. 100,000.
    c. 1,000,000.
    d. None of these

100. What is accreditation?
    a. A process whereby a counselor becomes certified or licensed to practice therapy
    b. A process whereby a researcher receives credit for his or her work in a publication
    c. A process whereby an institution or program receives public recognition for meeting standards
    d. A process whereby a doctoral student is credited for earning a counseling degree

101. Antony is a child who has lately been having tantrums. His pediatrician tells his mother that this is perfectly normal at his age as he is trying to assert his independence. At which of Erikson's developmental stages and resulting virtues would this child most likely be?
    a. Basic trust versus mistrust (positive resolution: hope)
    b. Autonomy vs. shame/doubt (positive resolution: will)
    c. Initiative versus guilt (positive resolution: purpose)
    d. Industry vs. inferiority (positive resolution: competence

102. A survey researcher has asked Larry and Carol about their attitudes toward obeying laws. They are asked what they would do in certain hypothetical situations. For example, if the only way to help someone and/or to avoid harming someone would involve breaking the law. "Law, schmaw, what's important is doing the right thing," said Carol. "True, we should do what's right, but we've also made an agreement with society to follow its rules. We should try to do that too, but I agree that a lot of it depends on the situation," said Larry. Identify where Larry and Carol fit in Kohlberg's stages of moral development:
    a. Larry is in Stage 1 and Carol is in Stage 2.
    b. Larry is in Stage 4 and Carol is in Stage 3.
    c. Larry is in Stage 5 and Carol is in Stage 6.
    d. Larry is in Stage 4 and Carol is in Stage 5.

103. Raphael's family has just moved to a new neighborhood where he is now culturally in the minority. In his old neighborhood, Raphael's culture was the predominant one. Now Raphael is feeling uncertain about his sense of self. He feels some conflict between depreciation and appreciation of his self. According to the racial/cultural identity development model, Raphael is experiencing
    a. conformity.
    b. dissonance.
    c. resistance and immersion.
    d. introspection.

104. Would Freud's psychodynamic approach and Albert Ellis' REBT favor the emic or the etic approach?
    a. They would both favor the etic approach.
    b. They would both favor the emic approach.
    c. Freud would favor the etic approach and Ellis the emic.
    d. Freud would favor the emic approach and Ellis the etic.

105. Eric's counselor uses narrative therapy. Eric has written a "story" to describe his life as his counselor asked him to do. Now the therapist helps Eric to find exceptions and strengths to write a new story that fits better with how Eric would like his life to be. This therapeutic technique is an example of
    a. clarification.
    b. deconstruction.
    c. re-authoring.
    d. documentation.

106. Which of the following is the most accurate statement regarding integrative counseling?
    a. Integrative counseling is another term for the same type of counseling as eclectic counseling.
    b. Integrative counseling begins with techniques and ends with the therapist's personal theory.
    c. Integrative counseling is a highly generalized theory which makes much use of incongruence.
    d. Integrative counseling synthesizes processes and techniques from various theoretical views.

107. In existential therapy, what do Umwelt, Mitwelt, and Eigenwelt mean respectively?
    a. Identity of self, physical system, relationships
    b. Physical system, relationships, identity of self
    c. Relationships, identity of self, physical system
    d. Identity of self, relationships, physical system

108. Christine's new therapist believes that clients' problems have social and political sources, and that one's personal and social identities are interconnected. The therapist also believes that the therapeutic relationship is a collaborative process between equals, and that androcentric norms are to be rejected. To what type of theory does Christine's therapist likely adhere?
    a. Solution-focused brief therapy
    b. Narrative therapy
    c. Feminist therapy
    d. Reality therapy

109. Justin has not always had problems, but currently needs some help adjusting to changes in college. His therapist sets specific goals right away. She tells him that he does not necessarily need to entirely understand his problems in order to find solutions. She also uses a scale of 1-10 to measure changes. What type of therapy is Justin undergoing?
   a. Solution-focused brief therapy (SFBT)
   b. Rational emotive behavior therapy (REBT)
   c. Person-centered/client-centered therapy
   d. Social constructionist narrative therapy

110. For a therapy group composed of adults with a single group leader, what is generally considered to be the optimum group size?
   a. 3
   b. 8
   c. 5
   d. 10

111. Which is most accurate statement regarding the duration of a therapy group?
   a. When a therapy group is first formed, nobody knows exactly how long the group will exist or run.
   b. When a therapy group is first formed, it is generally accepted that it will run for about six months.
   c. When a therapy group is first formed, the group members decide on how long they want it to run.
   d. When a therapy group is first formed, the leader should set its duration and advise the members.

112. Which of these groups does NOT represent three of Donald Super's nine major life roles?
   a. Mentor, employer, advisor
   b. Child, student, citizen
   c. Spouse, homemaker, parent
   d. Worker, leisurite, pensioner

113. According to Linda Gottfredson, young children around age 6 tend to choose occupations based upon
   a. their social values.
   b. their ability levels.
   c. their sex or gender.
   d. their personal traits.

114. Ann Roe believed that all BUT which of these elements influenced occupational selection?
   a. Genetic factors
   b. Environmental influences
   c. Parent-child relationships
   d. Cognitive development

115. Which of the following is the best synonym for the term appraisal?
   a. Assessment
   b. Evaluation
   c. Measurement
   d. Testing

116. If you give two tests and the correlation between them is 0.80, what is the true variance they have in common?
    a. 40%
    b. 64%
    c. 16%
    d. 80%

117. What are the coefficient of determination and the coefficient of nondetermination?
    a. The coefficient of determination is the degree of common variance, and the coefficient of nondetermination is the error variance or unique variance.
    b. The coefficient of determination is the degree of unique, variance and the coefficient of nondetermination is the degree of common variance.
    c. The coefficient of nondetermination is the result of squaring the correlation, and the coefficient of determination is the remainder after subtracting the coefficient of nondetermination.
    d. The coefficient of determination is equal to the correlation, and the coefficient of nondetermination is equal to the difference between the correlation and 100%.

118. Which of the following is NOT true about purposeful sampling?
    a. It may be comprehensive with every case or instance being selected.
    b. The researchers intend to generalize their findings to the population.
    c. The researchers may select examples of only the most extreme cases.
    d. The researchers may select examples of only the most typical cases.

119. What is stratified sampling?
    a. This refers to selecting naturally occurring groups of individuals.
    b. This refers to selecting samples of convenience or of volunteers.
    c. This refers to selecting from major subgroups of the population.
    d. This refers to selecting so that all individuals have equal chances.

120. Which group shows suggested minimum sample sizes for the kinds of research named?
    a. 25 for experimental research, 10 for correlational research, and 50 for survey research
    b. 5 for experimental research, 15 for correlational research, and 25 for survey research
    c. 20 for experimental research, 30 for correlational research, and 1000 for survey research
    d. 15 for experimental research, 30 for correlational research, and 100 for survey research

121. What is the difference between confidentiality and privileged communication?
    a. Confidentiality is a legal concept, and privileged communication is an ethical concept.
    b. Confidentiality is an ethical concept, and privileged communication is a legal concept.
    c. Confidentiality and privileged communication are both legal and are the same thing.
    d. Confidentiality and privileged communication are ethical concepts and are the same.

122. What is reciprocity?
    a. A process whereby the counselor and client take turns at speaking during counseling
    b. A process whereby each member of a therapy group takes an equal turn at speaking
    c. A process whereby one agency accepts another's credentials as equivalent to its own
    d. A process whereby one state board grants licensure to a counselor from another state

123. Jimbo decides to go for counseling and makes an appointment. When he gets there, the counselor gives him a statement of disclosure. Which is true regarding this document?
    a. A statement of disclosure is required by law in every state in the United States.
    b. A statement of disclosure is never required by law, but is highly recommended.
    c. A statement of disclosure may be required by law in some states and not others.
    d. A statement of disclosure should be given to a client after a course of therapy.

124. Which of these is correct regarding a release of information?
    a. This document is signed by the client before confidential information can be given to another professional or agency.
    b. This document is signed by the counselor and given to the client to disclose procedures before the counseling relationship starts.
    c. This document is signed by another professional or agency before a counselor can give confidential information to them.
    d. This document is signed by the client and given to the counselor before another professional or agency can give the counselor information.

125. Which of these is true about professional liability insurance for counselors?
    a. This insurance is always required by law in every state of the U. S.
    b. This insurance is required by law in some states, but not in others.
    c. This insurance is not required by law and is an unnecessary expense.
    d. This insurance is not recommended since it invites litigation.

126. Daniel Levinson's work has been criticized as being too limited because:
    a. His developmental life stages did not include any transitional periods.
    b. He only studied the structure of life for males and excluded females.
    c. He believed that there is a midlife crisis, but many do not see a crisis.
    d. He stated that people question their lives but did not include careers.

127. Roger Gould believed that there were different "protective devices" people have. Which of these is the most accurate definition of protective devices according to Gould?
    a. Coping strategies
    b. Defense mechanisms
    c. False assumptions
    d. Absolute truths

128. Mannie and Moe were Eastern European Jewish brothers who came to America in the early 1920s and both became naturalized U.S. citizens. Mannie worked in the garment district, enjoyed going to baseball games and eating (kosher) hot dogs, and proudly flew an American flag in front of his house. He also still attended shul (temple) in his new country, celebrated all Jewish holidays, and his wife would light candles every Friday night in observance of the Sabbath. Moe also flew an American flag, went to ball games and ate hot dogs; however, he also altered his last name so it would not sound Jewish, did not attend a synagogue, married a woman who was not Jewish, joined a non-Jewish country club, and worked on Wall Street as a stockbroker. He and his family would put up a Christmas tree and decorations every year. Which combination of terms correctly identifies each brother's process?
    a. Mannie's process was acculturation and Moe's process was assimilation.
    b. Mannie's process was assimilation and Moe's process was acculturation.
    c. Both Mannie and Moe underwent a process of acculturation in America.
    d. Both Mannie and Moe underwent the process of assimilation in America.

129. Juan is from a Hispanic culture and Mai is from an Asian culture. According to multicultural counseling theorists, they will have certain needs if seeking counseling. Of the following, which would likely be a more suitable counseling orientation for both of them?
    a. Traditional Freudian psychoanalysis
    b. Rogerian client-centered counseling
    c. Abraham Maslow's self-actualization
    d. Fritz Perls' Gestalt model of therapy

130. Andrew would like to talk to a counselor about some things he has on his mind. He wonders just what his life means and what the point is to our existence. He feels considerable anxiety over many things, and he frequently feels guilty as well. He is very introspective and is always seeking to understand himself better. Which type of therapy would probably make a good fit for Andrew?
    a. Reality therapy
    b. Behavioral counseling
    c. Existential therapy
    d. Transactional analysis

131. Robert Carkhuff categorized counselors' responses as all BUT which one of these?
    a. Additive
    b. Interchangeable
    c. Subtractive
    d. Multiplicative

132. Robert Carkhuff proposed a five-point scale to measure the quality of a counselor's empathic responses. Which level does the following example best represent? Client: Oh, my wife yelled at me so bad you wouldn't believe it! It just killed me!!! Counselor: What did she say?
    a. Level 1
    b. Level 2
    c. Level 3
    d. Level 4-5 (3)

133. Which of the following pairs do NOT have something notable in common between their respective theories of counseling?
    a. Carl Jung and Rollo May
    b. Gordon Allport and Kurt Lewin
    c. Sigmund Freud and Aaron Beck
    d. Alfred Adler and Joseph Wolpe

134. Madelyn has been in a long-term psychotherapy group for the past five years, and the group's leader often encourages members to explore issues originating in their childhoods. According to Gerald Caplan's model, this would be an example of
    a. a primary therapy group.
    b. a secondary therapy group.
    c. a tertiary therapy group.
    d. none of these group types.

135. Kathleen is not excessively troubled, but she is quite shy. She is a member of a counseling group with a focus on minimizing aspects of shyness and preventing their occurrence in social situations. According to Caplan, this would be an example of
    a. a primary group.
    b. a secondary group.
    c. a tertiary group.
    d. None of these

136. Ken belongs to a group whose aim is to prevent substance abuse among teens and young adults. In this group, the leader teaches members various coping skills and healthy behaviors. According to Caplan, this would be an example of:
    a. a primary group.
    b. a secondary group.
    c. a tertiary group.
    d. None of these

137. Donald Super identified four theaters of life in which we play roles. The home is one of them. Which of these is NOT one of the other three?
    a. Community
    b. School
    c. Workplace
    d. Church

138. Jason is a computer programmer. He is an excellent engineer but is not good at technical support, because he doesn't know how to converse easily people. His wife, Sallie, is a teacher and she is great at explaining things. Children and others love her. However, she can never get her computer to work. John Holland would identify Jason and Sallie respectively as which of his six personality types or styles?
    a. Jason is mainly a realistic type and Sallie is mainly an artistic type.
    b. Jason is mainly an investigative type and Sallie is mainly a social type.
    c. Jason is mainly a conventional type and Sallie is mainly an enterprising type.
    d. Jason is mainly an enterprising type and Sallie is mainly a conventional type.

139. Which of the following is true about Holland's RIASEC hexagon?
    a. Pairs of types that are not on adjacent sides are more psychologically alike.
    b. Pairs of types that are adjacent on the hexagon are less psychologically alike.
    c. An individual's six-type profile may be differentiated or undifferentiated.
    d. Congruence refers to similarity between pairs of types on different sides.

140. Which of the following pairs does NOT accurately represent one of Ann Roe's eight occupational fields?
    a. Unskilled labor, service work
    b. Managerial, general cultural
    c. Arts and entertainment, technology
    d. Outdoor work, scientific work

141. Tiedeman's decision-making model saw career decisions as being made up of two phases. What were these?
    a. Anticipation or examination and execution or fulfillment
    b. Anticipation or preoccupation and implementation or adjustment
    c. Preoccupation or examination and correction or adjustment
    d. Examination or definition and realization or completion

142. Which of the following is a good example of a standardized test?
    a. A checklist
    b. A rating scale
    c. A structured, scored test
    d. An open-ended interview

143. Which of these is NOT generally identified as a circumstance in which testing may be useful?
    a. Job or educational placement
    b. Counseling
    c. Diagnosis
    d. None of these

144. How can tests aid a counselor with a new client?
    a. They can help see if the client's needs are in the counselor's range of services.
    b. They can help the counselor to obtain a greater understanding of the client.
    c. They can help the client to obtain a greater degree of self-understanding.
    d. They can help with any or all of these purposes in the counseling process.

145. Dr. Miller wants to investigate certain variables in his college class. He is going to test his statement that all of the students in his class with IQ scores above 120 will finish the term with higher grades than all of the students in his class with IQ scores below 120. This statement is an example of a
    a. research question.
    b. directional hypothesis.
    c. nondirectional hypothesis.
    d. null hypothesis.

146. If you are conducting an experiment and you choose a significance level of .01, what does this mean?
    a. It means you are willing to accept the possibility of erring in accepting or rejecting the null hypothesis one time out of one hundred.
    b. It means that you are willing to accept the possibility of erring in conducting the experiment in one percent of the trials you make.
    c. It means that you are willing to accept the possibility that your instruments will err in their measurements one out of ten times.
    d. It means that you are willing to accept the possibility that your hypothesis will be wrong in ten out of one hundred experiments.

147. Which is correct regarding a type I (alpha) error or type II (beta) error?
    a. A type I error means accepting the null hypothesis when it is not true.
    b. A type II error means rejecting the null hypothesis when it is correct.
    c. A type I error means rejecting the null hypothesis when it is correct.
    d. A type II error means accepting the null hypothesis when it is correct.

148. What do "title and practice-control" laws mean?
   a. These are laws stating that one cannot practice counseling without using the title of LPC.
   b. These are laws stating that one can practice counseling without a license, but cannot use the title.
   c. These are laws stating that one cannot practice counseling without a professional counselor license.
   d. These are laws stating one may not get a professional counseling license without using the title.

149. Which of the following is NOT true of the FERPA?
   a. The acronym stands for the Family Educational Rights and Privacy Act of 1974.
   b. This law is also referred to as the Buckley Amendment.
   c. The intention of this act was to protect individuals' privacy.
   d. It gives students' parents access to their counseling records.

150. What does Title IX of the educational amendments provide?
   a. Remedial reading instruction
   b. A ban on sex discrimination
   c. Equal sports for both sexes
   d. Equal class sizes in schools

151. A formal mental status examination covers all BUT which of the following areas?
   a. Appearance and behavior
   b. Thought processes, mood and affect
   c. Intellectual functioning, sensorium
   d. Personality, brain dysfunctions

152. What are some examples of culture-bound values vs. class-bound values in counseling?
   a. Culture-bound values include strict adherence to a time schedule and an unstructured approach.
   b. Class-bound values include verbal expression, defined patterns of communication, and openness.
   c. Culture-bound values include individual-centered counseling, emotional expression, and intimacy.
   d. Class-bound values include a structured approach to problems and seeking short-term solutions.

153. Harry is a little boy whose parents have taken him to a behavior therapist. The parents want some help getting him to clean up his room, go to bed on time, get dressed for school in the morning, and complete other similar daily activities without a struggle or a big fight. The therapist makes a chart for Harry. Every time he completes a desired behavior, he gets a gold star on the chart for that activity. At the end of each week, he and his parents count his gold stars, and he gets a reward based on the number of stars—a pizza or ice cream treat, a movie, etc.—something he values. Which of the following is the most accurate name for the technique that Harry's therapist is using?
   a. Token economy
   b. Reinforcement schedule
   c. Systematic desensitization
   d. Negative reinforcement

154. Regarding principles of change related to the Johari Window, which pair listed is NOT true?
    a. A change in one quadrant effects all other quadrants; denying, covering up, or ignoring behavior all require energy.
    b. Threat and mutual trust both increase awareness; the smaller the upper left quadrant the poorer the communication.
    c. Regarding the unknown area, curiosity exists universally; social customs, training, and fears keep some parts unknown.
    d. In counseling, a goal is to make the lower right quadrant larger; another goal is to make the upper left quadrant smaller.

155. Which of the following does NOT correctly pair a model of consultation with the person who developed it?
    a. Caplan – mental health consultation model
    b. Bandura – social learning consultation model
    c. Bergan – process consultation model
    d. Schein – purchase consultation model

156. The acronym EMDR stands for which of the following?
    a. Eye movement desensitization and reprocessing
    b. Emotional-mental deconstruction and reconstruction
    c. Excessive movement disturbance remediation
    d. Executive mental decision-making and restructuring

157. Which of these is NOT included in the study of kinesics and proxemics?
    a. Facial expressions
    b. Verbal expressions
    c. Physical body gestures
    d. Seating arrangements

158. What is NOT one of the differences between individual counseling and family counseling?
    a. The change in locus of pathology
    b. The different focus of treatment
    c. The redirected unit of treatment
    d. The longer duration of treatment

159. Tuckman identifies the five states of a therapy group with all EXCEPT which of the following rhyming words?
    a. Forming, storming
    b. Conforming, swarming
    c. Norming, performing
    d. Mourning, adjourning

160. Irvin Yalom identified four stages of a therapy group. The first stage he identified was orientation. The other three include all BUT which of the following?
    a. Conflict
    b. Definition
    c. Cohesion
    d. Termination

161. In a decision-making model of career development, factors which could influence decision making include all BUT:
   a. One's vocational maturity
   b. The person's investment(s)
   c. Someone's personal values
   d. One's style of taking risks

162. In career self-efficacy theory, which of these is NOT one of the three elements that will be influenced by an individual's expectations?
   a. Choice
   b. Competence
   c. Performance
   d. Persistence

163. What is the difference between "undecided" and "indecisive" in terms of career counseling?
   a. There is no difference; they are simply synonyms.
   b. An undecided individual needs more information.
   c. The indecisive individual needs more information.
   d. An undecided person always has trouble deciding.

164. The standard error of measurement is NOT one of the following:
   a. A measure of reliability
   b. A measure of validity
   c. The confidence band
   d. Confidence limits

165. Which of the following is NOT an accurate statement about how the standard error of measurement is used?
   a. It is useful for the interpretation of individual test scores.
   b. It can help determine the range where a test score falls.
   c. Every test that is given has its own unique SEM value.
   d. It is calculated after the test has been taken and scored.

166. Which of these is NOT a condition for which testing should be used?
   a. Gaining self-understanding
   b. Licensure and certification
   c. Labeling some individuals
   d. For educational planning

167. Which of these tests has multiple forms for administration to differently aged subjects?
   a. Wechsler Intelligence Scales
   b. Stanford-Binet Intelligence Scales
   c. Miller Analogies Test (MAT)
   d. Scholastic Assessment Test (SAT)

168. Which of the following correctly states the relationship between significance level and type I error?
    a. As the significance level decreases, so does the level of type I error.
    b. As the significance level decreases, the level of type I error increases.
    c. There is no direct relationship between significance level and type I error.
    d. Type I error may increase or decrease as significance level increases.

169. Which of these correctly states the relationship between significance level and type II error?
    a. As the significance level decreases, so does the level of type II error.
    b. As the significance level decreases, the level of type II error increases.
    c. There is no direct relationship between significance level and type II error.
    d. Type II error may increase or decrease as significance level increases.

170. Which of the following correctly states the relationship between type I and type II errors?
    a. Type I error and type II error will both decrease if the significance level goes down.
    b. Type I error will increase and type II error will decrease if the significance level goes down.
    c. Type I error will decrease and type II error will increase if the significance level goes down.
    d. Type I error and type II error will both increase if the significance level goes down.

171. Which of these is NOT commonly cited as a reason for counseling program evaluation?
    a. The emphasis on accountability in the human services field
    b. A strong need to show the efficacy of counseling in general
    c. A need to show efficacy of specific theories and techniques
    d. A need to show the effectiveness of a particular counselor

172. What is NOT true of HIPAA?
    a. It is a law which varies from state to state.
    b. It protects the privacy of patient records.
    c. It regulates the sharing of information.
    d. It regulates electronic insurance claims.

173. What is true of an EAP?
    a. It is an educational assistance program.
    b. It is designed to help college students.
    c. It may be inside or outside a company.
    d. It does not have licensed counselors.

174. In the steps of developing a counseling program, which of the following should come FIRST?
    a. Operating the program
    b. Conducting a pilot study
    c. Evaluating the program
    d. Development of a plan

175. Which of these is a limitation to confidentiality in the ethical practice of counseling?
    a. Clerical staff in the counseling office will see client information.
    b. A health insurance company or HMO will see client information.
    c. A counselor gets helpful advice about a client from a colleague.
    d. All of these situations represent valid confidentiality limitations.

176. A couple presents for counseling. Evaluation reveals that the wife comes from a dysfunctional, neglectful, alcoholic home and has little trust or tolerance for relationships. Consequently, their marriage is marred by constant arguing and distrust, frequent demands that he leave, episodes of impulsive violence, alternating with brief periods of excessive over-valuation (stating that he is the "best thing that ever happened" to her, "too good" for her, et cetera. Which is the most likely diagnosis?
    a. Anti-social personality disorder
    b. Histrionic personality disorder
    c. Borderline personality disorder
    d. Narcissistic personality disorder

177. In Stanley Strong's social influence model of counseling, which of the following is NOT one of the characteristics of the counselor that Strong identified as those a client might view as valuable?
    a. Expertness
    b. Attractiveness
    c. Agreeableness
    d. Trustworthiness

178. In Murray Bowen's family systems theory of counseling, he identified eight theoretical concepts. Which of these is an accurate representation of one of these concepts?
    a. The basic building block of a family's emotional system is a quadrangle.
    b. Differentiation of self is how individuals distinguish between self and others.
    c. Nuclear family emotional systems with undifferentiated partners are more stable.
    d. Society is regressing by not distinguishing between emotional and intellectual decisions.

179. In Salvador Minuchin's structural family therapy, there are _____ between family subsystems; if these are too rigid, they lead to _____, and if they are too diffuse, they can lead to _____.
    a. transactional patterns; opposition; fragmentation
    b. boundaries; disengagement; enmeshment
    c. alignments; coalitions; conflicts
    d. structural maps; withdrawal; disorganization

180. What are major common features between Nathan Ackerman's psychodynamic theory of family counseling, Carl Whitaker's experiential family counseling, Salvador Minuchin's structural family therapy, and narrative family therapy?
    a. The goal of perceiving the situation differently and the counselor's position of neutrality
    b. The goal of maintaining the system's balance and the counselor's role as teacher/trainer
    c. The goal of making changes in the family and the counselor's interactive role in the family
    d. The goal of using knowledge the family has and the counselor's helping to find solutions

181. The psychodynamic model has a _____ unit of study; the experiential model has a _____ unit of study; the transgenerational model has a _____ unit of study; and the strategic model has a _____ unit of study.
    a. monadic; dyadic; triadic; dyadic and triadic
    b. dyadic; monadic; monadic and dyadic; triadic
    c. monadic; dyadic and triadic; triadic; dyadic
    d. triadic; monadic and dyadic; dyadic; triadic

182. By comparison, which of these is NOT as commonly identified as a cycle or period in the "life cycle of a family"?
    a. Leaving home
    b. Marrying
    c. Children
    d. Divorcing

183. Irvin Yalom specified that the functions of a therapy group leader should include: emotional stimulation, caring, meaning attribution, and executive leadership. Zander Ponzo found support for these same factors, and he also identified other factors found in successful groups. The factors Ponzo identified include all EXCEPT:
    a. Participation
    b. Risk-taking
    c. Neutrality
    d. Conflict-confrontation

184. Jacob Moreno is known for all of the following except:
    a. The theater of spontaneity
    b. The STEP Program
    c. Psychodrama
    d. Group psychotherapy

185. In career development and counseling, what is meant by the compensatory vs. spillover theory of leisure?
    a. Individuals who are dissatisfied with their jobs compensate by engaging in excessive leisure activities.
    b. Individuals whose leisure interests tend to spill over into the workplace are not as productive.
    c. Individuals may compensate for work with different leisure activities or their work may spill over into their leisure activities.
    d. Individuals may compensate for leisure by working harder or leisure activities may spill over to work.

186. Which of these is NOT an issue for adults in career transition which counselors should sensitively address during career counseling?
    a. Not wanting to undergo job transition
    b. Obsolete job skills/a need for retraining
    c. Lack of information/job-seeking skills
    d. Changes in physical abilities or values

187. Which of the following tests are most likely to be used in career counseling?
    a. Iowa Tests of Basic Skills
    b. Myers-Briggs Type Indicator
    c. Minnesota Importance Questionnaire
    d. All of the above are often used in career counseling.

188. Which of these is a LESS appropriate rationale for a counselor's use of testing?
    a. To help predict a client's future performance in school, work, or training
    b. To critique the client's performance in a school, work or training setting
    c. To help clients to make decisions regarding their school or work futures
    d. To help clients to identify interests they may not have known they had

189. What kind of tests are the Rotter Incomplete Sentences Blank and the Draw-A-Person Test?
    a. Specialized personality tests
    b. Specialized achievement tests
    c. Projective personality tests
    d. Inventory personality tests

190. The following are all examples of intrusive or reactive measurement EXCEPT:
    a. Questionnaires
    b. Records reviews
    c. Interviews
    d. Open observation

191. Dr. Stanwyck has used two different counseling approaches with two different groups of college students. Both groups had similar scores on a pre-test of self-efficacy. He gives each group the same post-test to measure their self-efficacy levels following the course of counseling. What kind of test would he most likely use to see if there is a statistically significant difference between the two groups' post-test scores?
    a. A t-test
    b. A one-way ANOVA
    c. A factorial ANOVA
    d. A MANOVA

192. Dr. Stanwyck has determined that his two groups of students have significantly different scores on the post-test of self-efficacy he gave to them after two different courses of counseling. Now he wants to find out whether there is also a statistically significant interaction between the two groups' mean scores. What kind of test would he be likely to use to determine this?
    a. A one-way ANOVA
    b. A factorial ANOVA
    c. A MANOVA
    d. An ANCOVA

193. Dr. Stanwyck has determined that not only was there a statistically significant difference in the scores of his two groups of students following two different courses of counseling, but also that these scores had a statistically significant interaction with each other. Now he wants to see if, in addition to tested levels of self-efficacy, his subjects' levels of optimism have changed following the two kinds of counseling. Accordingly, he gives both groups a questionnaire to assess their level of optimism. (Dr. Stanwyck had planned ahead and had given both groups a pre-test assessing their baseline optimism levels before the counseling courses began.) To make his analysis of the students' levels of both self-efficacy and optimism following the counseling, what kind of test will he need to use?
    a. ANOVA (one-way)
    b. ANOVA (factorial)
    c. MANOVA
    d. ANCOVA

194. Dr. Stanwyck has found a significant difference in the mean test scores of his two student groups. He has also found a significant interaction between their scores. He subsequently tested for significance on a second dependent variable as well. Now he wants to make one more analysis based on the information he has obtained related to the first dependent variable he tested—that of self-efficacy. In pretesting, he noticed that the college seniors in each group had higher average scores in self-efficacy than the college juniors in each group. Therefore, he now adjusts the groups' scores statistically to control for these initial differences before he compares his two test groups. What kind of test is he using?
    a. Factorial ANOVA
    b. MANOVA
    c. One-way ANOVA
    d. ANCOVA

195. Which of the following is true regarding payment for counseling?
    a. Payment to master's degree-level counselors is only automatic if they are licensed.
    b. Master's degree-level counselors do not receive payment even if they are licensed.
    c. Some counselors are reimbursed by insurance through a supervising psychologist.
    d. Counselors in private practice may not require direct payments from their clients.

196. Which of these is correct about insurance laws related to counseling?
    a. In some states, insurance laws now require licensed counselors to be reimbursed for treating certain mental illnesses.
    b. Insurance laws in all states now require that licensed counselors be reimbursed for treating certain mental illnesses.
    c. There is no law in any state of the U.S. requiring insurance companies to reimburse licensed counselors.
    d. Insurance laws in all states now require insurance companies to reimburse licensed counselors for all mental illnesses.

197. Many mental health professionals apply to HMOs and PPOs to be on their provider lists. What is the reason for their doing this?
    a. To enhance their professional reputations
    b. To allow clients to be referred to them
    c. To comply with national and state laws
    d. To gain membership in the organizations

198. Which of the following is true regarding legal standards of practice in counseling?
    a. Legal practices and ethical practices in counseling are easily separated.
    b. Ethical principles and the law each address all behaviors and practices.
    c. Privileged communication is a legal right of all counselors in every U.S. state.
    d. Sexual contact between counselors and clients is illegal in most, but not all states.

199. Which of these is correct regarding ethical issues in group counseling?
    a. Maintaining confidentiality is an ethical obligation, and confidentiality must be assured.
    b. Informed consent should be obtained from prospective group members before starting.
    c. Group members will naturally form social relationships during the course of counseling.
    d. With multicultural groups, it is the members' responsibility to respect different cultures.

200. Which of these is correct regarding ethical issues in family counseling?
    a. The counselor's attitude toward gender roles is irrelevant to family counseling.
    b. Due to confidentiality, the counselor should not report child abuse and incest.
    c. If the counselor diagnoses a family member, it could be used later on in a court of law.
    d. Family roles and family dynamics are the same, irrespective of a family's culture.

Answers and Explanations

1. B: Piaget's theory has the following stages: sensorimotor, preoperational, concrete operational, and formal operational (and later post-formal operations). Freud, Erikson and Kohlberg also have stage theories, but none of them includes a stage named Sensorimotor.

2. C: Counterbalancing is presenting stimuli in differing sequences to avoid influencing an experiment by the order of presentation. Countertransference is a process that can occur during therapy when an unresolved personal issue prevents a therapist from being objective. Counterculture is an alternative culture arising in opposition to the dominant values and behaviors of a society. "Countercounseling" is a made-up term.

3. A: A culture-specific disorder is one which is typical of a given culture. Culture shock is stress induced by living in a different culture. Culture free refers to a test whose score is not dependent on knowledge specific to a given culture. Cross-cultural means crossing more than one culture.

4. D: Group therapy, group counseling or group work refer to interventions done with more than three people at once. Group cohesion refers to the bond formed by group members. Group practice refers to a number of providers practicing in a single business entity. Group dynamics refers to the interactions between group members.

5. B: Carl Rogers is known for person-centered or client-centered counseling. Rollo May is known for existential counseling. Fritz Perls is known for Gestalt therapy. Aaron Beck is known for behavioral/cognitive-behavioral counseling.

6. A: Assigning diagnostic codes solely for the purpose of insurance reimbursement is NOT required by law. This practice may constitute insurance fraud. It is also unethical and moreover it is illegal.

7. C: Meta-analysis is research that compares the results of many studies in order to answer one or more research questions. A quasi-experiment is similar to experimental research but subjects cannot be randomized into treatment and control groups. A survey uses questionnaires and/or interviews to measure the attitudes and perceptions of respondents. Comparative research investigates any differences between groups without manipulating the conditions for each group.

8. A: Empathic understanding refers to the ability to perceive and appreciate a client's subjective feelings and thoughts. The term congruence is often used to refer to counselor openness and genuineness, meaning the therapist is authentic and integrated during the session. (Congruence can also mean agreement between a client's beliefs and behaviors.) Unconditional positive regard refers to acceptance, meaning the counselor is not judgmental of the client. Reflection refers to repeating what the client has said, emphasizing the emotional content of each statement.

9. B: Changes in human growth and development that are viewed as qualitative are changes in structure or organization (i.e. biological or sexual development). Changes in number, degree, or frequency are viewed as quantitative or as changes in content (i.e. intellectual development). Changes that are sequential are viewed as continuous and cannot be easily separated. Changes that

are discontinuous can be separated from others (i.e. language development) and these fit readily into stage theories of development.

10. C: Alfred Adler and Rudolph Dreikurs were proponents of individual psychology. All of the terms used in the question come from this approach. Client-centered or person-centered therapy was developed by Carl Rogers and includes concepts such as the process of becoming, the client-therapist relationship, unconditional positive regard, congruence or genuineness, and empathic understanding. Gestalt therapy, proposed by Fritz and Laura Perls, is based on existential principles. It has a viewpoint derived from holistic systems theory, and its focus is on the here-and-now of perceptions and feelings. Its name refers to a "unified whole," and it uses concepts of perception to understand and integrate the self. It makes use of the figure-ground concept (proposed by Edgar Rubin) in differentiating between focused figures (main issues) versus their ground (or background)) relationships. The analogy is that a foremost need is a figure and other needs are the ground, and as the main need is met, this completes the gestalt or whole. Transactional analysis was pioneered by Eric Berne, who posited that the personality has three ego states: parent, adult, and child. Berne states that a life script develops during childhood and influences one's behavior. He regarded many transactions between people as games played to avoid intimacy.

11. D: The NCC certification is considered a generic counselor certification. NCSC, CCMHC, and MAC are all specialty counselor certifications which may be obtained from the NBCC following certification of the NCC credential.

12. A: A norm is NOT a measure of central tendency. A norm refers to a typical behavior or an established standard of conduct. It may, however, be expressed by means of statistical averages. In group therapy, a norm is a written or unwritten rule of conduct or behavior. The mean is the arithmetic average of the scores or measurements of a number of individuals, and thus it is a measure of central tendency. The median is the middle score in a distribution of scores and is also a measure of central tendency. The mode is the most frequent score in a distribution and is another measure of central tendency.

13. D: Predictive is a type of validity, not of reliability. It means that predictions made by a test are confirmed by later behavior. Stability refers to test-retest reliability using the same testing instrument with the same group at different times. Equivalence is a type of reliability using alternate forms of the same test with the same group and correlating the results. Internal consistency refers to the degree of correlation between different aspects of a test intended to address the same characteristic. This measure of reliability is often measured via a split-half method – where items addressing a shared characteristic are divided into two test "halves" and then administered to involved subjects. The degree of correlation between the two halves measures the instrument's internal consistency.

14. C: Transition is a stage within the "tentative" period, not a main period itself. The three main periods are fantasy, tentative, and realistic.

15. B: Positive uncertainty is H.B. Gelatt's later model of career decision making. According to Bandura, personal agency reflects an individual's ability to achieve objectives. Self-efficacy is Bandura's term for an individual's belief that one can succeed at something. Vicarious learning is one of several learning experiences that Bandura states can strengthen self-efficacy.

16. D: Managing a counseling program can require skill in some or all of these areas: strategic planning, program design and development, budgeting, personnel management, supervision, evaluation, and marketing and public relations.

17. C: Informed consent and confidentiality are important ethical issues that must be considered in counseling, but they are not identified as underlying principles. Principles underlying ethical decision making are identified as beneficence (doing good and preventing harm); nonmaleficence (not doing harm); justice (treating people fairly); fidelity (being faithful to/honoring commitments); and autonomy (respecting others' freedom of choice and self-determination).

18. D: According to Yalom, a poor style of group leadership includes low or high emotional stimulation, low or high executive behavior, low use of caring function, and low use of meaning attribution. Yalom found that effective leaders used moderate amounts of emotional stimulation and executive direction, frequent use of caring functions, and consistent use of meaning attribution. Thus both group A's and group B's leaders have styles that fit Yalom's definition of poor group leadership. According to Yalom, it does not depend on which of these two leaders Sallie likes better since neither one uses the techniques of an effective group leader.

19. B: Albert Ellis' rational emotive behavior therapy (REBT) has all of the characteristics summarized prior to the question. Existential therapy (Rollo May, Victor Frankl, Irvin Yalom) is based on phenomenology, or the study of our direct experiences taken at face value rather than of our interpretations of them. William Glasser's reality therapy is based on choice theory and posits that we determine our own fates. Glasser states that we all have genetically based needs of survival, love and belonging, power or achievement, freedom or independence, and fun. Taking responsibility is a key concept of reality therapy. Arnold Lazarus' multimodal therapy is a holistic and eclectic approach with considerable behavioral influences. Lazarus identified seven interactive but discrete modalities for which he used the acronym BASIC ID: behaviors, affective responses, sensations, images, cognitions, interpersonal relationships, and drugs (i.e., biology, including nutrition).

20. C: Consultation is a voluntary problem-solving process, and it is also work-related. It uses the same skills as counseling does, but in a different context, role, and function than in counseling. It is for resolving existing problems and also for preventing future problems. It may be content-oriented or process-oriented, or both.

21. B: Autocratic is NOT a common role for a group member; it is a leadership style used by some group leaders. Answers A, C, and D are common roles for group members: A facilitative or building role is one wherein group members feel they contribute to the positive functioning of the group. A maintenance role contributes to the group by encouraging social and emotional bonding among members. A blocking role can hinder a group's attainment of goals by using negative or distracting behaviors.

22. A: Abraham Maslow's humanistic theory posits a hierarchy of needs. The more basic needs such as food/water, shelter and safety must be met before higher-order needs, such as love, belonging, and self-esteem can be addressed, according to Maslow. Edward Thorndike is known for formulating the Law of Effect, which says that a reward reinforces the connection between a stimulus and a response; this law is fundamental to behaviorism. Erik Erikson is known for his psychosocial stage theory, identifying eight (later nine) stages, each of which contains a central crisis/conflict/task which must be resolved in order to progress. Harry Stack Sullivan was a neo-Freudian theorist who stressed the importance of social/interpersonal relationships.

23. B: Kübler-Ross identified the five stages of the grieving experience as: denial (refusal to believe one is dying); anger (resentment, feeling it is unfair to be dying/objecting to dying); bargaining (trying to make deals with God or others—e.g., "I'll give everything to charity if I can just live/I'll treat my family members better if I just don't have to die now/I'll be a better person if I can just have some more time," etc.); depression (a feeling of hopelessness and/or helplessness in the face of one's mortality; sadness over leaving bodily life and loved ones behind); and, finally, acceptance (a feeling of peace at having to come to terms with the fact of one's imminent demise). Shock, panic, sorrow, stoicism, fear, withdrawal, resignation, and peace are all emotions that a dying person could certainly experience, but they are not named as stages in Kübler-Ross' theory.

24. C: The Hawthorne effect refers to the way experimental subjects' behavior can change when they receive attention and/or know that they are participating in research. Since Becky's disruptive behaviors were identified as attention-seeking, the extra attention she gets in the experiment likely satisfies her need for more individual attention. Knowing she is participating in research also may make her feel special, and thus motivate her to be on her best behavior for the scientists. The Rosenthal effect refers to changes in the subject's behavior caused by the researcher's expectations, attitudes, or behaviors. The Pygmalion effect is another name for the Rosenthal effect. There is no information in the question pertaining to any possible influence by the researchers' expectations. The placebo effect refers to the phenomenon of control subjects' behavior changing even though they have not been given any experimental treatment. The question does not state that Becky was a control subject.

25. D: Regression toward the mean, or reversion to the mean, expresses the fact that if an individual scores very high (85% or higher) or very low (15% or lower) on a pretest, that individual is likely to earn a score closer to the mean (average) on the posttest. The unusual pretest score is usually an error due to chance, personal and environmental factors, which are reliably likely to be different on the posttest. This term does not express that most individuals will score near the mean on standardized tests. It does not mean that posttest scores will be lower than pretest scores, since they could also be higher depending on the pretest score. It does not mean that individuals scoring close to the average on a posttest will score lower on the pretest.

26. C: Four key elements identified in building a helping relationship are: 1) Human relations core – empathy, respect, genuineness; 2) Social influence core – competence, power, intimacy; and (as identified by Stanley Strong in his social influence model), expertness, attractiveness, and trustworthiness; 3) Skills core – micro-skills (as identified by Allen Ivey): communication skills such as attending, inquiry, and reflection; and, 4) Theory core – theoretical knowledge that helps therapists to understand the self, interpersonal relationships, interpersonal skills, clients' problems, and to choose effective interventions. Answer B identifies empathy, which is included as part of the human relations core, but none of the other elements is correct. Answer D includes the core concepts of social influence and theory, but none of the other elements. Answer A contains all incorrect elements.

27. B: Harry Stack Sullivan favored a social systems approach to understanding human behavior. He felt that human behavior is best understood in terms of social interactions and interpersonal relationships. Erich Fromm believed that individuals could develop self-fulfillment, or social character, through joining with other people and could become lonely and unproductive if they did not. He felt that society offers opportunities to experience mutual love and respect. Wilhelm Reich contributed to the body therapy manipulation movement, and he believed that repeated successful orgasms were necessary for mental health. Karen Horney believed that security motivates every

individual and a lack of security causes anxiety. She felt that irrational attempts to repair disrupted relationships could turn into neurotic needs.

28. A: Object relations theory, which is based on Freudian psychoanalytic concepts, gives this chronology of stages: 1) Fusion with mother – sometimes called "normal infantile autism," and occurs in the first 3-4 weeks of life. 2) Symbiosis with mother – which takes place during the 3rd to 8th month of life. 3) Separation/individuation – which starts in the 4th or 5th month of life. 4) Constancy of self and object – which is achieved by the 36th month of life. This theory states that progressing through these consecutive stages gives a child a secure basis for later development by engendering trust in the infant that its needs will be met.

29. B: In Rogerian counseling, Rogers reacted against the directive psychoanalytic approach, which put the counselor in charge of advising, teaching, and interpreting, as described in Answer A. Rogers' focus was on the phenomenological reality of the individual client and the client's feelings. Answer C, which describes the therapeutic process as holistic, focused in the present, and based on existential concepts, reflects the bases of Fritz Perls' Gestalt therapy. Answer D, which describes the therapy process as helping clients to gain insights into themselves, describes a goal of Individual Psychology, pioneered by Alfred Adler and Rudolph Dreikurs.

30. C: Berne, who created transactional analysis (a cognitive model of therapy), believed that the personality has three ego states – parent, adult, and child. He felt that people will play various games, which he named in his book *Games People Play*, to avoid intimacy. The book *I'm OK – You're OK* was written by Thomas Harris. Harris extended Berne's transactional analysis by positing four basic life positions: "I'm OK – You're OK;" "I'm OK – You're Not OK;" "I'm Not OK – You're Not OK;" and "I'm Not OK – You're OK." The book *In And Out of the Garbage Can* was authored by Fritz Perls, the founder of Gestalt therapy. The book *On Becoming a Person* was written by Carl Rogers, whose therapy focused on the "process of becoming," which moves clients toward self-actualization.

31. D: In classical conditioning, an association is created between a stimulus that normally would not have a given autonomic effect on the animal and a stimulus that would. For example, a primary stimulus (such as food) evokes an involuntary response (such as salivation), or light evokes an involuntary contraction of the eye's pupil. During conditioning, a secondary stimulus, such as ringing a bell, is paired with the primary stimulus. With consistent repetition, the subject comes to associate the ringing bell with the involuntary response. Thus, when the primary stimulus of food or light is removed, the ringing bell alone evokes the same involuntary response of salivation or pupil contraction. In operant conditioning, an association is created between a behavior and a consequence. Thus, a positive stimulus presented following a voluntary response by the subject will reinforce or strengthen the recurrence of that response. For example, a child sits down and an adult praises the child. The child is then more likely to sit down again to receive praise. With repetition of reinforcement, the behavior will occur more often. Animals will also respond to operant condition. For example, they can learn that if they press a button or a lever they will receive a food reward, and will thus repeat the behavior to obtain more food. The key difference is that in operant conditioning a voluntary response is evoked, while in classical conditioning an involuntary (autonomic) response is evoked. Answer A is incorrect as the two processes are not the same. Answer B is incorrect as both processes involve a stimulus and response. Answer C is incorrect as concrete and formal operations are terms from Piaget's theory of cognitive development which have nothing to do with behaviorism. Also, both classical conditioning and operant conditioning have been successful with humans as early as Piaget's sensorimotor stage, as well as with animals.

32. A: According to Freud, the oral stage is from birth to 18 months; the anal stage is from 2 to 3 years; the phallic stage is from 3 to 5 years; the latency stage is from 6 to 12 years; and the genital stage is from 12 to 19 years of age. The infant's psychosexual focus is on the mouth as it nurses to obtain nourishment. The toddler's psychosexual focus moves to the anal area during toilet training as the child learns to control bowel movements. The early childhood psychosexual focus is on the phallus (the penis in males and the clitoris in females) as the child discovers his or her sexual organs. In middle childhood, the focus is on socialization, and Freud believed that children repress sexual urges until puberty. In adolescence, Freud said the psychosexual focus is on the genitals as sexual urges resurface and gain strength, and sexual activity begins.

33. C: It is projected that by 2050, all of the minority groups combined will total a larger number than all of the Non-Hispanic White people in the country. It is not projected that the Hispanic population alone will outnumber the White population. Since it is projected that all minority groups combined will outnumber Whites, it is incorrect that Whites will be the largest number in the population.

34. D: Individuals born after 1976 are known as Millennials; they are also variously known as Echo Boomers, the Internet Generation, Nexters, or Generation Y. Baby boomers are those born between 1946 and 1964. Baby Busters are those born between 1965 and 1976. Generation X is another term for Baby Busters.

35. B: In a heterogeneous group, if the members are too different from one another they may find it harder to relate. However, heterogeneous groups are more representative of the real world, so answer C is incorrect; heterogeneity is likely to stimulate interactions among members, so answer D is incorrect. Answer A is incorrect because homogeneity, or having similar members in a group, does not preclude having effective group dynamics – otherwise, homogeneous groups would never be indicated, but they are often successfully used.

36. C: Discussing members' problems is NOT an example of resistance. Discussing members' problems is a common activity in therapy groups. Seeming unable to set goals, talking too much or too little, and arriving late for group meetings are all examples of resistive behaviors that would impede group progress.

37. B: In an open group, if a member leaves, a new member is admitted to replace the one who left. New members can provide stimulation, new ideas, and new resources. An open group does not mean that anybody can join it; the member's needs and personality should be appropriate for the group, as determined by the leader with input from group members. A closed group does not mean that only certain people may join it; it means that new members are not admitted. This can facilitate group cohesion and maintain trust within the group. Since new members are not admitted to closed groups, it follows that members who leave are not replaced, as they are in open groups.

38. B: Specification = age 18-21. Super defined five vocational developmental tasks during different age periods: crystallization, from age 14-18; specification, from age 18-21; implementation, from age 21-24; stabilization, from age 24-35; and consolidation, from age 35 onward. (Note: Super's ages no longer apply, as they were originally based mostly on middle-class, white, college-educated males, and because people now more often have gaps and/or changes in their careers.)

39. D: Exploratory and directive are NOT included in Holland's personality types. The styles he identified are: 1) Realistic (aggressive; likes explicit tasks; poor interpersonal skills). 2) Investigative (intellectual; likes systematic, creative investigations; poor persuasive and social

skills). 3) Artistic (imaginative; likes self-expression; dislikes systematic, ordered activities). 4) Social (likes interpersonal activities; dislikes working with tools or machines). 5) Enterprising (extrovert; likes leadership and persuasive activities; dislikes abstract or cautious work). 6) Conventional (practical; likes structured, orderly activities; dislikes ambiguous or unsystematic work). Each person is said to possess all six types in varying proportions.

40. C: The Career Pattern Study was a study by Donald Super that investigated the vocational behavior of individuals from 9th grade into their 30s. He found that career maturity and achievement in high school were predictive of the same behaviors in adulthood. The Vocational Preference Inventory and the Self-Directed Search were both developed by John Holland for identifying a person's predominant vocational personality type according to his typology. The Career Assessment Inventory is an instrument developed by Charles B. Johansson which adopted Holland's typology. The Strong Interest Inventory is another instrument in which Strong also used Holland's typology.

41. C: Standard deviation is NOT the same as variance. Variance is the square of the standard deviation, or SD2. SD is a description of the variability within a distribution of scores. It is also the mean of all the deviations from the mean. SD is an excellent measure of the dispersion of scores; it describes the dispersion of scores better than the variance does.

42. A: In a normal bell-shaped curve, individual scores are distributed in six equal parts, three above the mean and three below it. Within the bell curve, 34% of scores are above the mean and 34% are below it, adding up to 68%, and this proportion is one standard deviation above or below the mean. 13.5% more of the scores fall two standard deviations above or below the mean, equaling 27%, so a total of 95% (68% + 27%) of scores fall within two standard deviations of the mean. Finally, 2% more of the scores fall three standard deviations above the mean and 2% more fall three standard deviations below the mean, equaling 4%, so 99% (68% + 27% + 4%) of scores are within three standard deviations of the mean. (Note: the 99% referred to is actually 99.7% but has been simplified here.) The rule of 68-95-99% is known as the empirical rule. It may help to look at a drawing of a normal bell curve with the percentages labeled to visualize this.

43. B: A correlation coefficient does show the relationship between two sets of numbers. A correlation coefficient ranges from -1.00, or a perfect negative correlation, to 1.00, or a perfect positive correlation. A perfect correlation can be either positive or negative. Correlation coefficients indicate the degree of relationship, but do not indicate any causal relationship between variables. When a very strong correlation exists between variables, knowing one score an individual got will enable fairly accurate prediction of another score that individual got.

44. D: Quantitative research is more focused on finding relationships, and often on showing cause and effect relationships if they can be statistically proven. Answers A, B, and C all describe characteristics of qualitative research.

45. C: In contrast to quantitative research, which assumes that social factors belong to a single objective reality, qualitative research assumes that individuals and groups construct a multiplicity of realities. Answers A, B, and D all describe characteristics of quantitative research.

46. D: To better understand these concepts, it is important to recognize that inductive reasoning draws upon specific concepts in pursuing more general (i.e., generalizable) understandings and insights. By contrast, deductive reasoning draws upon overarching general understandings in pursuing specific insights. Thus, inductive research often leads to the building of theory. It also

begins at the level of the real world and is practical in nature, so answer A is incorrect. By its nature, deductive research tends to come out of theory which already exists, so answer B is incorrect. In addition to predisposing theory formation, deductive research tends to be descriptive, correlational, and historical, so answer C is incorrect. Deductive research attempts to find relationships between the elements of a theory, and in doing so it often requires experimental research.

47. B: In seeking to determine causal relationships between variables, experimental research uses experimental groups (receiving an intervention or treatment) and control groups (receiving no intervention or treatment) to ensure that any observed changes are actually caused by the experimental treatment and not by some other intervening variable(s). Ideally all relevant factors in both groups should be being essentially equal except for the experimental treatment or intervention. Random subject assignment to either group helps ensure equivalent composition in each group in order to avoid biasing the results. Answers A, C, and D (survey research design, correlational research design, and descriptive research design) are all characteristics of non-experimental research designs.

48. A: Wundt established the first psychological laboratory in 1879. Sigmund Freud first used psychoanalysis to treat mental illness in 1890. Jesse Davis first began work as a counselor in a Detroit high school in 1898. Clifford Beers exposed conditions in mental health institutions in his book *A Mind That Found Itself*, published in 1908.

49. C: 1976 was the year that the State of Virginia passed the first general practice counselor licensure law. In 1954, the Office of Vocational Rehabilitation was created. In 1981, the Council for the Accreditation of Counseling and Related Educational Programs (CACREP) was established. In 1962, the State of California passed a law for the licensure of marriage, family, and child counselors.

50. C: It is possible for a counselor to be licensed in several different states of the country at the same time. Licensing requirements are established by the passage of law at the state level. There is no licensure at the national level. Licensure requirements are not the same from one state to another; there are variations in requirements depending upon the state. Counselors cannot move their licenses from one state to another if they relocate. However, a counselor can obtain licensure in more than one state.

51. D: Tatiana Tarasoff was murdered by Prosenjit Poddar, who was a client of a university psychologist, and her family subsequently sued the Board of Regents of the University of California. The court ruled that if a therapist has reason to believe that a client may pose a serious danger of violence to one or more third parties, that therapist must either confine the client under state laws of psychiatric involuntary hospitalization, or else break confidentiality to notify the police and warn the intended victim(s). This is known as the Duty to Warn. Since this case, decisions in other court cases in other states have reaffirmed this legal precedent.

52. D: The three broad areas of change identified by developmentalists are physical, cognitive, and psychosocial development. Sociocultural is not named as one of the areas of developmental change.

53. C: Incorporating additional objects or events into the infant's existing schema or structure such as sucking on things other than a nipple is assimilation. When the infant later modifies its organization by forming new schemas in response to the environment this is accommodation. Adaptation is Piaget's term for adjustment to the environment. Assimilation and accommodation are two processes which are parts of adaptation. Organization is how we organize our knowledge

and mental processes. Piaget said that we inherit two tendencies which are organization and adaptation.

54. D: Cultural pluralism refers to broad categories of individuals in society with special concerns or needs, and/or who are seeking greater representation in society. They include all of the groups listed in the question.

55. B: Linguistic is NOT one of the five different cultures. Language is often a common feature in a national culture, and language may be an aspect of our ecological culture. Language is also often one part of an ethnic culture, along with practices, learning, and style of living. A specific language does not constitute one of the five distinct culture types.

56. C: Free association is a technique commonly used in Freudian psychoanalysis. Guilt is a central concept of existential therapy; it occurs when we fail to reach our potential. Anxiety is also a central concept in existential therapy, and is considered to be the threat of non-being. Existentialists also believe that we search for meaning in life. They feel that we have freedom of choice and are responsible for our own fates. Thus we struggle with being alone/not connected to others, and we search for the meaning of our existence.

57. A: In his rational emotive behavior therapy (REBT) theory, Ellis stated that irrational belief systems, self-talk, and crooked thinking cause emotional disturbance and inappropriate affects and behaviors. While Ellis believed that self-talk is the source of emotional disturbance, it is not necessarily a symptom of neurosis or psychosis; Ellis was a cognitive-behavioral psychologist who had earlier subscribed to Freudian psychoanalysis but came to reject it by the early 1950s. In Ellis' paradigm, self-talk is not a problem-solving technique but a problem itself. While self-talk might be considered a kind of mental chatter, Ellis did not teach that it should be ignored, but rather that one should actively work to change irrational beliefs and behaviors through rational analysis and cognitive reconstruction.

58. B: William Glasser's reality therapy emphasizes that we determine our fate and are in charge of our lives. Rollo May's existential therapy says we have freedom of choice and are responsible for our fate. B. F. Skinner became the primary proponent of behaviorism which is deterministic and mechanistic in nature. Arnold Lazarus created multimodal therapy which is holistic and eclectic in its approach but also has strong behavioral influences. These both emphasize learning rather than freedom and responsibility. Carl Rogers had a humanistic and holistic approach. While he believed the individual is self-directed, he emphasized warmth, empathy, self-acceptance and self-exploration more than personal responsibility. Heinz Kohut was a proponent of neo-Freudian psychoanalysis wherein the counselor is directive and in charge. He followed Freud's belief in unconscious motivations and biological determinism, not freedom of choice. Albert Ellis focused more on rational self-analysis than on issues of freedom or responsibility, and Eric Berne viewed the counselor as a teacher who contracts with the client for positive change. He focused on analysis of transactions and on transformations.

59. C: Actually, Adler's therapy is considered to be versatile. It is also useful for treating specific disorders. Criticisms of Adlerian counseling include the lack of a firm research base; the vagueness of many of his terms and concepts and lack of "how-to" counseling instructions; and the inherent narrowness of his approach.

60. A: Glasser's reality therapy ignores the unconscious in favor of focusing on the here and now and the concrete. Rogerian or person-centered counseling emphasizes acceptance, empathy and the

therapeutic relationship, and deals more with surface issues disregarding innate drives and the unconscious. Behaviorism is famous for not caring about internal states, because what is learned can be unlearned, and only observable behaviors can be changed in this theory. Freud, Adler, and Jung all did a great deal of work regarding the unconscious. Karen Horney and Erich Fromm were neo-Freudians, and object relations theory (pioneered by Ronald Fairbairn, Melanie Klein, D.W. Winnicott, and others) is based on Freudian concepts. Existential theorists focus on internal motivations such as anxiety and guilt.

61. C: Jung coined these terms. He believed the collective unconscious is determined by the evolution of the human species, and that it contains universal brain response patterns he called archetypes. Adler was known for emphasizing birth order as a psychological influence, and he used the term "family constellation." Freud is famous for coining the terms id, ego, and superego as the basic personality structures. He also contributed many other terms, such as "ego defense mechanisms," "repression," "sublimation," "projection," "introjection," "reaction formation," etc. Aaron Beck coined the term "automatic thoughts" which are similar to Freud's "preconscious."

62. A: A structured group focuses on a central theme, which could be drinking/driving issues, dealing with loss and/or grief, anger management, learning job seeking skills and the like. A structured group has a leader. A self-help group has no leader and is a support system to help with psychological stress. A self-help group may also focus on loss or grief, weight loss, incest survivors, or parents who have lost a child. A psychoeducation group focuses on acquiring information and building skills. It can be preventive, growth-oriented, or remedial in nature. Psychoeducation groups are often at social service or mental health agencies and universities. A T-group, or training group, focuses on improving interpersonal skills. They often study the way a person functions in a group such as in a work environment.

63. D: Content is the subject under group discussion, and process is how the discussion or interaction is taking place. Context contrasts with content and means the setting in which the content exists. Product contrasts with process in that it is the result of a process.

64. B: Effective is NOT a term used to describe a group leader style. (It is, however, a term used in Virginia Satir's A-B-C-D-E family therapy model to describe a healthy way of interacting.) Group leadership styles are described as autocratic or authoritarian, democratic, or laissez faire. The autocratic style may not be liked by group members, but is best for making quick decisions. The democratic style may be liked better by group, but is not always the most productive. With a cohesive, committed group, the laissez faire style often gets superior results.

65. C: Donald Super developed the archway model as a graphic depiction of the many factors that determine an individual's self-concept. One pillar of the arch corresponds to internal variables such as aptitudes, interests, needs, and accomplishments. The other pillar represents external factors such as family, community, and the work market. The arch between the pillars is the self. John Holland developed a typology identifying six modal personality orientations. He also created the Vocational Preference Inventory and the Self-Directed Search for determining a person's predominant Holland personality type. Linda Gottfredson created a developmental theory of careers in the 1980s called "circumscription and compromise" which emphasizes vocational self-concept. John Krumboltz was responsible for the learning theory of career counseling (LTCC) which is based on Albert Bandura's social learning theory.

66. A: Gottfredson stated that orientation to size and power occurs from age 3 to 5 when children have neither; when they still think concretely; and when they are just beginning to understand

what being an adult means. Orientation to sex roles takes place from age 6 to 8 when children learn that adults have different roles and that many occupations are sex-typed. Orientation to social valuation happens from age 9 to 13 when children gain greater awareness of peer, family, and community values and of the variation among the social valuations of different occupations. Finally, orientation to the internal unique self transpires from age 14 on when children's aspirations, interests, and values influence their occupational preferences and choices.

67. D: Standardized scores are continuous and the units they use are equal. Standardized scores do enable us to compare several different test scores for the same person. They allow normative or relative meaning which enables comparisons between or among individuals. They do express the distance of an individual's score from the mean in terms of the particular standard score distribution's standard deviation.

68. C: An "n-score" is NOT a type of standardized score. Standard scores are obtained by converting raw score distributions into an accepted standardized format. The two most commonly used standardized scores are the z-score and the t-score.

69. B: A test may be reliable, meaning it is consistent and its results can be replicated, without being valid — meaning it does not test what it claims to test. Answer A is the definition of reliability, not validity. Answer C is not true because valid tests will normally be reliable (unless the variable being measured changes). Answer D is not true of reliability but is true of validity, which is situation-specific (i.e., a test can be valid for some purposes but not for others).

70. A: Historical analysis is analytical research done mainly via analysis of documents, and as such is not interactive in nature. Ethnographies and case studies are examples of interactive research, conducted via interviews and observation. Both interactive and non-interactive research designs are qualitative research designs.

71. C: Internal validity asks, "Did the treatment clearly cause the effect?" External validity ask the question, "Can you generalize the results?" Thus, the selection of subjects can affect both. Internal validity is compromised if comparison groups have different compositions (e.g., if they were not randomly selected), making it unclear if the outcome resulted simply from different kinds of persons in each group. Selection of subjects can also affect external validity if the subjects were not randomly selected, as the results may only apply to other similar individuals, such as college students, and cannot be generalized to the larger population. Attrition would affect internal validity if subjects drop out of the study since results could be very different without the continued presence of those subjects. External validity would not be as directly affected by attrition as internal validity. Instrumentation would affect internal validity if the measurement instruments are inaccurate or are changed during the study, or if there are human recording errors. In these cases, instrumentation would be a confounding variable and it would more pertinent to internal than external validity. Experimenter bias could influence subjects' responses, which would confound internal validity. External validity would be more confounded by subject reactions or lack of ecological validity if the setting or circumstances of the study are so unusual that generalization is impossible.

72. D: In nominal measurement, the numbers represent categories such as male and female. In ordinal measurement, the numbers show differences in magnitude such as from high to low or vice versa. In interval measurement, the numbers have equal quantities throughout so that the interval between them is always the same; the interval between 10 and 11 being the same as the interval between 2 and 3. In ratio measurement the numbers are on a scale with a true zero and can be

compared by ratios such as 400 being twice as much as 200. Random, stratified, cluster, and purposeful are types of sampling not types of measurement.

73. B: Frank Parsons, established Boston's Vocation Bureau in 1908. In his book, *Choosing a Vocation* (published in 1909), he established the trait-factor guidance approach. Jesse Davis was the first identified school counselor who he began working in a high school in Detroit in 1898. E. G. Williamson modified Frank Parsons' trait-factor approach in his book *How to Counsel Students* published in 1939. Clifford Beers published his book *A Mind That Found Itself* in 1908 exposing unethical and unhealthy conditions in mental health institutions of the time.

74. D: If a suicidal person has made a definite plan to commit suicide and also has means such as sleeping pills or a gun available, this is a sign of serious risk that the individual will attempt suicide. Another sign of suicide risk is depression and a sense of hopelessness, so a lifting or relief of depression is not correct. An unnatural sense of gaiety at giving up responsibilities is not a common sign of serious suicide risk. Frequent explosions of hostility or rage directed at others is a sign of disturbance, but this is more likely a sign of risk for murder or otherwise harming others than for suicide. Depression is anger turned inward at the self, and suicide is aggression against the self. A person who lashes out at others is less likely to commit suicide.

75. C: A client's dislike of a counselor's methods or techniques is NOT a criterion for filing a malpractice suit in court. As long as the methods are not inappropriate or unprofessional, malpractice cannot be established. If the client does not like the counselor's approach, the client should seek a different therapist. The conditions for a malpractice claim to succeed are: professional relationship was established; there was a breach of duty; the client suffered physical or psychological injury; and the injury was caused by the breach of duty.

76. A: Arnold Gesell was a maturationist who believed that given a normal environment a child's growth and development were predetermined by genetic makeup. He felt that children developed in a predictable, orderly way with little influence from the environment including the parents. A belief that development is most influenced by the environment would be akin to the position of a behaviorist. There are many other theories which hold that development is the product of both nature and nurture, but Gesell's was not one of them. The position that development is primarily influenced by either one or the other would be unusual for most developmental theories, which tend to apply their beliefs about development more uniformly to the majority of human beings.

77. B: Havighurst's stages of growth were not specifically focused on cognitive development alone. Developmental stages resulting in progressively higher levels of cognitive function would be a more accurate description of Jean Piaget's cognitive developmental theory. Havighurst did identify stages of growth; each one requiring completion to reach the next. Havighurst also believed that developmental tasks arise from a combination of physical maturation, cultural, and social influences, combined with the individual's values and desires. These tasks consist of knowledge, skills, attitudes, and behaviors which are attained via a combination of maturation, social learning, and personal effort.

78. D: Wrenn's term cultural encapsulation does not refer to staying isolated within one cultural context. It does refer to substituting model stereotypes for actual reality. It also refers to overlooking cultural variations in favor of believing in a universal idea of the truth, and it additionally refers to a technique-oriented approach to counseling. For example, a psychoanalyst might use only psychoanalytic techniques regardless of who the client was or what the client's problems were.

79. C: An etic world view puts more emphasis on our similarities than on our differences. An emic world view puts more emphasis on differences that we must understand in order to help different cultural groups from their specific perspectives. Thus, it is a specific rather than a global view. Therefore, the belief in taking each group's perspective is emic, not etic. The emic world view does not state that we need to transcend our differences, but rather to focus on them by taking each group's perspective in order to understand and help them.

80. B: One of Lazarus' modalities is sensations (i.e., vision, hearing, smell, taste, and touch). However, a perception is not a sensation, but rather the interpretation of a sensation. Further, the clarification that the perception is of a nonexistent odor suggests that it is either a hallucination or an aura (which some people experience preceding a migraine or seizure). Lazarus' seven modalities spell out the acronym BASIC ID. The acronym represents: behaviors; affective responses (emotions, moods); sensations; images (memories, dreams, and how we see ourselves); cognitions (ideas, thoughts); interpersonal relationships; and drugs (i.e., biology, including nutrition). The act of standing up or sitting down is a behavior. Having a conversation with an acquaintance is an interpersonal relationship experience (i.e., engaging in interactions with people). Having an idea about how to solve a problem involves cognition (an idea, thought, philosophy or insight).

81. A: An action or activity, defined as an external event, is the first step in therapy. This induces a belief, evident in the form of a self-verbalization. Third, there is a consequent affect (i.e., a feeling derived from the belief). This affect may be rational or irrational. (D and E stand for disputing and effect; see the "D-E" following question for further explanation.)

82. C: After action, belief, and the consequent affect, the remaining modalities are: 1) Disputing the belief that causes the affect (if it is irrational), and 2) the cognitive effect, which is defined as a change in the client's self-verbalization (evidencing understanding). According to Ellis, reconstructing one's irrational beliefs and self-talk will correct one's inappropriate feelings and behaviors.

83. B: Harrington and Glasser were proponents of reality therapy where the process of transference (i.e., when a client unconsciously expresses feelings toward the therapist which are really feelings toward a past significant other) is rejected. Reality therapists are solution-oriented and focus on the present. They feel transference is unnecessary if the therapist is authentic (i.e., being himself or herself in therapy). Answers A and D are positions typical of Freudian psychoanalysis, wherein transference is found beneficial to treatment. They believe it is inevitable in therapy, and encourage it so analysis of transference can be done to gain insights to the client's unconscious. Answer C is a position typical of a behaviorist; unconscious states are disregarded, and only observable behaviors are considered. In learning theories, external behaviors can be changed. According to Skinner, whatever internal feelings motivate the behavior will not matter because they cannot be seen and thus cannot be environmentally manipulated.

84. B: Concreteness is NOT one of the strengths of Rogerian counseling. One of its criticisms is its lack of concreteness. One of Rogers' techniques is the therapist's acceptance of the client, which benefits the client. Other strengths of Rogers' client-centered counseling include the openness of the theory, its evolution, and its applicability to a wide range of problems.

85. D: When group members hear different feedback from each co-leader, it may stimulate the energy of the group and lead to more multi-faceted discussions which can enhance the group process. Co-leaders should not always have the same amount of experience, because co-leading is a

good way to help newer, less experienced group leaders by pairing them with a more experienced co-leader. Co-leaders should not be of the same sex, as it is often more helpful if a male and a female are paired as co-leaders. For example, two men might be too competitive, and two women might be too cooperative. Thus, the dynamic between a male and a female would likely be more balanced and more likely to introduce discussion-stimulating differences in views. Co-leaders should have a good working relationship. Therefore, having markedly different theoretical orientations which could induce conflict is not a good idea.

86. D: Extinction is a behavioral technique of ignoring a behavior until the individual or group stops engaging in it. This is useful if the sole purpose of the behavior is to seek attention. Deprived of reinforcement (attention) long enough, the person(s) is/are likely to abandon their attention-seeking behaviors. However, in a group setting, ignoring a resistant behavior is not usually effective. (It might work with certain attention-seeking behaviors, such as talking too much or too loudly, interrupting, etc, but it would be unlikely to help in situations of resistance in the form of silence even if it is attention-seeking.) Confrontation has been identified as a powerful technique for dealing with resistance. Group leaders modeling ways to deal with resistance can also be effective. Discussion of resistive behaviors with the group before they occur is often a good way to prevent them.

87. C: Parsons' method did not include giving a prognosis. The three steps in his approach were: 1) study the individual for specific traits; 2) survey available occupations (factors); and, 3) match the individual with an occupation. Prognosis was, however, part of E. G. Williamson's approach.

88. A: Decision. This would be a part of decision-making models of career counseling. Williamson's approach included six steps: Analysis, synthesis, diagnosis, prognosis, counseling, and follow-up.

89. B: It is NOT one of Crites' three kinds of diagnoses. Crites is known for the idea of vocational maturity, but there is no "maturational" diagnosis in his approach. His three diagnoses are "differential", i.e., identifying what the problems are; "dynamic", i.e., identifying what has caused the problems; and, "decisional", i.e., identifying how the person is dealing with the problems.

90. C: Construct validity exists when a test successfully measures a hypothetical construct, such as locus of control, field dependency, creativity, etc. Convergent validation occurs when the construct being studied correlates highly with other constructs. Discriminant validation occurs when there is no statistically significant correlation with other constructs. Content validity refers to the instrument containing items from the proper domain of usable items. Predictive validity refers to the confirmation of a test's predictions by later behaviors or other measurable criteria. Concurrent validity refers to test results being successfully compared with other criteria or test results at the same time.

91. D: Norm-referenced tests compare the individual to others who took the same test. How one compares with others is more important in norm-referenced testing than how much one knows. Criterion-referenced tests compare one's score to an established criterion, such as the cut-off score on the NCE; they do not rank a score within a group. They also do not compare one's score to others as norm-referenced tests do.

92. C: Ipsative interpretation means comparing multiple subtest results for one individual with themselves only with no comparison to other people's results. Norm-referenced means comparing the individual's score(s) to others. Criterion-referenced means comparing the individual's score to a preset criterion. The WAIS-IV measures a number of different aptitudes. In this example, the tester

is comparing one individual's various scores on different subtests with each other which is an ipsative interpretation.

93. D: Covariate refers to analysis of covariance (ANCOVA) not ANOVA. In an ANCOVA, the influence on the dependent variable of one or more independent variables is controlled. A one-way ANOVA is used when there is only one variable at three or more levels (for example, if you had three or more experimental groups — because there are more than two, a t-test will not work.) A factorial ANOVA is used to determine at the same time whether mean scores on two or more variables have a significant difference, and also whether these variables have a significant interaction with one another. If you had one dependent variable and two independent variables, you would use a factorial ANOVA to measure those factors. If you had more than one dependent variable, the factorial ANOVA cannot be used. Instead you would use a multivariate analysis of variance (MANOVA). Multivariate means that you have both more than one independent variable AND more than one dependent variable. Finally, covariate means that you are controlling one or more of those independent variables.

94. B: You have a normal score distribution. You would use a nonparametric test when you are NOT able assume that your distribution of scores resembles a normal curve. If you have a normal distribution, parametric tests (such as analyses of variance or correlational tests) can be used. Nonparametric tests are indicated if: 1) your sample's variance is similar to the population's variance (i.e., the sample is homogeneous); 2) if you collected data from two samples which are independent of one another, in which case you could use the Mann-Whitney U test; or, 3) if your data are nominal (i.e., they are in groups or categories, such as male and female). In this case, you could use a Chi-square test to see whether your two distributions have a significant difference.

95. A: The Likert scale is the type of question where the answer choices are graduated in order of degree according to the strength of the respondent's opinion. A scatterplot is a graphic depiction of the relationship between two variables for a group of test respondents. It plots the respondent's scores on a graph. The Kruskal-Wallis test is a nonparametric test used when there are more than two mean scores on a single variable. It is a nonparametric version of an ANOVA. The Wilcoxen signed-rank test is a nonparametric measure used when there are scores for two samples that are correlated.

96. C: Wrenn stressed developmental needs as the focus of the counseling profession. Developmental needs are normal and hence not necessarily neurotic. He did not emphasize needs of the group over those of the individual or vice versa.

97. B: The Smith-Hughes Act (1917) granted federal funds for vocational education and guidance. The National Defense Education Act (1958) provided money for the training of school counselors. California passed a law in 1962 requiring that marriage, family and child counselors must be licensed. Counseling services to veterans in the Veterans Administration expanded following World War II.

98. A: The National Vocational Guidance Association founded in 1913 is known as the first professional counseling association. Though the Vocation Bureau in Boston, directed by Frank Parsons, began earlier in 1908, it is not known as the first professional counseling association. The APGA founded in 1951 and the OVR founded in 1954 were both founded later than the NVGA.

99. B: As of the 21st century, the number of certified and licensed counselors in the United States is approaching 100,000.

100. C: Accreditation is what an institution receives when it meets certain established standards or qualifications. Colleges, universities, and specialized programs of study may receive accreditation via regional agencies of the US Department of Education; health care facilities are accredited via the Joint Commission (formerly JCAHO). Accreditation is granted only to an institution or a program and not to individuals.

101. B: The stage of autonomy vs. shame and doubt typically occurs between ages 1-1½ and 3 years, and tantrums are manifested as the child tries to assert their independence. This period is often called the "terrible twos." Positive resolution of this conflict results in the child's development of the positive ego quality of "will" (the determination to exercise free choice). Basic trust vs. mistrust is the first stage (birth to 1-1/2 years of age) when an infant develops trust if their needs are met (e.g., being nursed when hungry and changed when needed, etc). Positive resolution results in developing a sense of hope. Initiative vs. guilt is the third stage from ages 3 to 6 when children learn to meet challenges, take responsibility, and identify others' rights. Positive resolution results in developing a sense of purpose. Industry vs. inferiority (6-11) is the fourth of the eight stages when children master social and school skills or develop a sense of inferiority if they do not. Positive resolution results in developing a sense of competence.

102. C: Larry is in Stage 5 (the first of Kohlberg's two postconventional stages) where social contracts exist and most rules are relative; Carol is in stage 6, the second of the postconventional level: universal ethical principles apply in a self-chosen orientation, and the individual may or may not obey a law depending on whether they believes it is the right or moral thing to do. Kohlberg's first preconventional level consists of stage 1 which has a punishment and obedience orientation (i.e., we must obey the law or be punished); and stage 2, which has a hedonistic and instrumental orientation (i.e., we must obey the law to get rewarded). Kohlberg's second conventional level consists of stage 3, where an interpersonal acceptance orientation is predominant (i.e., we must follow the rules to get approval); and stage 4, where a law and order orientation prevails (e.g., we must obey the laws to conform to authority). The postconventional and highest level with Stages 5 and 6 is the level and stages of Larry's and Carol's respective moral development.

103. B: Dissonance. The five stages of this theory are: conformity, dissonance, resistance and immersion, introspection, and synergistic articulation and awareness. In conformity, the individual depreciates his or her self and identifies with the majority. In dissonance, the individual's current self-concept is challenged and the person experiences a conflict between appreciating and depreciating the self. In resistance and immersion, the individual embraces minority views and rejects the majority which results in appreciation of the self. In introspection, the individual moves away from the intense feelings of resistance and immersion and becomes more concerned with appreciating the self. In synergistic articulation and awareness, the individual owns and appreciates elements of both the majority and minority cultures.

104. A: Both Freud's and Ellis' counseling styles would favor an etic approach as both types of counseling use the same techniques for everybody regardless of the individual client's personality or problems. An emic approach, which emphasizes individual differences rather than similarities. Thus, it would be favored by practitioners of Carl Rogers' person-centered counseling or Adler's individual psychology.

105. C: This therapeutic technique is referred to as "re-authoring," and it is used in narrative therapy to helping a client rewrite their story to make it more appropriate. Clarifications are observations made by the therapist to help discover and construct the client's story. Deconstruction

- 144 -

is externalizing and focusing on the problem rather than on the person (i.e., the person is not the problem, the problem is the problem) to help to deconstruct it. Documentation of the evidence is often done in narrative therapy by the therapist writing letters to the client. Done between sessions, these are found to be powerful supports to the therapy sessions.

106. D: Integrative counseling synthesizes existing theories and practices from a variety of theoretical perspectives (as opposed to just borrowing them). Thus, it implies that a model is being created. Integrative counseling is not the same as eclectic counseling which also uses a variety of techniques and theories. Integrative counseling goes beyond this to form a unique, synthesized theory. Integrative counseling begins with the counselor developing a personal theory rather than ending with it. The counselor's process of theory development results in a highly individualistic theory instead of a highly generalized one. Therefore, it is highly congruent and does not make much use of incongruity. The theory is also highly flexible.

107. B: Umwelt means the world of the physical or biological system. Mitwelt refers to the world of relationships. Eigenwelt is the world of self-identity. ("Welt" means "world" in German. "Um" means "around" and "umwelt" means "environment." "Mit" means "with," so "with-world" means one's relationships with others. "Eigen" means "one's own," so "Eigenwelt" is "one's own world" or the self.)

108. C: Feminist therapy. Feminist therapists believe that the personal is political, and that personal and societal identities are interdependent. They believe that intrapsychic, interpersonal, and contextual variables help in defining distress. Therefore, they use an integrated analysis of oppression including society's gender expectations and oppression based on race, ethnicity, culture, and sexual orientation. They believe that the counseling relationship is egalitarian and that women's perspectives are valued. They reject androcentric norms and accept subjective experience and feminist consciousness. The qualities listed in the question, when taken as a whole, do not uniquely relate to SFBT, narrative therapy, or reality therapy.

109. A: Solution-focused brief therapy (SFBT) emphasizes setting specific goals early in the therapeutic relationship and having a limited number of sessions. In SFBT, understanding the nature of the problem is not considered necessary to the generation of solutions to it. SFBT counselors often use scales to identify changes in the client's affect. The other three (B, C, D) are not necessarily short-term types of counseling. REBT focuses on correcting irrational beliefs and self-verbalizations by reconstructing and replacing them with rational thought. Rogerian or person-centered counseling focuses on empathy, warmth, unconditional acceptance and the relationship between the therapist and client. Narrative therapy is based on social constructionism and focuses on the client's "story," or their subjective perception of reality which is considered valid and socially constructed. It may be deconstructed and rewritten to help clients view their lives differently.

110. B: The optimum group size for an adult group with no co-leader is generally considered to be 8 people. With young children who are 5 or 6 years old, an optimum group size would be 3 or 4. Groups may be larger with older children. For adults, 5 may be too small and 10 too large.

111. D: When a therapy group is formed, the leader(s) should decide in advance how long it will run and should advise the members of this. The group's duration should not be unknown or indefinite. There is no generalization that therapy groups should run for six months. The group members should not decide on its length as they do not have the leader's knowledge or expertise.

112. A: Mentor, employer, and advisor are NOT roles defined by Super. The nine life roles he identified are: child, student, citizen, spouse, homemaker, parent, worker, leisurite, and pensioner. Super's theory is developmental and holistic. He formulated the concept of the "life-career rainbow," which encompassed his major stages of the life span and the life space (drawn from his interpretation these roles).

113. C: According to Gottfredson, younger children tend to choose occupations which fit their sex. Gottfredson's theory is developmental. She stated that since children of this age tend to identify certain occupations with either the male or the female gender, it follows that they will choose occupations based on gender roles or stereotypes. Orientation to sex roles is the name of her second developmental stage (ages 6-8). Preadolescents tend to choose occupations consistent with their social values since they are in Gottfredson's stage of orientation to social valuation (ages 9-13). Children of this age may also rule out occupations they feel are inappropriate to their intelligence or levels of ability. Adolescents, who are in Gottfredson's stage of orientation to internal unique self (age 14 and older), tend to choose occupations based on their awareness of their own personal characteristics.

114. D: Cognitive development was NOT identified as a major determinant in Ann Roe's theory which is a needs-based approach. She believed that occupational selection is a function of the needs developed by a child, whose structure were influenced by a combination of genetics, environmental experiences, and interactions between the parents and the child. Career development as a part of cognitive development is more closely identified with Tiedeman, O'Hara, and Miller-Tiedeman's decision-making model of career development.

115. B: Evaluation is synonymous with appraisal. Both terms imply going beyond measurement to make inferences or judgments about human behavior and characteristics. Assessment refers to processes and/or procedures for gathering data or information on human behavior. Testing is a type of assessment.

116. B: 0.64, or 64% = .80², or .80 squared. The amount of true variance (versus error variance), is measured by the square of the correlation of the tests. Response A would be the correlation halved; response C would be 20% of the correlation; and response D would be the correlation with no change.

117. A: The coefficient of determination equals the degree of common variance, or the square of the correlation. The coefficient of nondetermination is the unique, or error variance, or the variance which is not in common (i.e., the difference between 100 minus the coefficient of determination. If the correlation were .80, the common variance (coefficient of determination) would be 64%, and the error variance (unique variance/coefficient of nondetermination) would be 36%. Answer B is the opposite of the correct answer. Answers B and C are also opposites or reversed statements. Answer D is wrong because it is the correlation squared, not the correlation, which equals the coefficient of determination/common variance, and likewise the coefficient of nondetermination/error variance is the difference between 100% and the square of the correlation, not the correlation.

118. B: Purposeful sampling is only used when there is NO interest in generalizing the research findings to the population because it is not randomized. Purposeful sampling may be comprehensive, may involve extreme-case selection, or it may consist of typical-case selection.

119. C: Stratified sampling refers to selecting individuals who represent major subgroups in the population. The subgroups represented could be ethnic groups, age groups, gender, teenagers, married people, etc. Selecting naturally occurring groups is known as cluster sampling. The naturally occurring groups could be classrooms, apartment complexes, city blocks, neighborhoods, etc. Selecting samples of convenience or of volunteers refers to non-random or non-probability samples or "other" samples. These will not necessarily yield a normal score distribution, but may offer very valuable data. Selecting individuals so that each has equal chances of being selected is known as random sampling.

120. D: The suggested minimum sample sizes are a sample of at least 15 individuals for experimental and ex post facto research; a sample of at least 30 individuals for correlational research; and a sample of at least 100 individuals for survey research. Sample size influences statistical hypothesis testing. There are tables available for determining the appropriate sample size. In general, it is considered the rule that from 5% to 10% of the population is enough. The numbers suggested are a guideline for the smallest sample size to be selected for the respective types of studies as smaller numbers will not likely be representative nor give normal distributions.

121. B: Confidentiality is an ethical concept, derived from the need for an expectation privacy in order to have a successful working relationship (i.e., little positive work can be achieved if the client fears to reveal crucial information based upon fears the information may be divulged elsewhere). By contrast, privileged communication is a legal concept, as it is granted in specific circumstances by state law – for counselors, it is often found in state licensure laws. Answer A is the reverse of the correct answer. Answers C and D are incorrect because the two concepts are not the same, and they are not both legal (C) or both ethical (D) concepts.

122. C: Reciprocity is a process whereby one credentialing agency (such as a state licensure board) accepts the credential of another agency (such as the licensure board for another state) as equivalent to its own license. It does not mean that one state licensure board actually grants licensure to a counselor who is licensed in another state, but rather that the first state licensure board would accept that counselor's license from the other state as being equivalent to its own license. Answers A and B do not involve licensure or credentialing at all.

123. C: A statement of disclosure is not required by law in every state of the U.S., but may be required in some states. Since it is required by law in some states, answer B is incorrect. A statement of disclosure is given to a potential or new client before counseling begins, so answer D is incorrect.

124. A: A release of information form is to be signed by the client before confidential information can be released by their counselor to another professional or agency. It should specify what information can be released, to whom, and for what period of time. This is similar to the information release that patients sign for medical doctors to release their information to other doctors. A release of information is not a document given to a client by a counselor to disclose what procedures may be used before the counseling relationship begins, as this would be a statement of disclosure. The information release is not signed by the other professional or agency to receive the confidential information, but by the client who is giving permission. The information release is not for another professional or agency to give the client's information to the counselor. This would only happen if the other professional or agency were one that had also worked with the client in some capacity. In this case, the client would sign the release for the other professional or agency and give it to them not to the client's counselor.

125. B: Professional liability insurance is required by law in some states, but not others. It is highly recommended for counselors even in those states where it is not required, and it is not generally considered an unnecessary expense. There are several providers of this insurance. For example, the American Counseling Association (ACA) sponsors a professional liability insurance program for its members.

126. B: A major criticism of Levinson's work is that he only studied men. In fact, his most famous book is entitled *The Seasons of a Man's Life*. Critics argue that this limits his findings, since they cannot be applied to women. It is erroneous to say that his developmental periods did not include transitions. He actually named three major transitions between his four major eras of a man's life: the early adult transition, the mid-life transition, and the late adult transition. It is likewise false that many critics have argued against the existence of a midlife crisis. While there may be a few who would take this position, a far greater number agree that midlife is often a time of questioning and/or reevaluating one's life. It is also not true that Levinson's midlife crisis excluded questioning one's career. He actually made the point that career is one part of life that men tend to question in their 40s, and that this is a common time for some men to change their occupations.

127. C: Gould believe that what he called "protective devices" are false assumptions and are triggered at different ages. They may certainly be used as coping strategies or defense mechanisms by individuals, but these are not the most accurate definitions. The important point about these devices is that Gould thought they were false assumptions; therefore, misleading and not productive. Being false, they are in no way absolute truths.

128. A: Acculturation is how much an individual from a racial or ethnic minority adopts and incorporates the customs, values, and beliefs of the dominant culture. Assimilation is how much individuals from a minority change to the point that they are absorbed into the dominant culture, losing all traces of their original behaviors and values. Mannie became an American in following many American customs and behaviors, but retained his original minority religion and cultural values. Moe changed all of his behaviors and characteristics by wiping out his original ethnic and religious identity.

129. B: Rogerian counseling, of those listed, would be the most appropriate because it has an emic orientation—i.e., it emphasizes individual differences rather than similarities and would take into account the client's different cultural backgrounds and respect these. Traditional Freudian psychoanalysis has a more etic orientation—i.e., it uses the same techniques for everybody regardless of their individual backgrounds. As Atkinson (2004) suggested, traditional "time-bound, space-bound, cathartic psychotherapy" would probably not be as relevant to many cross-cultural clients. Maslow's theory of self-actualization is popular in American culture for its emphasis on individualism and realizing one's full potential. However, Juan's culture emphasizes familismo (familism), manifest in a strong identification with and attachment to one's family; and Mai's culture emphasizes collectivism, embodied in a strong identification with the good of the whole group over the needs of the individual. Thus, a Maslovian approach would likely be too individualistic and self-centered for these clients. Fritz Perls' Gestalt therapy also has a strongly self-centered orientation, and would also be less appropriate for multicultural counseling purposes.

130. C: Existentialism addresses the search for meaning which would be the best choice of these for Andrew. It would be a natural fit with his personality, since he already wonders and worries about the meaning of life and his role in it. Anxiety and guilt are also important concepts in existential therapy. Since Andrew often has these emotions, this form of counseling would help him to address his feelings and help explain why he has them. Andrew wants to understand himself better, and self

actualization is also a goal of existential counseling. Reality therapy would not be a good fit for Andrew as it is theoretically simplistic, whereas Andrew is very introspective and seeks understanding. Reality therapy ignores the client's personal history and is solution-focused. Andrew seems more interested in understanding himself than in finding immediate solutions. Behavioral therapy ignores inner states which would dissatisfy Andrew as he is so introspective. Behaviorism deals only with behaviors not the whole person, so this approach would fall short of meeting Andrew's needs. Transactional analysis would be too simplified for Andrew with its cognitive orientation and treatment contracts—and, like reality therapy, it is very goal-directed. Andrew is more inclined to explore questions of existence and to analyze his own psyche.

131. D: There is no "multiplicative" characterization of counselor responses in Carkhuff's theory. Additive refers to a response that adds noticeably (Level 4) or significantly (Level 5) to the client's affect. Subtractive refers to a response that does not attend to or detract significantly (Level 1) from the client's affect, or one that subtracts noticeably (Level 2) from the client's affect. Interchangeable refers to a response that is interchangeable (Level 3) with the client's affect.

132. A: This is typical of a level 1 response (i.e., a response that does not attend to or detracts significantly from the client's affect). In this example, the client is obviously very upset and expresses it. The counselor then responds with a simple, concrete question not reflecting the client's affect. A level 2 response is one that subtracts noticeably from the client's affect, and might be something like, "You seem a bit perturbed." A level 3 response is one that is interchangeable with the client's affect, and might be something like, "My goodness! You certainly are very upset about how she yelled at you." A level 4 or 5 response is one that adds noticeably (4) or significantly (5) to the client's affect, and might be, "I can see that you're really upset at how she yelled at you. Your feelings are terribly hurt by what she said and how she said it, and you feel crushed and destroyed by it. It has damaged your self-esteem and your relationship."

133. D: Adler cited birth order and the family as major influences on individual development. Wolpe developed a theory of reciprocal inhibition, which states that anxiety and relaxation cannot simultaneously coexist. Only Wolpe used systematic desensitization — a behavioral intervention which creates counter-conditioning by pairing aversive stimuli with more pleasant ones. Adler did view neuroses as failures in learning which caused distorted perceptions, but he did not use behavioral techniques to change them. He emphasized client responsibility and a collaborative relationship in counseling. Carl Jung and Rollo May had in common their emphases on the existential concepts of identity, meaning, and purpose. Gordon Allport and Kurt Lewin both believed in systems: Allport saw human behavior as fitting within interactional systems such as cultures, situations, and field theory. Lewin was a field theorist who saw "life space" as a function of the individual and the environment, and behavior as a function of life space. Sigmund Freud and Aaron Beck were both psychoanalysts. Freud founded psychoanalysis and proposed the concepts of the conscious, the unconscious, and the preconscious. Beck was a neo-Freudian who identified "automatic thoughts" similar to Freud's preconscious.

134. C: Caplan's model ranks groups according to their purpose. A tertiary group usually deals with more serious, longstanding individual difficulties.

135. B: In Caplan's model, a secondary group works to reduce the severity and/or duration of a problem which is usually not that severe, and this type of group generally includes some aspects of prevention.

136. A: In Caplan's model, a primary group emphasizes a healthy lifestyle and/or coping strategies aimed at reducing the incidence of a certain problem. In this case, it is substance abuse. This kind of group could also be aimed at preventing teen pregnancy, preventing divorce, etc.

137. D: Donald Super did NOT identify the church as one of the theaters in which we play out our roles. Home, community, school, and workplace are the four theaters he identified.

138. B: An investigative type prefers systematic, intellectual activities and has poor social skills. Examples include a computer programmer or a chemist. This is Jason's predominant type. A social type dislikes activities with tools or machines and prefers activities that inform or develop other people. This is Sallie's predominant type. A realistic type is aggressive, prefers explicit activities involving physical work and has poor social skills (examples could include a mechanic or a technician). An artistic type is imaginative, prefers self-expression, and dislikes systematic and ordered activities (examples could include an artist or an editor). A conventional type is practical, prefers structured activities, and dislikes ambiguous or unsystematic work (examples could include a file clerk or an accountant). An enterprising type is an extrovert who likes leadership roles and persuasive endeavors and dislikes abstract tasks or activities requiring caution. Enterprising types might be salespersons, entrepreneurs, or those in management roles.

139. C: An individual's profile of the six personality types may be differentiated (i.e., it has significant highs and lows among the types), or it may be undifferentiated (i.e., the profile tends to be more flattened among the various types). Pairs of types which are on adjacent sides of the hexagon are more psychologically alike, so answer A is incorrect. Pairs of types which are on non-adjacent sides of the hexagon are less psychologically alike, so answer B is incorrect. Congruence refers to similarity or sameness between the individual's personality type and the type of environment the individual is in not to pairs of personality types, so answer D is incorrect.

140. A: Unskilled labor represents one of Roe's six levels of occupations (not one of her eight fields). The eight fields she identified were: service (only this half of answer A is correct), business contact, managerial, general cultural, arts and entertainment, technology, outdoor, and science. The six levels she identified were: professional and managerial (highest level); professional and managerial (regular); semi-professional and managerial; skilled; semiskilled; and unskilled.

141. B: Tiedeman said that the continuous process of career decision making is made up of the first phase of anticipation or preoccupation, which includes the following sub-phases: exploration, crystallization, choice, and clarification. The second phase is implementation or adjustment, which includes these sub-phases: induction, reformation, and integration.

142. C: A test with a structured procedure for administration and a specified scoring system is a better example of a standardized test. A checklist, a rating scale, or an open-ended interview are all good examples of nonstandardized tests as they have no formalized or routinized directions for administering or scoring them.

143. D: ALL of these are circumstances in which testing may be useful to better inform such activities as job or educational placement, counseling, or diagnosis.

144. D: To help a counselor decide if a client's needs are within the counselor's range of services, to help a counselor gain understanding of the client, and to help a client gain self-understanding are only a few of the ways that test can inform the counseling process.

145. B: A hypothesis is a statement formulated by a researcher who then tests it to see if it is true or not. A directional hypothesis states that one group will have a significantly different score than another. (This is a hypothesis that would use a one-tailed test.) A research question is in the form of a question rather than a statement. A nondirectional hypothesis would state that there will be differences in the two groups, but will not state which group will have a higher or lower score. (This type of hypothesis would require a two-tailed test.) A null hypothesis would state that there is no difference between the two groups.

146. A: Significance level means the degree to which you are likely to make a mistake in either rejecting or accepting the null hypothesis when you should not (i.e., There is not a significant difference between your experimental groups but you reject the null hypothesis, or there is indeed a significant difference but you accept the null hypothesis that there is not). Conventions of experimental research tend to use significance levels of .05, .01, or .001. A level of .01, as in this question, means that you are willing to accept the possibility of error in one out of one hundred experimental trials. Significance level does not refer to actually executing the experiment itself wrongly, nor does it refer to errors of instrumentation or to the hypothesis itself being incorrect. Additionally, in answer D, "ten out of one hundred" is wrong. In answer C, "one out of ten" is also wrong.

147. C: A Type I or alpha error is rejecting the null hypothesis, which states that there is no difference in the results, when it is true. A type II or beta error is accepting the null hypothesis when it is wrong and there actually is a difference.

148. C: Title and practice-control laws state that one cannot practice counseling without a professional counselor license. Some states have laws saying that one may practice counseling without a license, but if doing so one may not legally use the licensed professional counselor (LPC) title. These are called "title-control" laws rather than "title and practice-control" laws. There is no law specifying that one cannot practice counseling without using the LPC title. Using the LPC title is not a requirement for obtaining a license.

149. D: This act does NOT give students' parents access to their counseling records. Rather, it gives them access to their educational records. It also gives the students themselves this access providing they are 18 years of age or older. Answers A, B, and C are all correct.

150. B: Title IX bans sex discrimination in academics and athletics in K-12 schools and colleges. Title IX has nothing to do with remedial reading. This law does not require that the same sports be available to both males and females, only that males and females be provided the same proportion of opportunities to participate in sports. This law has nothing to do with the sizes of classes in schools.

151. D: Personality characteristics are typically tested using psychological instruments such as the Minnesota Multiphasic Personality Inventory (MMPI) or the California Psychological Inventory which are personality tests. Brain dysfunctions are typically measured using neuropsychological assessments such as the Luria-Nebraska Neuropsychological Battery which measures organic damage and its location(s); the Bender® Visual-Motor Gestalt Test, which is often used with children to measure brain dysfunction. The five areas covered by a formal mental status examination are: appearance and behavior; thought processes; mood and affect; intellectual functioning; and, sensorium. Sensorium refers to orientation to self, place, time and environment.

152. C: Culture-bound values in counseling include the following: individually centered therapy; verbal, emotional, and behavioral expressiveness; defined communication patterns; openness, and intimacy. Class-bound values in counseling include strict adherence to a time schedule; ambiguous or unstructured approaches to problems; and, looking for long-range solutions or setting long-range goals. Answers A, B, and D are all reversed (i.e., elements of culture-bound values are identified as belonging to class-bound values, and vice versa).

153. A: The gold stars Harry receives are tokens. He gets to purchase rewards—privileges or items he values—with the tokens he receives for performing desired behaviors. A token economy is a type of behavior modification used for shaping behavior. A reinforcement schedule is a behavioral term referring to the criteria for giving reinforcements or rewards. It may relate to time or to number of occurrences (i.e., an interval schedule or a ratio schedule), and it may be fixed or variable. Systematic desensitization is another behavioral technique used to reduce unpleasant reactions to specific stimuli. This technique of counterconditioning, based on the theory of reciprocal inhibition, pairs the triggering stimulus with more pleasant events so that the client's association with that stimulus changes from negative to positive. It is useful with phobias, some anxiety disorders, and other learned negative responses. Negative reinforcement is also a behavioral term. It refers to removing a favored stimulus (NOT to introducing a punishment).

154. D: As the pair of inaccurate statements. Regarding the Johari Window, the goal in counseling is to make the lower right quadrant smaller (not larger) and to make the upper left quadrant larger (not smaller). The upper left quadrant represents what is known to the self and known to others. The lower right quadrant represents what is unknown to the self and unknown to others. The upper right quadrant is what is known to others but not known to the self, and the lower left quadrant is what is known to the self but not known to others. The goal is to make more information known to the self and to others and less unknown to both. The principles of change named in answers A, B, and C are all accurate.

155. C: Bergan's consultation model is behavioral, not process oriented. The process model was developed by Schein, who was also responsible for identifying the purchase model and the doctor-patient model. Caplan developed the mental health consultation model, and Bandura is known for the social learning model. Therefore, these other answers all correctly pair each consultation model with the person who developed it.

156. A: EMDR stands for the experimental counseling technique called eye movement desensitization and reprocessing. It is used to help the client to access memories of traumatic experiences and to reprocess those experiences via rapid eye movements (REM) similar to those seen during REM phases of sleep. This is when the sleeper is thought to be dreaming or otherwise processing mental images. Answers B, C, and D are all phrases made up to fit the initials.

157. B: Verbal expressions are NOT included. Kinesics refers to nonlinguistic or nonverbal communication such as facial expressions, physical gestures and body movements. Proxemics refers to spatial features of the environment such as seating arrangements, furniture placement, and how our personal space is affected by such arrangements.

158. D: It is NOT a correct statement of one of the differences: The duration of treatment in family therapy is usually shorter than in individual therapy. Family therapy generally tries to resolve current problems within a family via brief counseling. The locus of pathology in family counseling is viewed as being within the social context, typically the family, rather than as being within the individual. The focus of the interventions in family therapy is on the family rather than on the

individual even though one individual in the family may be the identified patient. The unit of treatment intervention is the family rather than an individual in family counseling.

159. B: "Conforming; swarming" is the one NOT written by Tuckman. The others refer to: 1) the formation of the group, or "forming"; 2) the processing and resolution of conflicts, or "storming"; 3) the process of conforming or not conforming to the group's norms, i.e., norming; 4) each member's participation and self-expression within the group and bonding with the group, i.e., performing; and 5) the termination of the group, i.e., mourning or adjourning.

160. B: "Definition" is NOT one of the stages Yalom identified. He named orientation, conflict, cohesion, and termination as the four stages of a therapy group. The first stage, orientation, is when members get to know one another as individuals and acclimate to the group as an entity. The second, conflict, is when group members experience differences of opinion and personalities clash resulting in disagreements, arguments, or other conflicted interactions among members. The third, cohesion, is when the group experiences bonding among the members and gains a sense group identity. The fourth, termination, is when the course of counseling and hence the group itself arrives at an end.

161. A: Vocational maturity is a concept associated with John Crites, who developed a comprehensive model of career counseling including three types of diagnoses (differential, dynamic, and decisional). Vocational maturity is not a term associated with decision models of career development. Factors associated with a decision-making model of career choice include the individual's risk-taking style; the individual's investment, such as money, time, or deferment of rewards; the individual's personal values; and the individual's self-efficacy or belief in one's ability to perform the required behavior(s).

162. B: The individual's relative competence is NOT one of the factors identified by career self-efficacy theory as likely to be affected by the individual's expectations. This theory states that the individual's expectations will influence: 1) choice or whether a behavior will be initiated; 2) performance, or how much effort will be expended; and, 3) persistence, or to what extent the individual will persevere when confronted by obstacles. Some theorists believe these explain gender differences in career choices. Higher self-efficacy seems related to choice and persistence in math and science careers.

163. B: Undecided means that the person needs more information before making a decision; it refers to a state of being. Being indecisive, by contrast, is a personality trait. An indecisive person may be given all the information there is on a subject, and may still be unable to decide. With indecisive clients, personal counseling may be needed before career counseling can be effective. Answer A is untrue since undecided and indecisive are not synonyms. Answers C and D are opposites of the correct definitions.

164. B: The SEM is NOT a measure of validity but of reliability. It is also known as confidence band or confidence limits.

165. D: The SEM is calculated in advance NOT after the test is taken. It also may be reported on the test's score profile. The SEM is useful for interpreting an individual's test scores. It helps to determine the range within which an individual's test score is likely to fall. Finally, each test does have its own unique SEM value.

166. C: Labeling is NOT a reason testing should be used. Even though some tests will yield scores which can assign a person to a level of giftedness or intellectual disability, using this categorization via scores for labeling a person should be avoided as it is stigmatizing and can limit the individual's educational, vocational, life options and ultimate success. Testing is useful for understanding oneself better, for obtaining licensure or certification via passing test scores, and for appropriately planning a person's educational programs.

167. A: The Wechsler Intelligence Scales include the WPPSI-III (Wechsler Preschool and Primary Scale of Intelligence), the WISC-IV (Wechsler Intelligence Scale for Children), and the WAIS-IV (Wechsler Adult Intelligence Scale)—the Roman numerals refer to edition numbers. The Stanford-Binet IQ test has a number of subtests to assess various abilities, but does not have different versions for different age groups as Wechsler does. The MAT is a test of analytical ability given to many college students as a standard for admission to graduate school. As such, it does not have versions for different ages. The SAT is a test commonly given to high school students to measure their verbal and quantitative abilities via subtests, and thus needs no age-accommodating versions. It is used to help determine their eligibility for admission to college.

168. A: As the level of significance goes down, type I error also goes down. A type I error is wrongly rejecting the null hypothesis. With a lower significance level, the chances of this are lower. Answer B is the reverse of the correct answer. Answer C is not true in that there is definitely a direct relationship between significance level and Type I error. It is not true that the amount of type I error can go either up or down as the significance level decreases.

169. B: Type II error has an inverse relationship with significance level (i.e., it will increase as the significance level decreases). Type II error is wrongly accepting the null hypothesis that there is no significant difference. The lower the significance level, the more chance there is of this happening. Answer A is the reverse of the correct answer. Answer C is not true in that there is definitely a direct relationship between significance level and type II error. It is not true that the amount of type II error can go up or down as the significance level decreases.

170. C: If the significance level of an experiment goes down, the type I error will also go down and the type II error will go up. Answers A and D are wrong because type I and type II errors will not both go in the same direction relative to the significance level. Type I and type II error have an inverse relationship (i.e., as one goes up the other will go down). Type I error is wrongly rejecting the null hypothesis and type II error is wrongly accepting the null hypothesis. Answer B is the reverse of the correct answer.

171. D: A need to show a particular counselor's effectiveness is NOT generally cited as a reason for counseling program evaluation. Evaluation goals are to demonstrate how well a technique, process, or program of treatment works rather than how well an individual therapist works. Program evaluation has been stimulated by the increasing emphasis on accountability in the field of human services, which arose in the 1970s and currently continues. Evaluation speaks to a crucial need to demonstrate the effectiveness of counseling in general and the effectiveness of specific theories, approaches, and therapeutic techniques as well.

172. A: HIPAA, the Health Insurance Portability and Accountability Act, is a national law and does NOT vary from one state to another. It dictates standards for protecting the privacy of patients' information in the health industry, including records of psychotherapy. It regulates the transmission of patients' or clients' records, and the exchange of information for insurance claims whether or not electronically transmitted.

173. C: An EAP may be located within a company or outside of it when the company contracts with a provider. An EAP is an employee assistance program, not an educational assistance program. It is designed to help employees of a company get counseling if they need it, not to help college students. An EAP does employ licensed professional counselors to counsel employees who are referred for counseling by their employers.

174. B: Conducting a pilot study comes before developing a plan, operating the program, and evaluating the program. Critical steps identified in developing a counseling program are: 1) conceptualizing the system; 2) establishing a philosophy and assessing needs; 3) developing goals and objectives; 4) processing information; 5) conducting a pilot study; 6) developing a plan; 7) implementing the program, which includes hiring and training; operating the counseling program; 8) evaluating the program; and, 9) modifying the counseling program based on the evaluation.

175. D: All of the situations listed are limitations to confidentiality. These limitations include: 1) danger to the client or to others (requiring certain reporting); 2) discussing a case with other professionals who can help; 3) discussing a case with superiors or teachers if the counselor is still a student; 4) client requests for release of records; 5) a lawsuit is filed against a counselor; 6) court orders for release of information; 7) clerical office staff working with client records; 8) managed care providers and health insurance companies' requests for client information.

176. C: Borderline personality disorder. The key features of BPD involved instability in relationships and affect, poor self-image, and high impulsivity. Violations of personal rights and apathy common to antisocial personality disorder are insufficiently pronounced. While evidence of histrionic behavior exists, the devaluation/over-valuation pattern common to BPD is not accounted for via histrionic personality disorder. Nor is the need for admiration, pervasive with narcissism, not otherwise addressed.

177. C: Strong did NOT state that the client needs to view the counselor as agreeable. The three qualities he named were "expertness" (i.e., the counselor has formal training, specialized knowledge, and counseling experience); "attractiveness" (i.e., the client perceives the counselor to be similar to the client and covets the counselor's approval); and "trustworthiness" (i.e., the client perceives the counselor as caring about and wanting to help the client).

178. D: Bowen applied his theory of families to the emotional functioning of society as well. His concept of societal regression expressed his belief that society is moving backwards, because it fails to differentiate between emotional decision making and intellectual decision making. Bowen stated that the basic building block of a family's emotional system is a triangle not a quadrangle. What Bowen called the differential of self refers to the degree to which individuals can distinguish between their thought processes and their emotional processes not between self and others. In the nuclear family emotional system, Bowen said people choose marital partners with equal levels of differentiation to their own; if partners are undifferentiated, they will produce similarly undifferentiated family members resulting in an unstable system, not a more stable one.

179. B: According to Minuchin, the family is made up of subsystems which have boundaries between them. If the boundaries are too rigid, it leads to disengagement of the subsystems. If the boundaries are too diffuse (loose or undefined), it can result in enmeshment. Insufficient boundaries can lead to unhealthy attachments and interactions. Overly strict boundaries can minimize healthy interactions. Transactional patterns are the evolved rules of the family structure which may be general or individual. Alignments are the way family members join with or oppose

one another. Coalitions are alliances between specific family members. Conflicts are disagreements or problems occurring within families. A structural map is a diagram or drawing showing the boundaries, alignments, coalitions, conflicts and other features or interactions within the family structure. The other terms in the answer choices are not specifically identified as terms used in structural family therapy.

180. C: In all of the therapies named, the goal is to make changes in the family's functioning, and in all of them the counselor takes an active role by interacting directly with the family. Strategic family therapy (Jay Haley, Cloe Madanes) has the goal of perceiving the existing situation differently (relabeling), and Murray Bowen, the creator of family systems theory, preferred taking a neutral position as a counselor. Maintaining the balance of the family system is a goal of Milan systemic family therapy, and counselors will most often have the role of a trainer in behavioral approaches to family therapy. Counselors in strategic family therapy often have teacher-like roles as their techniques include giving clients assignments. Social constructionist family therapy has the goal of helping the family to use the knowledge it already possesses. The social constructionist theory gave rise to DeShazer's and O'Hanlon's solution-based therapeutic approaches.

181. A: The psychodynamic model is monadic as it focuses on the individual's intrapsychic conflicts and their impact on familial relations. The experiential model is dyadic as it focuses on dysfunctional interactions between two family members such as marital partners or siblings. The transgenerational model is triadic as it focuses on conflicts in the interactions between more than two family members. The strategic model is both dyadic and triadic as it will focus on problems occurring both between two family members as well as among three members of reciprocal relationships in a family.

182. D: Divorce is not as commonly identified as the other choices as a period in the life cycle of a family. While theorists point out that there are many variations, the cycles generally identified are: 1) young adults leaving home and accepting responsibility; 2) getting married; 3) having children (which includes accepting new family members in the case of babies and young children, and increasing the flexibility of boundaries as children reach adolescence and grandparents age); 4) launching children as they grow up and leave the family unit; and, 5) accepting shifts in the roles of generations as family members move into later life.

183. C: Neutrality was NOT a factor identified by Ponzo or by Yalom as being present in leaders of successful groups. Ponzo identified caring support, and Yalom identified caring as characterized by warmth and concern. Yalom identified executive leadership, which includes giving direction, and Ponzo identified participation. All of these would tend to contradict neutrality in a group leader. The additional factors Ponzo cited were: openness, participation, risk-taking, conflict-confrontation, and caring support.

184. B: The STEP Program (Systematic Training for Effective Parenting program) is a psycho-educational model for parents developed by Don Dinkmeyer using Adlerian principles. Jacob Moreno started the Theater of Spontaneity in Vienna in 1921. He developed the concept of psychodrama which is used to enact conflicts or crises in a theatrical format with a director, actors, and an audience. Moreno was the first person to use the term group psychotherapy in the 1920s. Moreno also founded the American Society of Group Psychotherapy and Psychodrama in 1941.

185. C: This theory states that some people compensate for things they cannot do in their jobs by engaging in leisure activities which are markedly different from what they do at work, while other people use the same skills and do similar activities in their leisure time as they have at work, so that

their jobs are said to "spillover" into their leisure activity. This theory does not state that unhappy workers compensate with excessive leisure pursuits, nor does it state that people's preferences in leisure time reduce their job productivity. It also does not state that people try to make up for having leisure activities by working harder, nor that leisure interests spill over into their work lives.

186. A: Although resistance to change is a common human reaction and many adults in career transition may experience it, this is not identified as an issue in counseling adults in career transition. Thus, although it may certainly be an issue for counseling, it falls into the area of "identifying issues" as opposed to being a distinct issue of its own. Some people fear or resent change simply because it is a change. Others may resist change for more pragmatic reasons such as having outdated job skills. This can be remedied by counselors who can facilitate retraining. Still other individuals need to resolve issues around the changes in their physical capacities as they age learning to accept the reality that they may need a different kind of work or a different form of work in the same or a related field. Others will find that as they have grown older and times have changed, their values have changed as well. Finally, some may fear a transition because they lack the resources to obtain needed information and the skills to look for a new job. Career counseling can help people adjust to changes in themselves and their environment, as well as providing clients with the resources they need to make a successful transition.

187. D: All of these are tests routinely used in career counseling. The ITBS is an achievement test. Depending on the educational level, age, intelligence, and social and cultural background of the client, a career counselor might use the ITBS, SAT, Test of Adult Basic Education, ACT, GRE or a combination of several tests. The Myers-Briggs Type Indicator and MMPI are personality test. A counselor can use personality testing to get a better idea of which occupations would be a good fit with a client's personality characteristics. The Minnesota Importance Questionnaire is a test of values (i.e., what is most important to an individual). Other values tests include the O*Net Work Importance Profiler and Super's Work Value Inventory (revised). A counselor could use values testing to ascertain what things are most important to a client which would provide some direction in occupational choices.

188. B: Using testing to critique the client's performance in school, work, or training is a LESS appropriate rationale for a counselor to use testing. The client's teacher, employer, or trainer would be a more appropriate person to critique performance, and they will sometimes use tests to aid in their evaluations. When a counselor uses tests, it can often help to predict the client's future performance in educational, training, or workplace settings. Testing can also help clients to make decisions about their educational or occupational futures. A counselor can also administer and interpret certain tests to help clients discover other interests they have of which they may have been unaware. This can help give clients insight into things they might like to do which they had never previously considered.

189. C: These tests are projective in nature. The Rotter's Incomplete Sentences Blank prompts the subject to complete partial sentences in the testing process. The Draw-A-Person Test prompts the subject to make a drawing of a person. The results are evaluated and interpreted by the counselor. Both tasks are unstructured or open-ended allowing the subject to project individual feelings, ideas, states, needs, etc, onto it. From this, the tester may gain insights to the subject's internal consciousness. Specialized personality tests include the Tennessee Self- Concept Scale, the Bender® Visual-Motor Gestalt Test, and the Luria-Nebraska Neuropsychological Battery. Specialized achievement tests include the GED test, the College Board's AP Program test, and the College-Level Examination Program (CLEP) test. Inventory personality tests include the MMPI, the California

Psychological Inventory (CPI), the NEO Personality Inventory (revised), the Beck Depression Inventory, and the Myers-Briggs Type Indicator.

190. B: Reviewing records is an example of unobtrusive or nonreactive measurement (i.e., data collection occurs without the individual being aware of it). Intrusive or reactive measurement means that the individual is aware of the data collection. Examples include giving questionnaires, interviewing subjects, and openly observing subjects.

191. A: A t-test is used to see if the mean scores of two groups differ significantly. Since the researcher did not have more than two groups, he would most likely use this test. A one-way analysis of variance is used when there are, for example, three groups and a t-test can no longer be used. A factorial ANOVA is used not only to see if mean scores testing two or more factors (variables) differ significantly, but also to see if they interact with one another significantly. A multivariate analysis of variance is used with more than one dependent variable, therefore precluding the use of a factorial ANOVA.

192. B: A factorial analysis of variance is used to determine not only significant differences between mean scores on two or more variables, but also significant interactions of the factors with each other. A one-way ANOVA determines significant difference but not significant interaction. A multivariate analysis of variance involves more than one dependent variable, but since this researcher was only measuring self-efficacy he does not need to use it. An analysis of covariance is used when one or more independent variables are controlled with respect to their influence on the dependent variable. This research does not require such controls.

193. C: A multivariate analysis of variance (MANOVA) is needed when there is more than one dependent variable as in this case. An analysis of variance cannot be used when the experiment has two or more dependent variables. This researcher would not use an analysis of covariance unless he controlled how one or more independent variables affected the dependent variable(s).

194. D: Analysis of covariance (ANCOVA) is used when the influence of an independent variable or variables upon a dependent variable is statistically controlled. Since the seniors initially scored higher in self-efficacy than the juniors before the counseling, the researcher evens out the differences in their scores to control the effect of grade level on the dependent variable of self-efficacy. An ANOVA does not control the influence of an independent variable or variables on a dependent variable. It also cannot be used when you have more than one dependent variable, as is the case here. A MANOVA would work for this researcher's analysis of two dependent variables (self-efficacy and optimism), but would not control for the effect of grade level on self-efficacy the way the ANCOVA does.

195. C: Some counselors work under the supervision of a psychologist or psychiatrist (particularly those with Master's degrees rather than Ph.D. or M.D. degrees), and insurance companies reimburse the supervising psychologist or psychiatrist who then remits payment to the supervising counselor. Payment to master's degree-level counselors is NOT automatic even if they are licensed. However, it is also NOT true that counselors with Master's degrees must remain unpaid unless they are licensed. Their payment would depend on whether they have a supervising psychologist or psychiatrist and upon applicable state laws. Some counselors can practice without a license in certain states as long as they do not use the title of a licensed professional counselor and do not advertise that they are licensed. Some counselors in private practice will not see clients unless they pay them directly.

196. A: Laws have changed in only some states to require insurance companies to reimburse licensed counselors, but often for only certain mental illnesses. Newer laws do NOT exist in all states of the U.S. In the states where they do exist, they do NOT cover all mental illnesses.

197. B: HMOs (Health Maintenance Organizations) and PPOS (Preferred Provider Organizations) are managed care groups with strict policies regarding treatment including counseling. Professionals in private practice cannot receive referrals of clients whose health insurance is with one of these organizations unless the professionals have provider status with the organization. Counselors do not apply for provider status to enhance their reputations, but to increase the numbers of their potential clients. There are no national or state laws governing provider status in managed health care organizations. This is controlled by organizational policies. Counselors seeing clients insured through these organizations must obtain provider status (i.e., inclusion on the organization's list of allowed providers), not membership in the organization itself.

198. D: It is against the law for counselors and their clients to have sexual contact in most states of the U.S., but not in all states (which may be surprising to some people). There is a good deal of overlap between legal and ethical practices in counseling, so they are not always easily separated. Many ethical principles are built into the laws governing the counseling profession. There are some behaviors and practices that only the law addresses. Privileged communication is a right granted to counselors—usually through licensure statutes—but only in some states, not in all states.

199. B: Before beginning a counseling or therapy group, informed consent should be obtained. It requires the leader to provide adequate information to the prospective members about their rights and shared expectations, and it is complete only after the prospective members both understand and agree once they have been informed. Although maintaining confidentiality is an ethical obligation of group members, it can NOT always be assured and group members must be informed of this. Leaders should also identify specific exceptions to confidentiality for the members (e.g., court orders, individual and community safety, etc). In counseling or therapy groups, members are discouraged from forming outside social relationships and discussing group issues in such social groups. Members and leaders should agree on how they will deal with this if it does occur. In multicultural groups, the leader needs to model respect for cultural differences among the group members; it is not the responsibility of the members alone. Leaders may need to discuss their cultural values and assumptions early on within the group.

200. C: If a counselor applies some diagnostic label to a member of a family, this could be used later in court. For example, a counselor's information might be used in child custody hearings or divorce proceedings. This is an ethical issue that family counselors must consider. The counselor's attitude toward gender roles is NOT irrelevant. The counselor's idea of the role of women in families, for example, will make a meaningful difference in family counseling. Whether the counselor believes in traditional gender roles or not will also affect the course of counseling. Despite confidentiality, a counselor should NOT keep child abuse or incest a secret as the law requires such abuse to be reported. When a family is culturally different, the counselor needs to be aware that the family roles and family dynamics will also be different according to that family's culture of origin.

Secret Key #1 - Time is Your Greatest Enemy

Pace Yourself

Wear a watch. At the beginning of the test, check the time (or start a chronometer on your watch to count the minutes), and check the time after every few questions to make sure you are "on schedule."

If you are forced to speed up, do it efficiently. Usually one or more answer choices can be eliminated without too much difficulty. Above all, don't panic. Don't speed up and just begin guessing at random choices. By pacing yourself, and continually monitoring your progress against your watch, you will always know exactly how far ahead or behind you are with your available time. If you find that you are one minute behind on the test, don't skip one question without spending any time on it, just to catch back up. Take 15 fewer seconds on the next four questions, and after four questions you'll have caught back up. Once you catch back up, you can continue working each problem at your normal pace.

Furthermore, don't dwell on the problems that you were rushed on. If a problem was taking up too much time and you made a hurried guess, it must be difficult. The difficult questions are the ones you are most likely to miss anyway, so it isn't a big loss. It is better to end with more time than you need than to run out of time.

Lastly, sometimes it is beneficial to slow down if you are constantly getting ahead of time. You are always more likely to catch a careless mistake by working more slowly than quickly, and among very high-scoring test takers (those who are likely to have lots of time left over), careless errors affect the score more than mastery of material.

Secret Key #2 - Guessing is not Guesswork

You probably know that guessing is a good idea. Unlike other standardized tests, there is no penalty for getting a wrong answer. Even if you have no idea about a question, you still have a 20-25% chance of getting it right.

Most test takers do not understand the impact that proper guessing can have on their score. Unless you score extremely high, guessing will significantly contribute to your final score.

Monkeys Take the Test

What most test takers don't realize is that to insure that 20-25% chance, you have to guess randomly. If you put 20 monkeys in a room to take this test, assuming they answered once per question and behaved themselves, on average they would get 20-25% of the questions correct. Put 20 test takers in the room, and the average will be much lower among guessed questions. Why?
1. The test writers intentionally write deceptive answer choices that "look" right. A test taker has no idea about a question, so he picks the "best looking" answer, which is often wrong. The monkey has no idea what looks good and what doesn't, so it will consistently be right about 20-25% of the time.
2. Test takers will eliminate answer choices from the guessing pool based on a hunch or intuition. Simple but correct answers often get excluded, leaving a 0% chance of being correct. The monkey has no clue, and often gets lucky with the best choice.

This is why the process of elimination endorsed by most test courses is flawed and detrimental to your performance. Test takers don't guess; they make an ignorant stab in the dark that is usually worse than random.

$5 Challenge

Let me introduce one of the most valuable ideas of this course—the $5 challenge:

You only mark your "best guess" if you are willing to bet $5 on it.
You only eliminate choices from guessing if you are willing to bet $5 on it.

Why $5? Five dollars is an amount of money that is small yet not insignificant, and can really add up fast (20 questions could cost you $100). Likewise, each answer choice on one question of the test will have a small impact on your overall score, but it can really add up to a lot of points in the end.

The process of elimination IS valuable. The following shows your chance of guessing it right:

If you eliminate wrong answer choices until only this many remain:	Chance of getting it correct:
1	100%
2	50%
3	33%

However, if you accidentally eliminate the right answer or go on a hunch for an incorrect answer, your chances drop dramatically—to 0%. By guessing among all the answer choices, you are GUARANTEED to have a shot at the right answer.
That's why the $5 test is so valuable. If you give up the advantage and safety of a pure guess, it had better be worth the risk.

What we still haven't covered is how to be sure that whatever guess you make is truly random. Here's the easiest way:

Always pick the first answer choice among those remaining.

Such a technique means that you have decided, **before you see a single test question**, exactly how you are going to guess, and since the order of choices tells you nothing about which one is correct, this guessing technique is perfectly random.

This section is not meant to scare you away from making educated guesses or eliminating choices; you just need to define when a choice is worth eliminating. The $5 test, along with a pre-defined random guessing strategy, is the best way to make sure you reap all of the benefits of guessing.

Secret Key #3 - Practice Smarter, Not Harder

Many test takers delay the test preparation process because they dread the awful amounts of practice time they think necessary to succeed on the test. We have refined an effective method that will take you only a fraction of the time.

There are a number of "obstacles" in the path to success. Among these are answering questions, finishing in time, and mastering test-taking strategies. All must be executed on the day of the test at peak performance, or your score will suffer. The test is a mental marathon that has a large impact on your future.

Just like a marathon runner, it is important to work your way up to the full challenge. So first you just worry about questions, and then time, and finally strategy:

Success Strategy

1. Find a good source for practice tests.
2. If you are willing to make a larger time investment, consider using more than one study guide. Often the different approaches of multiple authors will help you "get" difficult concepts.
3. Take a practice test with no time constraints, with all study helps, "open book." Take your time with questions and focus on applying strategies.
4. Take a practice test with time constraints, with all guides, "open book."
5. Take a final practice test without open material and with time limits.

If you have time to take more practice tests, just repeat step 5. By gradually exposing yourself to the full rigors of the test environment, you will condition your mind to the stress of test day and maximize your success.

Secret Key #4 - Prepare, Don't Procrastinate

Let me state an obvious fact: if you take the test three times, you will probably get three different scores. This is due to the way you feel on test day, the level of preparedness you have, and the version of the test you see. Despite the test writers' claims to the contrary, some versions of the test WILL be easier for you than others.

Since your future depends so much on your score, you should maximize your chances of success. In order to maximize the likelihood of success, you've got to prepare in advance. This means taking practice tests and spending time learning the information and test taking strategies you will need to succeed.

Never go take the actual test as a "practice" test, expecting that you can just take it again if you need to. Take all the practice tests you can on your own, but when you go to take the official test, be prepared, be focused, and do your best the first time!

Secret Key #5 - Test Yourself

Everyone knows that time is money. There is no need to spend too much of your time or too little of your time preparing for the test. You should only spend as much of your precious time preparing as is necessary for you to get the score you need.

Once you have taken a practice test under real conditions of time constraints, then you will know if you are ready for the test or not.

If you have scored extremely high the first time that you take the practice test, then there is not much point in spending countless hours studying. You are already there.

Benchmark your abilities by retaking practice tests and seeing how much you have improved. Once you consistently score high enough to guarantee success, then you are ready.

If you have scored well below where you need, then knuckle down and begin studying in earnest. Check your improvement regularly through the use of practice tests under real conditions. Above all, don't worry, panic, or give up. The key is perseverance!

Then, when you go to take the test, remain confident and remember how well you did on the practice tests. If you can score high enough on a practice test, then you can do the same on the real thing.

General Strategies

The most important thing you can do is to ignore your fears and jump into the test immediately. Do not be overwhelmed by any strange-sounding terms. You have to jump into the test like jumping into a pool—all at once is the easiest way.

Make Predictions

As you read and understand the question, try to guess what the answer will be. Remember that several of the answer choices are wrong, and once you begin reading them, your mind will immediately become cluttered with answer choices designed to throw you off. Your mind is typically the most focused immediately after you have read the question and digested its contents. If you can, try to predict what the correct answer will be. You may be surprised at what you can predict.

Quickly scan the choices and see if your prediction is in the listed answer choices. If it is, then you can be quite confident that you have the right answer. It still won't hurt to check the other answer choices, but most of the time, you've got it!

Answer the Question

It may seem obvious to only pick answer choices that answer the question, but the test writers can create some excellent answer choices that are wrong. Don't pick an answer just because it sounds right, or you believe it to be true. It MUST answer the question. Once you've made your selection, always go back and check it against the question and make sure that you didn't misread the question and that the answer choice does answer the question posed.

Benchmark

After you read the first answer choice, decide if you think it sounds correct or not. If it doesn't, move on to the next answer choice. If it does, mentally mark that answer choice. This doesn't mean that you've definitely selected it as your answer choice; it just means that it's the best you've seen thus far. Go ahead and read the next choice. If the next choice is worse than the one you've already selected, keep going to the next answer choice. If the next choice is better than the choice you've already selected, mentally mark the new answer choice as your best guess.

The first answer choice that you select becomes your standard. Every other answer choice must be benchmarked against that standard. That choice is correct until proven otherwise by another answer choice beating it out. Once you've decided that no other answer choice seems as good, do one final check to ensure that your answer choice answers the question posed.

Valid Information

Don't discount any of the information provided in the question. Every piece of information may be necessary to determine the correct answer. None of the information in the question is there to throw you off (while the answer choices will certainly have information to throw you off). If two seemingly unrelated topics are discussed, don't ignore either. You can be confident there is a relationship, or it wouldn't be included in the question, and you are probably going to have to determine what that relationship is to find the answer.

Avoid "Fact Traps"

Don't get distracted by a choice that is factually true. Your search is for the answer that answers the question. Stay focused and don't fall for an answer that is true but irrelevant. Always go back to the question and make sure you're choosing an answer that actually answers the question and is not just a true statement. An answer can be factually correct, but it MUST answer the question asked. Additionally, two answers can both be seemingly correct, so be sure to read all of the answer choices, and make sure that you get the one that BEST answers the question.

Milk the Question

Some of the questions may throw you completely off. They might deal with a subject you have not been exposed to, or one that you haven't reviewed in years. While your lack of knowledge about the subject will be a hindrance, the question itself can give you many clues that will help you find the correct answer. Read the question carefully and look for clues. Watch particularly for adjectives and nouns describing difficult terms or words that you don't recognize. Regardless of whether you completely understand a word or not, replacing it with a synonym, either provided or one you more familiar with, may help you to understand what the questions are asking. Rather than wracking your mind about specific detailed information concerning a difficult term or word, try to use mental substitutes that are easier to understand.

The Trap of Familiarity

Don't just choose a word because you recognize it. On difficult questions, you may not recognize a number of words in the answer choices. The test writers don't put "make-believe" words on the test, so don't think that just because you only recognize all the words in one answer choice that that answer choice must be correct. If you only recognize words in one answer choice, then focus on that one. Is it correct? Try your best to determine if it is correct. If it is, that's great. If not, eliminate it. Each word and answer choice you eliminate increases your chances of getting the question correct, even if you then have to guess among the unfamiliar choices.

Eliminate Answers

Eliminate choices as soon as you realize they are wrong. But be careful! Make sure you consider all of the possible answer choices. Just because one appears right, doesn't mean that the next one won't be even better! The test writers will usually put more than one good answer choice for every question, so read all of them. Don't worry if you are stuck between two that seem right. By getting down to just two remaining possible choices, your odds are now 50/50. Rather than wasting too much time, play the odds. You are guessing, but guessing wisely because you've been able to knock out some of the answer choices that you know are wrong. If you are eliminating choices and realize that the last answer choice you are left with is also obviously wrong, don't panic. Start over and consider each choice again. There may easily be something that you missed the first time and will realize on the second pass.

Tough Questions

If you are stumped on a problem or it appears too hard or too difficult, don't waste time. Move on! Remember though, if you can quickly check for obviously incorrect answer choices, your chances of guessing correctly are greatly improved. Before you completely give up, at least try to knock out a couple of possible answers. Eliminate what you can and then guess at the remaining answer choices before moving on.

Brainstorm

If you get stuck on a difficult question, spend a few seconds quickly brainstorming. Run through the complete list of possible answer choices. Look at each choice and ask yourself, "Could this answer the question satisfactorily?" Go through each answer choice and consider it independently of the others. By systematically going through all possibilities, you may find something that you would otherwise overlook. Remember though that when you get stuck, it's important to try to keep moving.

Read Carefully

Understand the problem. Read the question and answer choices carefully. Don't miss the question because you misread the terms. You have plenty of time to read each question thoroughly and make sure you understand what is being asked. Yet a happy medium must be attained, so don't waste too much time. You must read carefully, but efficiently.

Face Value

When in doubt, use common sense. Always accept the situation in the problem at face value. Don't read too much into it. These problems will not require you to make huge leaps of logic. The test writers aren't trying to throw you off with a cheap trick. If you have to go beyond creativity and make a leap of logic in order to have an answer choice answer the question, then you should look at the other answer choices. Don't overcomplicate the problem by creating theoretical relationships or explanations that will warp time or space. These are normal problems rooted in reality. It's just that the applicable relationship or explanation may not be readily apparent and you have to figure things out. Use your common sense to interpret anything that isn't clear.

Prefixes

If you're having trouble with a word in the question or answer choices, try dissecting it. Take advantage of every clue that the word might include. Prefixes and suffixes can be a huge help. Usually they allow you to determine a basic meaning. Pre- means before, post- means after, pro - is positive, de- is negative. From these prefixes and suffixes, you can get an idea of the general meaning of the word and try to put it into context. Beware though of any traps. Just because con- is the opposite of pro-, doesn't necessarily mean congress is the opposite of progress!

Hedge Phrases

Watch out for critical hedge phrases, led off with words such as "likely," "may," "can," "sometimes," "often," "almost," "mostly," "usually," "generally," "rarely," and "sometimes." Question writers insert these hedge phrases to cover every possibility. Often an answer choice will be wrong simply because it leaves no room for exception. Unless the situation calls for them, avoid answer choices that have definitive words like "exactly," and "always."

Switchback Words

Stay alert for "switchbacks." These are the words and phrases frequently used to alert you to shifts in thought. The most common switchback word is "but." Others include "although," "however," "nevertheless," "on the other hand," "even though," "while," "in spite of," "despite," and "regardless of."

New Information

Correct answer choices will rarely have completely new information included. Answer choices typically are straightforward reflections of the material asked about and will directly relate to the question. If a new piece of information is included in an answer choice that doesn't even seem to relate to the topic being asked about, then that answer choice is likely incorrect. All of the information needed to answer the question is usually provided for you in the question. You should not have to make guesses that are unsupported or choose answer choices that require unknown information that cannot be reasoned from what is given.

Time Management

On technical questions, don't get lost on the technical terms. Don't spend too much time on any one question. If you don't know what a term means, then odds are you aren't going to get much further since you don't have a dictionary. You should be able to immediately recognize whether or not you know a term. If you don't, work with the other clues that you have—the other answer choices and terms provided—but don't waste too much time trying to figure out a difficult term that you don't know.

Contextual Clues

Look for contextual clues. An answer can be right but not the correct answer. The contextual clues will help you find the answer that is most right and is correct. Understand the context in which a phrase or statement is made. This will help you make important distinctions.

Don't Panic

Panicking will not answer any questions for you; therefore, it isn't helpful. When you first see the question, if your mind goes blank, take a deep breath. Force yourself to mechanically go through the steps of solving the problem using the strategies you've learned.

Pace Yourself

Don't get clock fever. It's easy to be overwhelmed when you're looking at a page full of questions, your mind is full of random thoughts and feeling confused, and the clock is ticking down faster than you would like. Calm down and maintain the pace that you have set for yourself. As long as you are on track by monitoring your pace, you are guaranteed to have enough time for yourself. When you get to the last few minutes of the test, it may seem like you won't have enough time left, but if you only have as many questions as you should have left at that point, then you're right on track!

Answer Selection

The best way to pick an answer choice is to eliminate all of those that are wrong, until only one is left and confirm that is the correct answer. Sometimes though, an answer choice may immediately look right. Be careful! Take a second to make sure that the other choices are not equally obvious. Don't make a hasty mistake. There are only two times that you should stop before checking other answers. First is when you are positive that the answer choice you have selected is correct. Second is when time is almost out and you have to make a quick guess!

Check Your Work

Since you will probably not know every term listed and the answer to every question, it is important that you get credit for the ones that you do know. Don't miss any questions through careless mistakes. If at all possible, try to take a second to look back over your answer selection and make sure you've selected the correct answer choice and haven't made a costly careless mistake (such as marking an answer choice that you didn't mean to mark). The time it takes for this quick double check should more than pay for itself in caught mistakes.

Beware of Directly Quoted Answers

Sometimes an answer choice will repeat word for word a portion of the question or reference section. However, beware of such exact duplication. It may be a trap! More than likely, the correct choice will paraphrase or summarize a point, rather than being exactly the same wording.

Slang

Scientific sounding answers are better than slang ones. An answer choice that begins "To compare the outcomes..." is much more likely to be correct than one that begins "Because some people insisted..."

Extreme Statements

Avoid wild answers that throw out highly controversial ideas that are proclaimed as established fact. An answer choice that states the "process should be used in certain situations, if..." is much more likely to be correct than one that states the "process should be discontinued completely." The first is a calm rational statement and doesn't even make a definitive, uncompromising stance, using a hedge word "if" to provide wiggle room, whereas the second choice is a radical idea and far more extreme.

Answer Choice Families

When you have two or more answer choices that are direct opposites or parallels, one of them is usually the correct answer. For instance, if one answer choice states "x increases" and another answer choice states "x decreases" or "y increases," then those two or three answer choices are very similar in construction and fall into the same family of answer choices. A family of answer choices consists of two or three answer choices, very similar in construction, but often with directly opposite meanings. Usually the correct answer choice will be in that family of answer choices. The "odd man out" or answer choice that doesn't seem to fit the parallel construction of the other answer choices is more likely to be incorrect.

Special Report: How to Overcome Test Anxiety

The very nature of tests caters to some level of anxiety, nervousness, or tension, just as we feel for any important event that occurs in our lives. A little bit of anxiety or nervousness can be a good thing. It helps us with motivation, and makes achievement just that much sweeter. However, too much anxiety can be a problem, especially if it hinders our ability to function and perform.

"Test anxiety," is the term that refers to the emotional reactions that some test-takers experience when faced with a test or exam. Having a fear of testing and exams is based upon a rational fear, since the test-taker's performance can shape the course of an academic career. Nevertheless, experiencing excessive fear of examinations will only interfere with the test-taker's ability to perform and chance to be successful.

There are a large variety of causes that can contribute to the development and sensation of test anxiety. These include, but are not limited to, lack of preparation and worrying about issues surrounding the test.

Lack of Preparation

Lack of preparation can be identified by the following behaviors or situations:

Not scheduling enough time to study, and therefore cramming the night before the test or exam
Managing time poorly, to create the sensation that there is not enough time to do everything
Failing to organize the text information in advance, so that the study material consists of the entire text and not simply the pertinent information
Poor overall studying habits

Worrying, on the other hand, can be related to the test-taker, or many other factors around him or her that will be affected by the results of the test. These include worrying about:

Previous performances on similar exams, or exams in general
How friends and other students are achieving
The negative consequences that will result from a poor grade or failure

There are three primary elements to test anxiety. Physical components involve the same typical bodily reactions as those to acute anxiety (to be discussed below). Emotional factors have to do with fear or panic. Mental or cognitive issues concern attention spans and memory abilities.

Physical Signals

There are many different symptoms of test anxiety, and these are not limited to mental and emotional strain. Frequently there are a range of physical signals that will let a test taker know that he or she is suffering from test anxiety. These bodily changes can include the following:

Perspiring
Sweaty palms

Wet, trembling hands
Nausea
Dry mouth
A knot in the stomach
Headache
Faintness
Muscle tension
Aching shoulders, back and neck
Rapid heart beat
Feeling too hot/cold

To recognize the sensation of test anxiety, a test-taker should monitor himself for the following sensations:

The physical distress symptoms as listed above
Emotional sensitivity, expressing emotional feelings such as the need to cry or laugh too much, or a sensation of anger or helplessness
A decreased ability to think, causing the test-taker to blank out or have racing thoughts that are hard to organize or control.

Though most students will feel some level of anxiety when faced with a test or exam, the majority can cope with that anxiety and maintain it at a manageable level. However, those who cannot are faced with a very real and very serious condition, which can and should be controlled for the immeasurable benefit of this sufferer.

Naturally, these sensations lead to negative results for the testing experience. The most common effects of test anxiety have to do with nervousness and mental blocking.

Nervousness

Nervousness can appear in several different levels:

The test-taker's difficulty, or even inability to read and understand the questions on the test
The difficulty or inability to organize thoughts to a coherent form
The difficulty or inability to recall key words and concepts relating to the testing questions (especially essays)
The receipt of poor grades on a test, though the test material was well known by the test taker
Conversely, a person may also experience mental blocking, which involves:
Blanking out on test questions
Only remembering the correct answers to the questions when the test has already finished

Fortunately for test anxiety sufferers, beating these feelings, to a large degree, has to do with proper preparation. When a test taker has a feeling of preparedness, then anxiety will be dramatically lessened.

The first step to resolving anxiety issues is to distinguish which of the two types of anxiety are being suffered. If the anxiety is a direct result of a lack of preparation, this should be considered a normal reaction, and the anxiety level (as opposed to the test results) shouldn't be anything to worry about. However, if, when adequately prepared, the test-taker still panics, blanks out, or seems to overreact, this is not a fully rational reaction. While this can be considered normal too, there are many ways to combat and overcome these effects.

Remember that anxiety cannot be entirely eliminated; however, there are ways to minimize it, to make the anxiety easier to manage. Preparation is one of the best ways to minimize test anxiety. Therefore the following techniques are wise in order to best fight off any anxiety that may want to build.

To begin with, try to avoid cramming before a test, whenever it is possible. By trying to memorize an entire term's worth of information in one day, you'll be shocking your system, and not giving yourself a very good chance to absorb the information. This is an easy path to anxiety, so for those who suffer from test anxiety, cramming should not even be considered an option.

Instead of cramming, work throughout the semester to combine all of the material which is presented throughout the semester, and work on it gradually as the course goes by, making sure to master the main concepts first, leaving minor details for a week or so before the test.

To study for the upcoming exam, be sure to pose questions that may be on the examination, to gauge the ability to answer them by integrating the ideas from your texts, notes and lectures, as well as any supplementary readings.

If it is truly impossible to cover all of the information that was covered in that particular term, concentrate on the most important portions, that can be covered very well. Learn these concepts as best as possible, so that when the test comes, a goal can be made to use these concepts as presentations of your knowledge.

In addition to study habits, changes in attitude are critical to beating a struggle with test anxiety. In fact, an improvement of the perspective over the entire test-taking experience can actually help a test taker to enjoy studying and therefore improve the overall experience. Be certain not to overemphasize the significance of the grade - know that the result of the test is neither a reflection of self worth, nor is it a measure of intelligence; one grade will not predict a person's future success.

To improve an overall testing outlook, the following steps should be tried:

Keeping in mind that the most reasonable expectation for taking a test is to expect to try to demonstrate as much of what you know as you possibly can.
Reminding ourselves that a test is only one test; this is not the only one, and there will be others. The thought of thinking of oneself in an irrational, all-or-nothing term should be avoided at all costs.
A reward should be designated for after the test, so there's something to look forward to. Whether it be going to a movie, going out to eat, or simply visiting friends, schedule it in advance, and do it no matter what result is expected on the exam.

Test-takers should also keep in mind that the basics are some of the most important things, even beyond anti-anxiety techniques and studying. Never neglect the basic social, emotional and biological needs, in order to try to absorb information. In order to best achieve, these three factors must be held as just as important as the studying itself.

Study Steps

Remember the following important steps for studying:

Maintain healthy nutrition and exercise habits. Continue both your recreational activities and social pass times. These both contribute to your physical and emotional well being.
Be certain to get a good amount of sleep, especially the night before the test, because when you're overtired you are not able to perform to the best of your best ability.
Keep the studying pace to a moderate level by taking breaks when they are needed, and varying the work whenever possible, to keep the mind fresh instead of getting bored.
When enough studying has been done that all the material that can be learned has been learned, and the test taker is prepared for the test, stop studying and do something relaxing such as listening to music, watching a movie, or taking a warm bubble bath.

There are also many other techniques to minimize the uneasiness or apprehension that is experienced along with test anxiety before, during, or even after the examination. In fact, there are a great deal of things that can be done to stop anxiety from interfering with lifestyle and performance. Again, remember that anxiety will not be eliminated entirely, and it shouldn't be. Otherwise that "up" feeling for exams would not exist, and most of us depend on that sensation to perform better than usual. However, this anxiety has to be at a level that is manageable.

Of course, as we have just discussed, being prepared for the exam is half the battle right away. Attending all classes, finding out what knowledge will be expected on the exam, and knowing the exam schedules are easy steps to lowering anxiety. Keeping up with work will remove the need to cram, and efficient study habits will eliminate wasted time. Studying should be done in an ideal location for concentration, so that it is simple to become interested in the material and give it complete attention. A method such as SQ3R (Survey, Question, Read, Recite, Review) is a wonderful key to follow to make sure that the study habits are as effective as possible, especially in the case of learning from a textbook. Flashcards are great techniques for memorization. Learning to take good notes will mean that notes will be full of useful information, so that less sifting will need to be done to seek out what is pertinent for studying. Reviewing notes after class and then again on occasion will keep the information fresh in the mind. From notes that have been taken summary sheets and outlines can be made for simpler reviewing.
A study group can also be a very motivational and helpful place to study, as there will be a sharing of ideas, all of the minds can work together, to make sure that everyone understands, and the studying will be made more interesting because it will be a social occasion.

Basically, though, as long as the test-taker remains organized and self confident, with efficient study habits, less time will need to be spent studying, and higher grades will be achieved.

To become self-confident, there are many useful steps. The first of these is "self talk." It has been shown through extensive research, that self-talk for students who suffer from test anxiety, should be well monitored, in order to make sure that it contributes to self confidence as opposed to sinking the student. Frequently the self talk of test-anxious students is negative or self-defeating, thinking that everyone else is smarter and faster, that they always mess up, and that if they don't do well, they'll fail the entire course. It is important to decreasing anxiety that awareness is made of self talk. Try writing any negative self thoughts and then disputing them with a positive statement instead. Begin self-encouragement as though it was a friend speaking. Repeat positive statements to help reprogram the mind to believing in successes instead of failures.

Helpful Techniques

Other extremely helpful techniques include:

Self-visualization of doing well and reaching goals
While aiming for an "A" level of understanding, don't try to "overprotect" by setting your expectations lower. This will only convince the mind to stop studying in order to meet the lower expectations.
Don't make comparisons with the results or habits of other students. These are individual factors, and different things work for different people, causing different results.
Strive to become an expert in learning what works well, and what can be done in order to improve. Consider collecting this data in a journal.
Create rewards for after studying instead of doing things before studying that will only turn into avoidance behaviors.
Make a practice of relaxing - by using methods such as progressive relaxation, self-hypnosis, guided imagery, etc - in order to make relaxation an automatic sensation.
Work on creating a state of relaxed concentration so that concentrating will take on the focus of the mind, so that none will be wasted on worrying.
Take good care of the physical self by eating well and getting enough sleep.
Plan in time for exercise and stick to this plan.

Beyond these techniques, there are other methods to be used before, during and after the test that will help the test-taker perform well in addition to overcoming anxiety.
Before the exam comes the academic preparation. This involves establishing a study schedule and beginning at least one week before the actual date of the test. By doing this, the anxiety of not having enough time to study for the test will be automatically eliminated. Moreover, this will make the studying a much more effective experience, ensuring that the learning will be an easier process. This relieves much undue pressure on the test-taker.
Summary sheets, note cards, and flash cards with the main concepts and examples of these main concepts should be prepared in advance of the actual studying time. A topic should never be eliminated from this process. Omitting a topic because it isn't expected to be on the test is only setting up the test-taker for anxiety should it actually appear on the exam. Utilize the course syllabus for laying out the topics that should be studied. Carefully go over the notes that were made in class, paying special attention to any of the issues that the professor took special care to emphasize while lecturing in class. In the textbooks, use the chapter review, or if possible, the chapter tests, to begin your review.

It may even be possible to ask the instructor what information will be covered on the exam, or what the format of the exam will be (for example, multiple choice, essay, free form, true-false). Additionally, see if it is possible to find out how many questions will be on the test. If a review sheet or sample test has been offered by the professor, make good use of it, above anything else, for the preparation for the test. Another great resource for getting to know the examination is reviewing tests from previous semesters. Use these tests to review, and aim to achieve a 100% score on each of the possible topics. With a few exceptions, the goal that you set for yourself is the highest one that you will reach.

Take all of the questions that were assigned as homework, and rework them to any other possible course material. The more problems reworked, the more skill and confidence will form as a result. When forming the solution to a problem, write out each of the steps. Don't simply do head work.

By doing as many steps on paper as possible, much clarification and therefore confidence will be formed. Do this with as many homework problems as possible, before checking the answers. By checking the answer after each problem, a reinforcement will exist that will not be on the exam. Study situations should be as exam-like as possible, to prime the test-taker's system for the experience. By waiting to check the answers at the end, a psychological advantage will be formed, to decrease the stress factor.

Another fantastic reason for not cramming is the avoidance of confusion in concepts, especially when it comes to mathematics. 8-10 hours of study will become one hundred percent more effective if it is spread out over a week or at least several days, instead of doing it all in one sitting. Recognize that the human brain requires time in order to assimilate new material, so frequent breaks and a span of study time over several days will be much more beneficial.

Additionally, don't study right up until the point of the exam. Studying should stop a minimum of one hour before the exam begins. This allows the brain to rest and put things in their proper order. This will also provide the time to become as relaxed as possible when going into the examination room. The test-taker will also have time to eat well and eat sensibly. Know that the brain needs food as much as the rest of the body. With enough food and enough sleep, as well as a relaxed attitude, the body and the mind are primed for success.

Avoid any anxious classmates who are talking about the exam. These students only spread anxiety, and are not worth sharing the anxious sentimentalities.

Before the test also involves creating a positive attitude, so mental preparation should also be a point of concentration. There are many keys to creating a positive attitude. Should fears become rushing in, make a visualization of taking the exam, doing well, and seeing an A written on the paper. Write out a list of affirmations that will bring a feeling of confidence, such as "I am doing well in my English class," "I studied well and know my material," "I enjoy this class." Even if the affirmations aren't believed at first, it sends a positive message to the subconscious which will result in an alteration of the overall belief system, which is the system that creates reality.

If a sensation of panic begins, work with the fear and imagine the very worst! Work through the entire scenario of not passing the test, failing the entire course, and dropping out of school, followed by not getting a job, and pushing a shopping cart through the dark alley where you'll live. This will place things into perspective! Then, practice deep breathing and create a visualization of the opposite situation - achieving an "A" on the exam, passing the entire course, receiving the degree at a graduation ceremony.

On the day of the test, there are many things to be done to ensure the best results, as well as the calmest outlook. The following stages are suggested in order to maximize test-taking potential:

Begin the examination day with a moderate breakfast, and avoid any coffee or beverages with caffeine if the test taker is prone to jitters. Even people who are used to managing caffeine can feel jittery or light-headed when it is taken on a test day.
Attempt to do something that is relaxing before the examination begins. As last minute cramming clouds the mastering of overall concepts, it is better to use this time to create a calming outlook. Be certain to arrive at the test location well in advance, in order to provide time to select a location that is away from doors, windows and other distractions, as well as giving enough time to relax before the test begins.

Keep away from anxiety generating classmates who will upset the sensation of stability and relaxation that is being attempted before the exam.

Should the waiting period before the exam begins cause anxiety, create a self-distraction by reading a light magazine or something else that is relaxing and simple.

During the exam itself, read the entire exam from beginning to end, and find out how much time should be allotted to each individual problem. Once writing the exam, should more time be taken for a problem, it should be abandoned, in order to begin another problem. If there is time at the end, the unfinished problem can always be returned to and completed.

Read the instructions very carefully - twice - so that unpleasant surprises won't follow during or after the exam has ended.

When writing the exam, pretend that the situation is actually simply the completion of homework within a library, or at home. This will assist in forming a relaxed atmosphere, and will allow the brain extra focus for the complex thinking function.

Begin the exam with all of the questions with which the most confidence is felt. This will build the confidence level regarding the entire exam and will begin a quality momentum. This will also create encouragement for trying the problems where uncertainty resides.

Going with the "gut instinct" is always the way to go when solving a problem. Second guessing should be avoided at all costs. Have confidence in the ability to do well.

For essay questions, create an outline in advance that will keep the mind organized and make certain that all of the points are remembered. For multiple choice, read every answer, even if the correct one has been spotted - a better one may exist.

Continue at a pace that is reasonable and not rushed, in order to be able to work carefully. Provide enough time to go over the answers at the end, to check for small errors that can be corrected.

Should a feeling of panic begin, breathe deeply, and think of the feeling of the body releasing sand through its pores. Visualize a calm, peaceful place, and include all of the sights, sounds and sensations of this image. Continue the deep breathing, and take a few minutes to continue this with closed eyes. When all is well again, return to the test.

If a "blanking" occurs for a certain question, skip it and move on to the next question. There will be time to return to the other question later. Get everything done that can be done, first, to guarantee all the grades that can be compiled, and to build all of the confidence possible. Then return to the weaker questions to build the marks from there.

Remember, one's own reality can be created, so as long as the belief is there, success will follow. And remember: anxiety can happen later, right now, there's an exam to be written!

After the examination is complete, whether there is a feeling for a good grade or a bad grade, don't dwell on the exam, and be certain to follow through on the reward that was promised...and enjoy it! Don't dwell on any mistakes that have been made, as there is nothing that can be done at this point anyway.

Additionally, don't begin to study for the next test right away. Do something relaxing for a while, and let the mind relax and prepare itself to begin absorbing information again.

From the results of the exam - both the grade and the entire experience, be certain to learn from what has gone on. Perfect studying habits and work some more on confidence in order to make the next examination experience even better than the last one.

Learn to avoid places where openings occurred for laziness, procrastination and day dreaming.

Use the time between this exam and the next one to better learn to relax, even learning to relax on cue, so that any anxiety can be controlled during the next exam. Learn how to relax the body. Slouch in your chair if that helps. Tighten and then relax all of the different muscle groups, one group at a time, beginning with the feet and then working all the way up to the neck and face. This will ultimately relax the muscles more than they were to begin with. Learn how to breathe deeply and comfortably, and focus on this breathing going in and out as a relaxing thought. With every exhale, repeat the word "relax."

As common as test anxiety is, it is very possible to overcome it. Make yourself one of the test-takers who overcome this frustrating hindrance.